THE NEW LATIN AMERICAN CINEMA
A Continental Project

Texas Film Studies Series
Thomas Schatz, Editor

CINEMA
C I N E
CINEMA

CINEMA
C I N E
CINEMA

CINEMA
C I N E
CINEMA

CINEMA
C I N E
CINEMA

CINEMA
C I N E
CINEMA

CINEMA
C I N E
CINEMA

CINEMA
C I N E
CINEMA

CINEMA
C I N E
CINEMA

CINEMA
C I N E
CINEMA

CINEMA
C I N E
CINEMA

CINEMA
C I N E
CINEMA

THE NEW
LATIN AMERICAN CINEMA

A Continental Project

Zuzana M. Pick

 UNIVERSITY OF TEXAS PRESS, AUSTIN

First edition, 1993

Requests for permission to reproduce material from this work
should be sent to Permissions, University of Texas Press, Box 7819,
Austin, TX 78713-7819.

∞ The paper used in this publication meets the minimum requirements of American National Standard for Information Sciences—
Permanence of Paper for Printed Library Materials, ANSI Z39.48-1984.

Library of Congress Cataloging-in-Publication Data

Pick, Zuzana M.
    The new Latin American cinema : a continental project /
Zuzana M. Pick. — 1st ed.
        p.   cm. — (Texas film studies series)
    Includes bibliographical references and index.
    ISBN 0-292-76545-2 (alk. paper). — ISBN 0-292-76549-5 (pbk. :
alk. paper)
    1. Motion pictures—Social aspects—Latin America.
    2. Motion pictures—Political aspects—Latin America.   I. Title.
II. Series.
PN1995.9.S6P5   1993
302.23'43'098—dc20   93-73

Contents

Preface and Acknowledgments

My initial encounter with the cinemas of Latin America was accidental rather than planned. As a Colombian, I had never seen any Latin American films other than some Mexican comedies that were regularly exhibited at the Cine Mexico in Bogotá. But in the late sixties, when I arrived in Canada, I discovered some of those films still recognized today as the most representative of the New Latin American Cinema. These films gave me the first taste of what later became my dissertation topic. I discovered the baroque magic of Brazil through the films of Ruy Guerra and Glauber Rocha, the decadent expressionism of Buenos Aires in the films of Leopoldo Torre-Nilsson, the desolate beauty of Bolivia through the films of Jorge Sanjinés, and the victorious realism of revolutionary Cuba through the documentaries of Santiago Alvarez and the dialectical fictions of Tomás Gutierrez Alea.

The images spoke to me about places I knew without having ever been there and offered the opportunity to travel back to South America. Looking back at the tropics, the mountains, and the metropolis of the South, I began shedding those unpleasant prejudices that nationalism so often imposes on Latin Americans before they ever leave their countries. I began appreciating the diversity of cultures that had so far been only a name: Latin America. With these images came the discovery of social and political struggles provoked by social injustice. I realized that my upbringing—as a middle-class daughter of European immigrant parents—had shielded me from conflict like the smog that cloaks the poverty of the shantytowns skirting Bogotá.

In Paris, as a graduate student in film, I encountered other Latin Americans who, like me, had left their countries to study and work. My earliest critical pieces dealt with the Chilean cinema of the Popular Unity movement and with the work of filmmakers who arrived from Santiago in the winter of 1974 following the military coup. Upon my return to Canada in 1975, work on my doctoral dissertation took me back for the first time since 1966 to Latin America—this time to Cuba. This trip was a long-delayed rendezvous with a region I left as a young woman and a possibility to rebuild bonds that I felt were lost when I emigrated.

This book is the result of academic interests solidified since 1983 when Chilean friends in exile, some of them filmmakers, encouraged me to continue writing on Chilean cinema in exile as part of my teaching and research on Latin America. This study on the New Latin American Cinema also acknowledges my personal history of transcultural and cross-cultural wanderings. Writing about Latin American films in Canada has given me the chance to reassess my own sense of belonging to cultures only accessible through their representations. Throughout the years I have lived and worked here, my approach to the New Latin American Cinema has remained grounded in an intellectual, yet introspective, journey into identity and cultural affiliation. Whereas geographical distance has meant a detachment from the day-to-day experience of Latin American cultures, it has given me a better understanding of how individuals and communities struggle to maintain an idea of self. My work on exile, in particular, has allowed me to explore the complexities of cultural exchange.

Therefore, my own background has been crucial for the design of this book. I have endeavored to retain a personal perspective designed to reflect on and explore the interrelationships between place and representation, territory and culture, while drawing on the extensive body of critical and historical research on the New Latin American Cinema. This book grows out of existing studies by critics and academics from Latin America, Europe, and North America. All of them deserve an acknowledgment for their prolific and outstanding work. Furthermore, I have relied on the critical essays and manifestos written by filmmakers themselves who participated and continue to intervene in the ideological and conceptual framework of the movement.

In particular I would like to mention the scholars and writers whom I have met throughout the years and who have supported my own work: Julianne Burton, Michael Chanan, Michel Ciment, Ambrosio Fornet, Randal Johnson, Julia Lesage, Ana López, Lino Micciché, Paulo-Antonio Paranagua, Peter Schumann, Robert Stam, and Thomas Waugh. Among the Latin American filmmakers, and in addition to the Chileans living inside and outside their country, I want to mention especially Walter Achugar, Ambrosio Fornet, Pedro

Chaskel and Fedora Robles, Tomás Gutierrez Alea, Fernando Birri, María Luisa Bemberg, Jorge Fraga, Aldo Francia, Edgardo Pallero, Fernando Solanas, Mayra Vilasís, and Tizuka Yamasaki.

The first outline for this book came out of a course taught in the Film Studies Department of the University of Iowa. My appreciation goes to Professors Dudley Andrew and Thomas Lewis for asking me to go there as a visiting professor, to students for their contributions and insights into the materials of the course, and especially to Anne-Marie Gill, Raúl Ferrera, and Adriana Zuanic. In my own department at Carleton University in Ottawa, I want to thank my colleagues Christopher Faulkner, Mark Langer, George McKnight, Patrick MacFadden, William Straw, and Patricia Goodspeed, who for more than fifteen years have encouraged my scholarship, and the students who have taken courses on Latin American cinema. Also thanks to many other colleagues at Carleton who are too numerous to mention without risking embarrassing omissions.

Financial assistance for the different stages of this project was made available by the offices of Graduate Studies and Research and the Faculty of Arts of Carleton University. Teaching release time was provided through a research stipend of the Social Sciences and Humanities Research Council of Canada and a research achievement award of Carleton University. Special appreciation goes to Professor John ApSimon (Dean of Graduate Studies and Research) and to Anne Burgess (Research Administration) for continuous support, and to Professor Janice Yalden (Dean of the Faculty of Arts) for her confidence in my work on Latin American cinema. I hope she will not be disappointed.

Colleen Kong has been my research assistant and copy editor for three years. She helped me to write better by patiently revising my prose. My colleagues and friends Peter Harcourt and Michael Dorland at Carleton University have given generously of their time to discuss and read through the different stages of the manuscript. They encouraged me all the way and guided me through the difficult task of making this material conceptually and critically sound. To them a deep-felt acknowledgment and an apology if I have not always followed their constructive criticism. My gratitude to Julianne Burton, whose scrupulous reading of the completed manuscript helped me with the final revisions; to Saida Abdi and David Heath of Carleton University for editing assistance; to Professor Thomas Schatz and Frankie W. Westbrook of the University of Texas Press for their confidence and kind encouragement; and to Alison Tartt for excellent copyediting and Judith Hammill for indexing.

And a very special thanks to Leutén Rojas, who, as my partner for so many years, has so lovingly contributed with his comments and questions improving my work. I dedicate this book to Simone Millaray Rojas-Pick and Olga Rojas-Zech for no other reason than because I love them.

THE NEW LATIN AMERICAN CINEMA
A Continental Project

Introduction. The New Latin American Cinema: A Continental Project

A desire to unveil the conflicting realities of their own countries has led young directors in Latin America since the early 1950s to explore the political potential of the medium. Responding to the climates of social and political crises that prevailed across the continent, the filmmakers of the Documentary Film School of Santa Fé (Argentina), the Ukamau Group (Bolivia), the *cinema nôvo* (Brazil), as well as those of revolutionary Cuba and others in Colombia, Chile, Uruguay, and Venezuela sought committed ways to use film as an instrument of social awareness. By the end of the decade and through a concerted effort, these filmmakers sought to join diverse radical projects developed within specific national contexts into a broader ideological and cultural agenda capable of encompassing the territorial expanse of the continent. This ideological agenda was initiated by and developed through a cinematographic movement known as the New Latin American Cinema.

Constituted in 1967 during the historic festival of Latin American cinema in Viña del Mar (Chile), the New Latin American Cinema has over the last three decades produced an impressive body of work that bridges the gap between theory and practice and consists of films, critical essays, and political manifestos. The circulation of this body of work has disseminated the objectives and goals of the predominantly political cinemas of Latin America.

One of the goals of this book is to explore the institutional and aesthetic foundations of the New Latin American Cinema while recognizing that its history and its practices owe as much to the self-defining consciousness of the movement as to the social, political, and cultural formations that made its growth possible. Another goal is to sketch out the possible points of intersection between the politically oriented cinematic practices developed in different national contexts and the conceptual framework of the New Latin American Cinema.

To consider the virtually simultaneous emergence and growth of diverse national-oriented practices and a unified continental project is, in my view, a potentially productive critical approach to an otherwise complex cinematographic movement. It tolerates a concurrent consideration of contextual and ideological factors that constitute the movement's history, and allows for a diachronic layering of instances that have mediated the movement's unfolding growth. Furthermore, the burgeoning of radical cinematic tendencies within specific countries has as much to do with elements specific to national formations as with the capacity of the New Latin American Cinema to anchor itself concurrently within national and supranational projects.

Whether it currently exists as a unified entity, or merely as a naming practice that consolidates what otherwise would not be subject to consolidation, the New Latin American Cinema can be seen as the site that empowers and controls the inevitable variety of regional cinematographic practices, within and across national boundaries. As a movement, it accommodates diverse practices into a whole in the same way as the term Latin America organizes the heterogeneous formations that stretch from the Rio Grande to Tierra del Fuego. The New Latin American Cinema has nourished itself on the concept of Latin America which (although still contested) is informed by shared histories of underdevelopment and modernization and shared struggles to name a continental experience of modernity.

By invoking a continental ideal of unity grounded in Latin America's distinctiveness, the movement has aligned itself with the discourses and representations through which Latin American histories and cultures have been mediated. Moreover, the ideals of continental solidarity—its unity within diversity—have enabled the movement to incorporate the political goals of its constituting cinematic practices into a continental and modernist project. This supranational ideal constitutes the ideological foundation of the movement. This ideal has also been the basis of the process of self-definition that has characterized the New Latin American Cinema.

Simultaneously, this ideology of a continental unity within diversity has allowed the movement to expand and consolidate itself by incorporating the most heterogeneous manifestations with the most homogeneous sense of purpose. In this way, the movement has reinserted itself into the societies from which it has emerged. Insomuch as the New Latin American Cinema has been altered by the distinct cinemas of the region, it has also sought to influence their national histories.

The unfolding of the New Latin American Cinema—as an ideological project and a cinematographic practice—is the result of its capacity to conceptualize the social and political impact of cinema as a cultural practice. The modernist impulses of the movement have been crucial to the manner in which films and filmmakers have adopted cinema as a critical tool. It has been ultimately up to individual filmmakers, working within the national components of the movement, to evaluate the relevance of their own attempts to align artistic expression with social change. Through the achievements and shortcomings of individual practices, the movement has managed to rearticulate itself and to pursue its project in spite of institutional and political drawbacks.

Concurrently, the movement has served to contest traditional accounts of the specific national cinemas of the region. Most histories of Latin American cinemas have validated industrial strategies and modes capable of reflecting unifying, rather than contestational, forms of national expression and, in general, marginalized nonmainstream practices. Historians have systematically promoted an aesthetic canon based on the identification of films seen as authentically representative of national cinemas. Yet other historians have advocated alternative and oppositional modes, those that make up the backbone of the New Latin American Cinema.

The practices of the New Latin American Cinema have historically located themselves outside the traditional paradigms of national cinemas. As the movement has challenged the homogenizing accounts of national cinemas, it has simultaneously sought to provide a place where diverse national and regional practices can converge. Yet specific national practices—like those of Cuba—have been formulated as chief, if not politically indispensable, agents of the movement's continental agenda. In this way, the movement has been the site where consensual models of industrial growth and creative merit can be de-centered and where new affiliations can be forged.

The longevity of the movement, its sustained development over the last three decades, is just one of the traits that distinguishes the New Latin American Cinema from other cinematic movements that have emerged internationally since the mid-1940s. The movement has consistently defined its political pertinence by inserting itself in social change, and its ideology and aesthetics are articulated in historical and contemporary forms of cultural struggle. The dynamic heterogeneity of the New Latin American Cinema has cinematically contributed to redefining the narrow limitations of political filmmaking by exploring alternative modes of production and consumption.

The specific production methods and aesthetic options promoted by the New Latin American Cinema movement may have been modified periodically to accommodate contextual conditions, and filmmakers may have adjusted to changing social, political, and personal situations. What remains stable is the movement's resolve to use film as a tool for social change, a vehicle to transform national and regional expressions, support international differences, and assert regional forms of cultural autonomy. Therefore, the movement has sought to oppose the dominance of Hollywood models of production and reception, to devise alternatives to traditional systems of production, distribution, and exhibition capable of altering existing patterns of cinematic culture.

The distinct characteristics of this movement call for the mobilization of critical tools to account for its diversity and uniqueness. The development of the movement, and of the practices that have emerged in different Latin American countries since the 1960s, suggests an alliance between cultural politics and social history. Moreover, this development has as much to do with an ideological agenda as with institutional arrangements designed to promote and aesthetic options developed to sustain the New Latin American Cinema.

Therefore, I have mapped out six areas of inquiry—history, authorship, gender, popular cinema, ethnicity, and exile—to investigate the complex interrelation between the supranational goals of the New Latin American Cinema and the national tendencies that have contributed to shape the movement's ideology. To achieve the objectives of this study, and rather than opting for an exhaustive approach, I have taken a narrower approach capable of dealing with specific aspects of this multifaceted and intellectually challenging field of study. To the extent that the growth of the New Latin American Cinema is bound to a commonality of purpose, I am examining a variety of critical issues in terms of the relevance they hold within the movement. This examination provides a blueprint for an in-depth study of particular films produced in different countries. The study of individual films details the pertinence of political and aesthetic issues for the movement and its national components. Selected for their analytical usefulness, rather than for their representability, the films of María Luisa Bemberg, Fernando Birri, Octavio Getino, and Fernando Ezequiel Solanas (Argentina); Jorge Sanjinés and the Ukamau Group (Bolivia); Jorge Bodanzky, Carlos Diegues, Ruy Guerra, and Tizuka Yamasaki (Brazil); Marta Rodríguez and Jorge Silva (Colombia); Marilú Mallet, Valeria Sarmiento, and Raúl

Ruiz (Chile); Tomás Gutierrez Alea, Sara Gómez and Hector Veitía, Mayra Segura, Mayra Vilasís, Mario Crespo, and Ana Rodríguez (Cuba); and Paul Leduc (Mexico) serve to further connections between different films and notions identified as crucial to the New Latin American Cinema.

The first chapter of this book considers how the New Latin American Cinema constructed its ideological and aesthetic agenda and how it consolidated itself as a continental project. A general overview of three decades of the movement describes the institutional and historical factors that affect the movement's distinctive history and cohesion. Notwithstanding the prevalent distrust for synchronic modes of historical study, I recognize the usefulness of a condensed account that situates the movement's emergence against the background of nationally oriented projects and a supranational goal (the New Latin American Cinema).

Therefore, this chapter describes the significance of film festivals—at Viña del Mar (Chile) and Mérida (Venezuela) in the late 1960s and in Havana (Cuba) since 1979—in supporting creative endeavor, discussions, and exchanges between filmmakers working in different countries. The emergence of the movement in the 1960s, and its growth in the 1970s and (to a certain extent) into the 1980s, is explained in the alignment of innovative strategies of filmmaking with political and cultural struggles. The constitution of the New Latin American Cinema, its historical consciousness as a movement, is traced through its retroactive naming and its designation of certain films, events, and organizations as shaping instances of an institutional undertaking.

The incorporation of an astounding variety of modes of production, consumption, and reception within the New Latin American Cinema is related as much to its self-definition as to its affiliation to alternative tendencies within national cinemas and modernizing projects in various Latin American countries. Hence, this chapter deals with social processes and organizations that have sustained national initiatives and patterned cinematic production in different countries. National practices are emphasized as active mediating agencies in the ever-expanding agenda of the New Latin American Cinema disseminated through organizations (like the Committee of Latin American Filmmakers and subsequently the New Latin American Cinema Foundation) that have initiated and furthered the movement's conceptual framework and historiographic enterprise.

The second chapter deals with authorship and with the manner in which the New Latin American Cinema has armed itself with a critical framework to shift the agency of meaning away from narrowly defined notions of creativity. The definition of a revolutionary cinema—conceived as always open, never complete—was linked to oppositional strategies capable of challenging mainstream modes of cinematographic production and consumption. Filmmakers assumed consciously their role as initiators of change. Through critical writings and manifestos, they proposed modes suitable to distinct forms of creative and political militancy.

Although these writings responded to conditions affecting specific national cinematic practices, some of the premises advanced by filmmakers were incorporated into the movement. This chapter takes into account how the New Latin American Cinema has sought to rearticulate authorship. Connecting aesthetics and politics, creative process and social relations, the movement debated the social and cultural function of the author and acknowledged authorial agency as one instance within the diverse range of elements that mediate cinematographic practice and cultural production. In this way, authorship in the New Latin American cinema operates across a variety of fields and is anchored in the joint engagement of subjective and collective positions.

Each one of the films examined in this chapter seeks to intervene ideologically in favor of social change through aesthetic strategies that link interactively the process of production and the moment of reception. *The Brickmakers* (Marta Rodríguez and Jorge Silva, Colombia, 1967–1972) emerges from a sociological project to denounce the dehumanization of a family in a brickmaking community on the outskirts of Bogotá. Produced by stages and with modest resources, it promotes solidarity and dialogue between working-class and progressive middle-class groups. *Up to a Point* (Tomás Gutierrez Alea, Cuba, 1983) arises from relatively stable production methods and the changing demands of creative activity within the Cuban Revolution. It draws attention to gender and class inequality by shifting between videotaped interviews with workers and the love affair between a female dockworker and a scriptwriter.

The Hour of the Furnaces (Fernando Ezequiel Solanas and Octavio Getino, Argentina, 1965–1968) is a landmark of militant cinema. This polemical documentary explores the ideological antagonisms between nationalist populism and bourgeois liberalism and their implications for the politics of Argentina since 1956. Like *The Sons of Fierro* (Solanas, 1973–1978), *The Hour of the Furnaces* acknowledges authorship as a collective agency whereby representation and spectatorship are regulated by discursive rather than aesthetic formations. The *Sons of Fierro* narrates twenty years of Peronist resistance, without overlooking the ambiguities of the Peronist movement, through an innovative structuring of musical and cinematographic protocols.

The third chapter deals with issues of gender and representation and seeks to identify new expressive territories that not only subvert accepted aesthetic standards but claim a public space for issues censored from the private sphere. These feminist-oriented practices reflect the importance of reshaping notions of social and gendered experience, history, and memory within the New Latin American cinema.

This chapter presents mostly, but not exclusively, the work of women filmmakers who are seeking to contest existing discourses on femininity, to deconstruct gender inequality, and to rearticulate the politics and practices of gendered representations. The feminist approaches of the films studied indicate how filmmakers are redressing the omission of women from history within a comprehensive critique of power and authority capable of rearranging the place of gender within representation.

A Man, When He Is a Man (Valeria Sarmiento, Chile, 1982) fractures the iconography and mythology of the Latin lover. Folklore, film, and popular music serve to unmask *machismo* and contest the gratifying symbols of romance. This documentary breaks the silence that surrounds the ingrained violence of gender relations and denounces *machismo* through a powerful exposition of its highly mediated representations. *Mujer transparente* (1990) includes five short films directed by Hector Veitía, Mayra Segura, Mayra Vilasís, Mario Crespo, and Ana Rodríguez (Cuba, 1990). It valorizes fantasy and desire and offers a timely corrective to women's representation in Cuban cinema by stressing interiority. This film empowers the intimate and private feelings of female characters and opens a distinctive space for the feminine voice within the New Latin American Cinema.

In addition, women filmmakers are challenging traditional constructions of femininity. To free gender from its problematic appropriation in national allegories, women filmmakers are inserting personal politics into gender-neutral representations of history. *Camila* (María Luisa Bemberg, Argentina, 1984) reconstructs the story of Camila O'Gorman and takes a political view of power and gender relations by drawing on the affective protocol of melodrama. *Frida: Naturaleza viva* (Paul Leduc, Mexico, 1984) is a nontraditional biography of painter Frida Kahlo. It explores the complex alliances between gender, class, and ethnicity that inform Mexican national-ism. Through its modernist options, the film rearticulates the place of subjectivity in biography, of memory in history.

Through an oppositional notion of popular cinema, the New Latin American Cinema has explored social experiences marginalized and excluded from class-based and homogeneous representations of na-tionhood. Chapter 4 explains how popular cinema has integrated tra-ditional and avant-garde expressions of popular culture and how film-makers have deconstructed and reconstructed the subversive power of popular traditions and historical memory. The notion of popular cinema, as an agent of change, is imbedded in the imagination of collective traditions. This notion entails political choices and inno-vative aesthetic options capable of releasing popular creativity.

The films analyzed, albeit with different emphasis, are inflected by class and location, history and memory. *Los inundados* (Fer-nando Birri, Argentina, 1962) bypasses the predominantly urban fo-cus of the traditional genres of Argentine popular cinema and the methods of production sanctioned by the industrial models of Ar-gentine cinema. The film is reflective and ironic: its mode of address empowers the collective expressivity of popular culture. *The Guns* (Ruy Guerra, Brazil, 1964) deconstructs the representations through which the Brazilian Northeast has been interpreted and the dis-courses that have limited the self-representation of the people of the backlands. The film takes into account popular culture as an expres-sive agency and establishes a dialectic between powerlessness and alienation, revolt and apathy.

The Courage of the People (Jorge Sanjinés and the Ukamau Group, Bolivia, 1971) is considered one of the most important films of the New Latin American Cinema. It reconstructs a massacre of miners in the town of Siglo XX on the night of June 24, 1967, with the participation of some of the survivors. Shooting on the actual sites of the historical event, the filmmakers discarded traditional film-making methods to preserve the emotional and expressive authen-ticity of popular memory. The political impact of this film comes from a conscious attempt to rethink historical reconstruction where-by a cinematographic sense of authenticity intensifies, rather than intrudes upon, history.

In its project to rearrange the terms that have served to construct national identities, especially through popular cinema, the New Latin American Cinema has tended to overlook the racial underpin-nings of national identity constructs. In the late 1970s and into the 1980s filmmakers within the movement have begun addressing cul-tural difference and ethnicity. Chapter 5 deals with the way in which

Brazilian and Cuban filmmakers, in particular, are struggling to articulate the paradox of an intellectual legacy that has censored the history of racial inequality in Latin America.

Rather than posing ethnicity as an alternative to stereotyped images, this chapter explores how cinematographic treatments of ethnicity contest *mestizaje* and replot race relations, how representation is mobilized to reimagine history. The films analyzed in this chapter reflect (in spite of their shortcomings) the struggle to come to terms with the mythologies of *mestizaje* and the master narratives of national identity. These films present different ways of dealing with ethnicity, either by exploring the dialectics of cultural difference or questioning ahistorical presumptions and romantic celebrations of cultural diversity.

One Way or Another (Sara Gómez, Cuba, 1974–1978) draws attention to social relations. It places Afro-Cuban culture in a contemporary context and promotes reflection on prejudices which are rooted in patriarchal, religious, and racial ideologies. *Iracema* (Jorge Bodanzky, Brazil, 1974) questions the romantic underpinnings of race relations amid the forlorn destruction of the Amazon forest. The film uses metaphor to construct a critical intertext on Brazil's self-image as a nation struggling to enter modernity by alluding to a foundational novel and questioning a contemporary master text of national and territorial consolidation.

Quilombo (Carlos Diegues, Brazil, 1984) reconstructs the history of Palmares (the legendary settlement of runaway slaves) and connects ethnicity to an emerging black-consciousness movement. It draws on elements of Afro-Brazilian popular culture (music, carnival, and *candomblé*) through which the practices forcibly transplanted to Brazil have been preserved and revitalized. *Gaijin: The Road to Liberty* (Tizuka Yamasaki, Brazil, 1979) presents the struggle of a young woman to overcome gender inequality, racial prejudice, and class exploitation. The film empowers the female immigrant experience by representing the traumatic confrontation of cultures and landscapes to provide an alternative account of early Japanese immigration in Brazil.

The sixth chapter deals with exile (as notion and experience) to explain how geographic and cultural displacement have fostered decentered views on identity and nationality and how the practices of exiled filmmakers have been transformed and rearticulated into the New Latin American Cinema. Filmmakers forced to leave their countries, even temporarily, were driven to seek new ways of communicating with and engaging in new cultural (and sometimes linguistic) contexts. Hence, this chapter considers how exile produces a new political agency whereby community associations are relocated, cultural specificity is renegotiated, and cultural affiliations are reconstructed. The practices of Chilean and Argentine exiled filmmakers in the 1980s have stressed the dialectics of historical and personal circumstance and have validated autobiography as a reflective site.

The trauma of exile alters creativity: no longer grounded in one's own homeland, creativity thrives in contact with new milieus. In this way, filmmakers have ventured into new expressive territories where the lines of demarcation between the old and the new become extremely fluid. As narratives originating in one place are transferred to another, representation enters into an intercultural and international dialogue. The films in this chapter provide an opportunity to understand how territorial relocation has (in turn) underwritten diversity and difference within the movement.

Unfinished Diary (*Journal inachevé, 1982*), made in Canada by Marilú Mallet, rescues the fragmented and fragmenting elements of exile through a self-reflective aesthetic that privileges the personal. The Chilean filmmaker has reshaped the literary mode of diary writing by juxtaposing fiction and documentary and has imagined exile as a scrapbook on which memory is constantly being rewritten. The film's autobiographical impulse seeks a new place to represent the conflicts and crisis of the exile experience. *The Three Crowns of the Sailor* (1982) and *Tangos: The Exile of Gardel* (1986), made in France by Raúl Ruiz (Chile) and Fernando Ezequiel Solanas (Argentina) respectively, relay the perplexing forms that national identity takes in exile and evidence a relentless obsession with national idioms. Although both films are engaged with memory, they are also marked by a staunch refusal to be engulfed by nostalgia. Both are incursions into cross-cultural landscapes and reclaim a Latin American imagination.

To conclude, I have linked the New Latin American Cinema to the discourses that have served to negotiate the continent's distinctive identity. Insofar as the movement has developed historically within the dialectical interactions of regional expressions, national projects, and continental ideals, its ideology is affiliated to the idea of Latin America as a historical entity that has been integral to the continent's modernity.

Therefore, the movement has furthered critical and reflective approaches to cultural production and representation, identity and social change. What is at stake here is the manner in which most filmmakers identified with the movement have systematically addressed national identity through the pervading usage of an all-encompassing notion of national reality. Yet the films studied in this book, in contrast to the writings of Latin American filmmakers, problematize the erasure of regional, social, racial, and sexual differences implied by the term *national reality* and privilege subjective and collective identities as embattled sites of representation and discourse.

Through its conceptual framework, the New Latin American Cinema has placed modernity at the service of experimentation and heterogeneity. Moreover, as I argue in the concluding section of this book, the critical modernism of some of the films produced by the New Latin American Cinema operates within a conscious awareness of yet untold and multiple narratives of cultural identity. This is the principle upon which Latin Americans have challenged fixed ideas of identity and imagined new utopias. This principle is exemplified in the movement's characteristic logic and longevity: its belief that its ideological project remains unfinished.

ONE
UNO
UMO

Convergences and Divergences

The constitution of the New Latin American Cinema cannot be traced to a single foundational occurrence. The movement has sought to engage in the continuous struggles for cultural and political autonomy, freedom of expression, and social change, but always as an active agent of diverse yet similar histories of violence and discontinuity. As Ana López suggests, "It is precisely as a movement that stresses a particular set of nationalist positions and that articulates these positions across a terrain much broader than the national sphere that the New Latin American Cinema acquires its revolutionary cultural significance."[1]

The practices that have flourished in Latin America during the last three decades disclaim a linear treatment of their historical development and confront film historians with their particular brand of eccentricity. This eccentricity is constituted by an astounding variety of modes of production, consumption, and reception that emerged in different countries and were incorporated into the movement. The New Latin American Cinema has also systematically sought to set up the necessary structures to sustain itself as a continental project. In historical terms, the movement owes a great deal to the way in which diverse groups fostered the circulation of ideas and films by establishing effective networks for exchange and distribution.

The acknowledgment of certain events played a pivotal role in the retroactive naming of the New Latin American Cinema. These historical milestones have been crucial to the discursive organization of the New Latin American Cinema. They have radically shaped the consciousness of a movement whose endurance depends not only on cinematographic and institutional paradigms but on an ideological agenda that transcends the local or national orientations of its constituting practices to encompass the whole continent.

The International Festival of the Latin American Cinema at Viña del Mar in Chile (1967 and 1969) and the First Encounter of Latin American Documentary Film at the University of Mérida in Venezuela (1968) inaugurated contacts among the filmmakers who worked in different countries. In a parallel initiative, the Cinematheque of the Third World (1969) in Montevideo (Uruguay) initiated the distribution and exhibiting of films and a film festival with the periodical *Marcha*. These organizations, together with filmmaking collectives set up mainly inside Latin American universities, provided the settings to discuss cinematographic strategies. More recently the Committee of Latin American Filmmakers (1974), subsequently expanded and reorganized as the New Latin American Cinema Foundation (1985), and the International Festival of the New Latin American Cinema in Havana (1979–   ) have been instrumental in supporting creative endeavor and circulating ideas. These organizations have played (through their most visible participants) a crucial role in the development of the movement, both as a strategy for cultural production and a historiographic enterprise.

In the 1960s the films made by the Documentary Film School of Santa Fé in Argentina and the Ukamau Group in Bolivia, the *cinema nôvo* in Brazil, and the revolutionary cinema of Cuba exemplified the transformation of cinematic practices in Latin America. As a whole, these practices expressed a collective reaction to the chronic effects of underdevelopment, a dialectical alliance of cultural and social militancy. Seen from a historical perspective, the movements or tendencies that developed within specific national contexts represented an alternative to the modernization projects taken up by Latin American states. These nationally based tendencies gave a political coherence to a cinematic movement that aligned innovational strategies with the struggle against cultural dependency and illiteracy.

At present, assuming a manageable understanding of what the New Latin American Cinema is, it is useful to explore how the movement acquired a distinct identity and a historical consciousness. "The New Latin American Cinema," to quote Ana López again, "represents an attempt to impose unity on a diverse number of cinematic practices; a political move to create an order out of disorder and to emphasize similarities rather than differences."[2]

History and Institutions

The identification of the historical milestones of the New Latin American Cinema is bound as much to an institutional undertaking as to the establishment of organizational structures in different

Latin American countries. The instances of self-definition and the social processes—those which have served to define the cohesiveness
of the movement—are mutually intersecting operations whereby
patterns of cultural production are affected by ideology. The elements
that constitute the coherence of the New Latin American Cinema
have had effects more far-reaching than the predominantly aesthetic
elements usually associated with other cinematic movements.[3]

The New Latin American Cinema, as it completes its third decade
in the 1990s, no longer yields to an appraisal based exclusively on
the filmmakers' political responses to social and political change.
The transformations of the different organizations set up to sustain
the movement, at the national and continental levels, are crucial to
the development of Latin American cinemas and the consolidation
of the movement. From this perspective it might be possible to view
the diverse national practices as active mediators for the redefinition of cinema in Latin America and to draw attention to the manner in which the movement disseminated its political agenda.

Latin American filmmakers in different countries, in the absence
of solid infrastructural and budgetary structures, have adjusted their
cultural and economic strategies and operated within viable alternatives, testing intrinsic political contradictions in the cultural
arena. If traditional histories have failed to consider the role of oppositional modes of filmmaking within various national cinemas, it
is precisely in the written histories of the New Latin American
Cinema that the convergence between national considerations and
pan-continental solidarity has been established.

The oppositional strategies advocated by filmmakers in Latin
America (frequently marginalized from national histories of film)
served to define the institutional framework of the New Cinema of
Latin America. Notwithstanding positional shifts, these oppositional strategies, which became central to the movement's agenda,
are intrinsically grounded in distinct forms of cultural nationalism.
As Patricia Aufderheide points out, the New Latin American
Cinema proposed—with its inception in 1967—a synthesis of cultural nationalism and leftist ideology, and "film came to be seen as
not simply an arm of political struggle, but a staging ground of the
battle for political power."[4]

In order to make sense of the occurrences that marked the historical consciousness of the New Latin American Cinema, I will simultaneously trace nationally based initiatives and a continentally oriented enterprise. To demonstrate how isolated cinematic strategies
grew into a continental movement, I will focus on the mechanisms
contributing to this convergence during four specific stages of the

movement's development, beginning in the mid-1950s and ending in 1987, the twentieth anniversary of Viña del Mar.

Aware of the potential risk of generalization, I have chosen this approach as a way of presenting a broad historical view of the New Latin American Cinema. By acknowledging the dialectic interactions of regional expressions, national projects, and continental ideals, this method has the potential to address, as Ana López has stated, "the solidarity between the national and the Latin American that has so often been cited as a key characteristic of the New Latin American Cinema."[5]

Pioneers and Early Manifestations

It was in the mid-1950s that Latin American documentary filmmakers had the first opportunity to evaluate their experiences. In 1958 the International Festival of Documentary and Experimental Film, organized by the Radio-Electric Broadcasting Society (SODRE) in Montevideo since 1954 by Danilo Trelles, invited Fernando Birri (Argentina), Jorge Ruiz (Bolivia), Nelson Pereira dos Santos (Brazil), Patricio Kaulen (Chile), and Manuel Chambi (Peru). In different countries filmmakers were pursuing remarkably similar objectives by producing images of a rarely seen social reality. These filmmakers were working toward a documentary of social inquiry by breaking away from the predominantly ethnographic model which had characterized the Latin American documentaries of the fifties.[6]

Although documentary had traditionally occupied an important place, alongside fictional filmmaking in Latin America, most of the work had centered around the activity of private companies which produced newsreels or sponsored documentaries. However, the pioneering impetus of the social documentary rested on the activity of small groups laboring within film societies and universities, or within other educational agencies that offered new spaces for artistic expression. This new approach to documentary also encouraged the development of alternative modalities of production and reception to the models instituted by mainstream documentary. To the extent that directors of fiction film could rely on more public and established venues for critical exposure, it would take a few more years before any of these documentarists would be considered the forerunners of a film movement.

The Latin American films presented at prestigious film festivals—Cannes, Venice, San Sebastián, and Moscow—drew the attention of European critics. In the early 1960s, critics in Europe and the

Americas began naming new film movements. Even before the New Latin American Cinema could recognize itself as a movement, film critics in Britain, France, Italy, and later North America were fascinated by a younger generation of Latin American directors. European critics regarded these filmmakers from Argentina, Brazil, and Cuba as having turned the cinematographic establishment upside-down with their irreverent treatment of the medium.

In this way, the film reviews and interviews published in European and North American film magazines contributed to the founding of a new Latin American film canon. The endorsement of these films, outside the region where they were produced, was sustained by film festivals and circulated predominantly as an art cinema in spite—and perhaps because—of its explicit political goals. However, some of these festivals—in particular Sestri Levante (Italy) and Karlovy Vary (Czechoslovakia)—allowed attending filmmakers to establish initial contacts among themselves and discover, in the words of Cuban critic and screenplay writer Ambrosio Fornet, "the infinite artistic and ideological possibilities of a new cinema as a principled expression of Latin American reality."[7]

If the New Latin American Cinema initially had to seek critical recognition outside the region, by the mid-1960s some of the filmmakers associated with the movement became skeptical of the European and North American accolades. Filmmakers from the Argentine *nueva ola*, for instance, were forced to recognize that European critical approval after the release of their first features did not automatically guarantee either widespread critical acceptance or financial success at home. Although production was backed by protective legislation instituted by the Frondizi regime, this movement faced a variety of problems. *Los inundados* (Fernando Birri, Argentina, 1962), for example, received an award in Venice, but its distribution was limited by a system unfavorable to nationally produced films. Yet the renovating aims of the movement were far from homogeneous and encouraged a political debate on cinematic representation.[8]

Grounded in the contested terrain of national identity, the Brazilian *cinema nôvo* represented the violence of urban and rural misery that challenged the modernist image constructed by the state, symbolized by the new capital city Brasilia. The films of Nelson Pereira dos Santos, Glauber Rocha, and Carlos Diegues drew simultaneously on Italian neorealism and nationalist options. While their avant-garde agenda sealed the critical recognition of the *cinema nôvo* outside Brazil, the circulation of its films inside the country was extremely limited. Yet the political objectives of the movement

(to locate cinematic practices within the changing parameters of nationhood and cultural development) broadened the debate on national cinema in Brazil.

In this period, the traditional film industries in Latin America
were thrown into disarray by their inability to sustain a level of production sufficient to defray financial losses. National governments
began responding to the lobbying of producers, distributors, and exhibitors, and protective legislation was instituted to revitalize the
fledgling industries of Argentina (1962), Brazil (1961), and Mexico
(1960). As the younger generation of Latin American filmmakers
joined the debates centered around the need to safeguard national
cinemas, they began challenging the arguments advanced by mainstream producers and coined the term "old"—in opposition to the
"new"—cinema. As Ana López writes, "Vehemently criticized, the
old cinema was rejected as imitative of Hollywood, unrealistic,
alienating and sentimental. Over the years, it became little else than
a clichéd straw man in all arguments for cinematic and cultural
renovation."[9]

Inasmuch as filmmakers realized the importance of promoting
their work more widely, and eventually benefited from European
funding for their films, they also took it upon themselves to define
the political objectives of their films and relate these objectives to
specific national situations. Fernando Birri published "Cinema and
Underdevelopment" (1962) and Glauber Rocha wrote a polemical
manifesto entitled "The Aesthetics of Hunger" (1965). Their arguments centered on a politics of representation grounded in the consciousness of underdevelopment.

Appealing to the understanding that "cinema is a cultural product, a product of the superstructure," Fernando Birri wrote that "it
is subject to all the superstructure's distortions. In the case of
cinema these are exacerbated even further than in other arts due to
its nature as an industrial art. In countries like ours, which are in
the throes of incipient industrialization, political shocks make this
condition chronic."[10] Glauber Rocha called for a radical aesthetic
that would subvert the glossy images of a Latin American cinema
that had so far turned its back on the realities of colonization and
underdevelopment. Recognizing that *cinema nôvo* "cannot develop
effectively while it remains marginal to the economic and cultural
processes of the Latin American continent," he argued for a New
Latin American Cinema "belonging to new peoples everywhere and
not a privileged entity of Brazil."[11]

Eventually these political proposals (rather than the formal affinities of national components) were central to the construction of the

identity of the New Latin American Cinema. The impact of these (and other) texts written by Latin American filmmakers for the historical consciousness of the movement does not bear exclusively on their programmatic value. These texts mapped out the discursive engagement of ideology and aesthetics as a necessary condition for revolutionary change. Guided by the desire to transform the established modes of production and reception, filmmakers based their propositions on the conditions affecting their singular national context. By concurrently grafting these instances onto experiences shared by others, filmmakers began a merging process that located their work within a hemispheric context.

The filmmakers of this New Latin American Cinema, unlike those of any other cinematic movement in the history of film, were actively involved in the definition of the movement's genealogy. In 1983 Fernando Birri recalled that the New Latin American Cinema was born because "in the middle of the 50's, in different places in Latin America, a generation of filmmakers was growing up who wanted to provide a reply to some of the problems of the moment, and who brought with them more questions than answers."[12] Films such as *The Charcoal Worker* (Julio García Espinosa and Tomás Gutierrez Alea, Cuba, 1955); *Tire dié* (Fernando Birri, Argentina, 1956), and *Rio, North Zone* (Nelson Pereira dos Santos, Brazil, 1957) provided important terms of reference for the filmmakers and critics of the movement. Seen at the vanguard of a radically new practice, the emblematic value of these films grew well into the 1970s and contributed to the constitution of the New Latin American Cinema.

Birth of a Movement

The year 1967 eventually became a momentous date for the New Latin American Cinema, marking the official emergence of a continental project during the First International Festival of the New Latin American Cinema in Viña del Mar. Headed by Aldo Francia, this festival promoted extensive exchanges between filmmakers from Argentina, Brazil, Bolivia, Cuba, Chile, Uruguay, and Venezuela, most of whom met there for the first time. The round tables that followed the screenings produced the appellation *new cinema.* This term would slightly displace (but not supplant) the national orientation of former debates and articulate them into a continental project. Nationally based initiatives were strengthened insofar as their overall problematic could be fitted into a larger context.[13]

The delegations attending the festival presented reports outlining the historical context of their respective practices at a series of round-table discussions. Given that filmmakers were laboring under similar conditions, they debated sociocultural and political rather than formal issues. Henceforth, the New Latin American Cinema named practices that proposed to revolutionize the cinema by breaking away from the tenets of mainstream national productions. To mark the twentieth anniversary of Viña del Mar, Alfredo Guevara—who attended as a member of the Cuban delegation and director of the Cuban Film Institute (Instituto Cubano del Arte e Industria Cinematográficas, ICAIC)—wrote that after this event "we stopped being independent or marginal filmmakers, promising filmmakers or amateurs experimenting and searching, in order to discover what we were without yet knowing: a new cinema, a *movement*."[14]

The establishment of a socialist state in Cuba in 1960, and later the escalation of anti-imperialist struggles in most Latin American countries, inspired many young Latin Americans. Progressive artists and intellectuals visited Cuba in this period and spearheaded a vast movement of pan–Latin American solidarity.[15] In addition, the Cuban Revolution took on a symbolic value and, in the words of John King, "demonstrated a need for commitment and for political clarity" and represented the possibility "of fusing the artistic and political vanguards."[16] This context explains not only the admiration of the young generation of Latin American filmmakers for Cuban cinema but also the important role that Cuban filmmakers played in the movement's process of self-definition. They actively promoted the term New Cinema of Latin America by initiating critical debates, informal exchanges, and later formal collaborative efforts. At the same time, the movement allowed Cuban filmmakers to break out of the political isolation of the U.S.-imposed blockade against Cuba endorsed by most Latin American countries through the Organization of American States.

The movement's adoption of an anti-imperialist rhetoric was a means of establishing connections between the protosocialist and antibourgeois movements in Latin American countries and the Cuban Revolution. These connections were crucial to the definition of the cultural and political objectives of the New Cinema of Latin America. In the declaration signed by filmmakers at the closing of the Viña del Mar festival, the movement outlined the principles of its revolutionary practice by embracing a pan–Latin American and anticolonial ideology of cultural nationalism. Ambrosio Fornet summarizes the movement's ideological commitment to three basic principles (later ratified in Mérida in 1968) as follows "1) To contribute to the development and reinforcement of national culture and, at the same time, challenge the penetration of imperialist ideology and any other manifestation of cultural colonialism; 2) to assume a continental perspective towards common problems and objectives, struggling for the future integration of a Great Latin American Nation; and 3) to deal critically with the individual and social conflicts of our peoples as a means of raising the consciousness of the popular masses."[17]

The circulation of films beyond national borders furthered a sense of creative solidarity that eventually led to the consolidation of political options. The debates on the continental project of the New Latin American Cinema, initiated at Viña del Mar and pursued at Mérida one year later, were characterized by attempts to systematize the radical aesthetics of the movement. The impulse to prescribe a unique strategy was hampered by the range of options available, particularly because they were grounded in differing contexts and national initiatives.

In 1968 the Argentine documentary *The Hour of the Furnaces* (Fernando Solanas and Octavio Getino, 1965–1968) was given its Latin American premiere at the First Encounter of Latin American Documentary Film, organized by the University of the Andes in Mérida (Venezuela). The showing of this film engaged filmmakers and critics in considering the national peculiarities of Latin American cultural production.[18] A broader strategic realignment included the naming of politically informed aesthetic choices. The terms *cine de denuncia, cine testimonio,* and *cine de agitación,* among others, were coined to signify the distinctive traits of new documentary tendencies that, in the words of Julianne Burton, were becoming increasingly militant in their "search for the underrepresented aspects and underrealized potentials of national-cultural identity."[19]

Although filmmakers had already altered the social modalities of documentary, the New Latin American Cinema—as a movement—provided them with the opportunity to define a radical conceptual framework for their practices. In the next few years, politically motivated documentarists demonstrated the capacity of cinema to mobilize. They would not only define the goals of political documentary but explain its bearing on specific forms of political and cultural struggle. Hence the publication in 1968 of "Towards a Third Cinema" by Argentine filmmakers Fernando Solanas and Octavio Getino. This manifesto was conceived as a critical appendix to their film *The Hour of the Furnaces,* which received its world premiere at the International Festival of New Cinema in Pesaro (Italy).

This festival, held during the spring of 1968, disrupted the usual calm of this holiday resort on the Adriatic coast. As Walter Achugar (a producer and distributor from Uruguay) recalls: "When they screened *The Hour of the Furnaces,* director Fernando Solanas was carried out into the streets on the shoulders of the crowd in a spontaneous demonstration of support. As the festival repeatedly spilled out into the street, there were many confrontations with the police. I remember tearing out telephones and throwing them at the police through the windows of the second story of the festival office. I remember fleeing en masse down the narrow cobbled streets of Pesaro with the police in hot pursuit."[20]

Bolstered by the presence of films in European festivals and the unprecedented cinematographic output by Latin American filmmakers, the movement embarked on an inevitable process of canon formation. Filmmakers and critics retroactively identified, through films produced in different countries from the mid-1950s, the practices that could be seen as prototypical of the New Latin American Cinema. In addition, practices of the films produced in the brief period from 1967 to 1969 were incorporated insofar as they were seen as embodying either the ideals of a Latin American revolution or the achievements of national cinemas.

Furthermore, the movement sought to establish a distinctive critical vocabulary. Terms such as *imperialism* and *decolonization* were used in the manifestos and declarations written, and collectively signed, by filmmakers. These terms confirmed the movement's explicit endorsement of insurgent tactics and radical-left politics. Filmmakers viewed cinema as an ideological agent and rejected standard assumptions about filmmaking as a nonpartisan activity, as entertainment. At the same time, filmmakers adopted terms such as "third cinema," "imperfect cinema," and "aesthetics of hunger," taken from the manifestos written by Fernando Solanas and Octavio Getino, Julio García Espinosa, and Glauber Rocha respectively. Although these terms originated within specific contexts and nationalist options, they were used as all-encompassing categories, capable of accounting for the ideological and aesthetic characteristics of the movement.[21] Confronted with a new cultural phenomenon, film practitioners in Latin America engaged in what Ambrosio Fornet has called a "taxonomic fever" that was not exempt from polemics.[22]

The establishment of a critical nomenclature and a cinematographic canon provided a general framework to the movement's pancontinental project. While the particularities of national tendencies or movements were made explicit in some of the documents of the New Latin American Cinema, this aspect was not always clearly articulated. In a sense, the anti-imperialist and pan-nationalist rhetoric used by practitioners and critics associated with the movement did not always adequately reflect the movement's project of acknowledging, rather than overruling, the political and cultural agendas of particular national tendencies or movements.

In 1969, when Viña del Mar hosted the Second Festival of New Cinema, the screening of *The Hour of the Furnaces* prompted discord as well as solidarity. During the round-table sessions, some of the objections raised to the labeling of exemplary practices were not necessarily signs of dissent but appeals for the recognition of differences. As Hans Ehrmann wrote at the time, some of the attending Chilean filmmakers selected Raúl Ruiz as their spokesperson to argue against the political dogmatism of some interventions.[23] These filmmakers were disinclined to endorse a cinema exclusively based on partisan action. The feature films of the Chilean *nuevo cine* shown in Viña del Mar, such as *The Jackal of Nahueltoro* (Miguel Littín, 1968), *Valparaíso mi amor* (Aldo Francia, 1968), and *Three Sad Tigers* (Raúl Ruiz, 1969), incorporated a variety of strategies which represented a variety of options, rather than a unique agenda, for political change.[24]

The film program of the Viña del Mar festival of 1969 was far more extensive than that of 1967 with 110 short films and features representing ten countries, including a large selection of Chilean films. Some of these films became the cornerstones of the movement's canon.[25] These films also demonstrated that, in addition to the overwhelming strength of Cuban revolutionary cinema or the Brazilian *cinema nôvo*, other modes of militant cinema were emerging in countries where production was more modest. As a result, filmmakers began to address a range of problems that were seen as reflecting both the contemporary and historical underdevelopment of cinematic practices in Latin America. As John King points out, these were some of the questions that filmmakers confronted: "the development of cinema under the auspices of a socialist state; the relationship between film-makers and the state in a dependent capitalist context; the problems not only of production in conditions of scarcity, but also the possibility of either entering the established distribution and exhibition networks or creating alternative structures for dissemination. . . ."[26]

In addition, as the movement expanded, the filmmakers themselves recognized the need to engage in the heightened sociopolitical tensions that played themselves out in the cultural arena. Not only were filmmakers prepared to turn their cameras toward the dark side of underdevelopment and neocolonialism, denouncing their effects and causes through their films. They also questioned the illusion of progress and democracy, scrutinizing the realities of discourses that benefited few but disenfranchised the majority of Latin Americans. In their films, Latin American filmmakers celebrated class struggle, recalling past and present victories and defeats, and looked toward the people themselves as the revolutionary vanguard. To make a film "with an idea in the head and a camera in hand," as Glauber Rocha said, also implied transforming the modes of production and reception of cinema. Adopting new ways of communication either to attract viewers accustomed to mainstream cinemas or audiences only occasionally exposed to film, Latin American filmmakers were searching to make cinema a tool of social criticism.

Thus, filmmakers in the various countries began establishing mechanisms to project their work into the social fabric, to transform their cinema into a popular, revolutionary, and collective practice. The movement served to promote the radical cinematic strategies adopted by filmmakers and provided these same filmmakers with a sense of community and history in which they could recognize themselves. But ultimately the New Cinema of Latin America organized a discursive field whereby processes of politization and historical reevaluation could converge in a rhetoric of cultural nationalism and continental revolution. In other words, the movement provided a site where cinema could, as I have written elsewhere, "through the politization of culture . . . increase national awareness and collective values. A 'decolonized aesthetic' originated in the affirmation of living traditions."[27]

State Intervention and Growth

From 1967 on, the films of the New Latin American Cinema reflected the cultural and political fortunes of the continent, and by 1969 the political effects of the movement began to be felt in opposing ways. Cinema in Cuba, the only socialist country in Latin America, celebrated the achievements of its first decade in 1969. The most innovative practitioners of the *cinema nôvo* in Brazil were stifled by the repressive measures instituted by the military that seized power in 1964.[28] Yet individual filmmakers were using cinema—and documentary in particular—to register the effervescence and reversals of political processes in different countries, not only in their own.[29] But as Ambrosio Fornet points out, these filmmakers "clearly saw in [these processes] the expressions of the same continental will."[30]

By 1970 the New Latin American Cinema had already established itself as a revolutionary cinema. Focusing on a limited, but expanding, and remarkable body of films, Latin American filmmakers associated with the movement had defined the movement's critical referents and strategies. While the New Cinema of Latin America served as a rallying point for a community of practitioners who in different countries shared similar concerns, the movement's capacity to sustain this creative and political energy was channeled through different groups and organizations.

In the subsequent three years, the intercontinental effects of the movement began to be felt as films circulated in Europe and North America, and filmmakers obtained crucial support from organizations outside the region. The notoriety of the movement also paid off in regard to production. In Europe, RAI-TV (the Italian state-run broadcasting system) co-produced a series of films entitled Latin America Seen by Its Filmmakers with Edgardo Pallero (Argentina) and Walter Achugar (Uruguay) as managing producers. Changes in the political climate meant that, of the six films initially projected, only one was completed as planned. This film was *The Courage of the People* (Jorge Sanjinés and Ukamau Group, Bolivia, 1971).[31]

Notwithstanding the auspicious mood that inaugurated the second decade of the movement, warning signs of uncertainty were not far behind. The effervescence surrounding the election of Salvador Allende—and the cinematographic policies established by the Popular Unity government—brought hope for the burgeoning *nuevo cine* until most of the Chilean filmmakers were forced into exile after the military coup of 1973.[32] Although the exile of Chilean filmmakers was probably the most dramatic example of the power that right-wing military regimes were intent on using to dismantle all forms of opposition, filmmakers in other countries were equally affected by political repression.

The New Latin American Cinema reacted as a movement by setting up solidarity committees (in collaboration with progressive groups in Europe and North America) and establishing support systems like the Committee of Latin American Filmmakers. Constituted in Caracas during a meeting of filmmakers in 1974, this committee reiterated the movement's ideological stand, its commitment to the popular struggles of the continent. It denounced the widespread use of torture and the disappearance of filmmakers like Jorge Müller and Carmen Bueno (Chile, 1974) and Raymundo Gleyzer and Rodolfo Walsh (Argentina, 1976).

To counter the negative impact of events upon the nationally based components of the New Latin American Cinema, distribution companies were set up by producers and filmmakers living in exile. The first attempts at comprehensive distribution date from this period. Dicimoveca (headed by Edmundo Aray, Carlos Rebolledo, and Walter Achugar) and Palcine (founded by Sergio Trabucco, a Chilean exile) in Venezuela, later Cineal (established by Walter Achugar) and Primer Plano in Spain and Zafra in Mexico, expanded the initiative begun by the Cinemateca del Tercer Mundo in Uruguay (1969–1972). In addition, Tricontinental Films (later renamed Unifilm), a company established by Gino Lofredo and Rodi and Carlos Broullon, began distributing Latin American films in the United States.[33]

In addition, filmmakers and critics met while attending film festivals in Europe. They also had the opportunity to get together in Latin America during special events highlighting either specific national productions (like Cuba) or special retrospectives of Latin American cinema. Responsible for the coordination of these meetings were some of the most visible members of the movement.[34] These gatherings provided the opportunity to ratify the movement's commitment to a pan–Latin American agenda. The circulation of the movement's self-defined agenda, either by its practitioners or supporters in Latin America and elsewhere, in the Americas and Europe had several purposes. It served to publicize the movement, generate a sense of community, collaboration, and solidarity, and disseminate the films of Latin America at a time when many filmmakers and critics were living in exile.

The effect of political events on the movement was felt most apparently as the exile of filmmakers and the breakup of collectives altered the interrelationship between producers and audiences. Jorge Sanjinés, for instance, continued working and developing the revolutionary strategies of a popular cinema in other Latin American countries. He produced The Principal Enemy (1973) in Peru, Get Out of Here! (1976) in Ecuador, and That's Enough (1979) in Colombia. Although Sanjinés had to reconstitute a filmmaking collective, his efforts were underwritten by the political legitimacy of the New Latin American Cinema.

The cohesion manifested by the movement, the intent to construct an organic link between cultural practice and political action, was challenged between 1973 and 1979. As Paulo-Antonio Paranagua suggests, this period signals the beginning of major structural changes for the New Latin American Cinema as it faced the contradictory effects of "dictatorial repression and state sponsorship."[35] In order to maintain a sense of purpose at the continental level, the movement had to negotiate the effect of institutional changes on its historical framework.

This aspect of the movement's evolution can be understood only in relation to the historical peculiarities of its formation. The community of filmmakers—who were part of the New Latin American Cinema—had sought to theorize, since the movement's inception in 1967, the interrelationship between representation and social change, cultural practices, and historical and social processes. As a self-defining community, the filmmakers of the New Latin American Cinema remained committed to this self-imposed mandate: to engage in the changing conditions of cinematographic production both in their own countries and elsewhere in Latin America.

The "dirty war" (in Argentina, Chile, and Uruguay, but also in Colombia) and the tactics used by the military to silence dissent (in Bolivia, Brazil, and Uruguay) forced a redefinition of strategies. In the mid-1970s the institutional framework of the movement was altered by the conditions confronted by filmmakers working in the different countries. The chronic vulnerability of Latin American film industries—sharpened by political uncertainty and more or less lengthy periods of reentrenchment—led to changes in modes of production.

The most important infrastructural changes took place in Brazil, where policies first proposed in the 1960s were activated in the 1970s. In 1972 the Brazilian military regime established a state-funded organization with a mandate to produce, distribute, and exhibit the national cinema. Roberto Farias, the chosen candidate of the *cinema nôvo* group, became the first director of Embrafilme. This first step was followed by an increase in exhibition quotas, according to a nationalist model that had already been established in the 1940s during the government of Getulio Vargas.[36]

The independent Brazilian filmmakers who had been part of the *cinema nôvo* (with the exception of Glauber Rocha, then in exile in Europe) took advantage of the policies established by Embrafilme. In spite of the political limitations of the period, the former members of the *cinema nôvo* pursued their activity. Yet major directors were affected by the whimsical verdicts of the Brazilian censorship board and saw their films delayed by long legal battles as a result of their critical outlook on the effects of right-wing policies during the military regime. Moreover, the diversity of films produced suggested a radical rearrangement of cinematic strategies earlier proposed by *cinema nôvo*. This production suggested a relative permanence of the principles espoused by *cinema nôvo* and the New Latin American Cinema in the 1960s, while the conditions of production placed this cinema within a renewed institutional framework.[37]

In Argentina filmmakers had to contend with the fluctuating policies of the Peronist party during a brief period of political stability. While attempting to combine the militant principles defined in *The*

Hour of the Furnaces (1965–1968) with the nationalist motivations of Perón's second presidency, the agenda of Argentine cinema temporarily reconverged with the New Latin American Cinema. Given the exile of the major figures of the movement, and the ambivalent conditions under which national practices were developing, this convergence validated the continental project of the New Latin American Cinema. After the military coup of 1976, filmmakers sought a reprieve from stringent censorship regulations in the adaptation of literary works.[38] While Rodolfo Walsh and Raymundo Gleyzer disappeared and were (presumably) assassinated, Jorge Cedrón, Octavio Getino, Fernando Solanas, and Gerardo Vallejo were forced into exile.[39]

The New Latin American Cinema saw the emergence of a dynamic cinema in exile, particularly in the work of Chilean filmmakers. This cinema in exile would become the sole representative of Chilean cinema until a nonofficial production inside Chile emerged slowly in the late 1970s.[40] The military assumed control of censorship and abolished all modalities of state support for the cinema. Amid the extreme repressiveness of the regime, filmmaking activity was further restricted by free-market policies that eroded the systems of distribution and exhibition. Video production eventually grew and its circulation was guaranteed by alternative networks set up to provide an oppositional space for cultural expression.

In Cuba the highly innovational period of filmmaking in the late 1960s was followed by a period of theoretical self-questioning after the publication of Julio García Espinosa's "For an Imperfect Cinema" (1969). The patterns of production set up in 1959 by the Cuban Film Institute provided a relatively stable environment for the creative development of the movement's only socialist cinema, to which the years after 1969 brought a relative thematic and stylistic diversification.[41]

In other countries, the conditions fluctuated between important breakthroughs or relative progress. In Venezuela, on the one hand, new financing structures opened the way for greater autonomy for local producers-directors and promoted the slow development of a feature film industry while encouragement for alternative forms of filmmaking (such as the documentary) was entrusted to university-based groups. Thus, filmmakers, critics, and academics were in a position to take on an important number of projects, some of which—as I have already pointed out—were directly related to supporting the New Cinema of Latin America. In Mexico, on the other hand, the nationalization of the film industry (under the aegis of the National Bank of Cinematography) brought about an author-oriented production represented by Felipe Cazals, Jaime Humberto Hermosillo, Alberto Isaac, Paul Leduc, and Arturo Ripstein, among others, until succeeding government policies devastated the gains made between 1971 and 1976. The fate of socially conscious cinemas in these countries was activated by the newfound prosperity of petro-dollars and depended on the inherent ambiguity of state legislation.

The government-initiated measures would have important strategical effects on the ongoing development of the New Latin American Cinema. The enlarged heterogeneity of nationally based cinemas, particularly in terms of alternative practices, was the result of institutional realignments. To the extent that film legislation was established, the lobbying efforts of filmmakers—motivated by political rather than financial considerations—were finally paying off. Monetary incentives and funds reallocated by taxation of box-office revenue benefited national producers. Resources for film production (including publicity), made available through private investors, streamlined the financial base of cinema and contributed to increase production. Although screens were still occupied by foreign films, national films gained audience exposure through exhibition quotas. Independent filmmakers worked within a more or less solid production and distribution infrastructure. In this context, nationally based initiatives sought to reconcile their aims within changing sociocultural environments.

This institutional realignment affected the New Latin American Cinema. Given that the debates on national cinemas were increasingly framed by concerns developed within the movement, cultural nationalist issues would in turn reactivate the process of canon formation. Consequently, the filmmakers of the New Latin American Cinema began broadening the conceptual framework of the movement, reclaiming the historical processes that had shaped its development.

By the end of the 1970s, the New Latin American Cinema had expanded its self-chosen mandate. If the anti-imperialist rhetoric was less prominent in the manifestos and declarations, the movement saw itself as having produced "millions of meters of celluloid on which our contemporary history, as a mobilizing agency capable of forging consciousness, is imprinted."[42]

Turning Point and Consolidation

In the 1980s filmmakers and critics sought to assert the movement's distinctiveness and dispel concerns about an aesthetic crisis. While

films appeared to deviate from the oppositional options and the socialist rhetoric characteristic of the 1960s, filmmakers were determined to use the cinema to address the always-provisional and unfolding histories of the continent. The extensive growth of the
movement and the move toward semi-industrial modes of production within some of its national components puzzled some of its
most committed supporters.[43] Seeking to address accusations about
the movement's decline in 1982, Ambrosio Fornet asked this question: "Has the New Cinema, deadlocked, restricted itself to use
these new resources to restate the same ideas, or is [the movement],
conscious of its limitations, trying to renovate its language without
betraying its objectives?"[44]

The International Festival of the New Latin American Cinema in
Havana and the Cuban Film Institute would play a pivotal role in
what I have chosen to call a process of consolidation. This yearly
event, hosted and organized by the Cuban Film Institute, was an
important turning point for the movement. Between 1979 and 1991
filmmakers, producers, and critics from Latin America have met to
celebrate the achievements of the New Latin American Cinema (and
later television and video) and promote discussion and cross-cultural exchanges.

The first festival, held in 1979, consisted of a retrospective programming of films and a series of seminars. Designed in part to measure the developments of the decade, it took place only months after
the victory of the Sandinistas in Nicaragua. The historical awareness of the movement was heightened by the presence of filmmakers from the Nicaraguan Institute of Cinematography who added
their youthful voices to those of veteran directors such as Fernando
Birri, Nelson Pereira dos Santos, Julio García Espinosa, Miguel Littín, and Glauber Rocha. Alfredo Guevara, founding director of the
Cuban Film Institute, addressed the audience at the closing of the
festival in the following terms:

> The New Latin American cinema has proven in its festival that
> it rightfully belongs to the marvellous tide that rises from our
> national cultures. Not from the bourgeois culture but from the
> culture of its struggling peoples; no matter in what context, or in
> what level of its modalities of struggle. The New Latin American
> Cinema belongs rightfully to that marvellous tide, let me repeat,
> of the rebirth of our artistic culture which is one and diverse,
> popular and epic, picaresque and militant, tormented and rebel-
> lious, testimonial and apocalyptic, but also and without losing
> its popular characteristics, naturally sumptuous and astonishing.

It is in that creole culture, born of the "mestizaje" of ancient civilizations that converged precisely at the moment of their utmost splendor, that the New Latin American cinema grounds its roots.[45]

Confronted with an increasingly diverse production, the movement had to accommodate the diversity of its national components once again. Latin America's *mestizo* essence, invoked by Guevara, would become a powerful symbol of solidarity for the movement. It called attention to the diversity of the movement, served to counteract the adverse conditions faced by filmmakers in the 1970s, and reasserted the political resolve of a movement.[46]

As filmmakers sought to pursue their cultural-political project, the Havana festival became the primary forum for a series of debates. These debates were increasingly centered on the need to evaluate the changing context of Latin American filmmaking through a simultaneous interest in broader technological, institutional, and cultural determinants. The ideological realignment of the New Latin American Cinema (which began in the 1970s and continued into the 1980s) was an infrastructural accommodation, a controlled response to changes within its national components. Unable to resolve the ambiguous relationship between the movement's continental agenda and the nationally based projects to develop an appropriate industrial foundation, Latin American filmmakers debated the paradox of integrating partial solutions into an overall continental project.[47]

Furthermore, practitioners and supporters (filmmakers and critics, and more recently administrators, festival organizers, and curators) who met in Havana contributed to the movement's projection inside and outside Latin America, cemented its aesthetic canon, and reinforced its historical relevance. The festival also provided the opportunity for expanded international contacts, increased coproductions, and dissemination through specialized programming and retrospectives that have given an unprecedented exposure to Latin American films and videos.

The process of consolidation, then, needs to be understood in terms of the three basic trends that characterized this decade. These trends served concurrently to solidify the movement's history and respond to changing conditions. The filmmakers and supporters of the New Latin American Cinema undertook to strengthen existing pan-continental organizations (and to establish new ones), to reassess current practices in light of historical forms of cinematic production, and to regulate the movement's diversity through support of new agendas and negotiation of complex infrastructural ambiguities.

The movement's agenda was sustained by a growing number of organizations, some enlarging already-defined objectives and others responding to new issues and concerns. The role of the Committee of Latin American Filmmakers, for example, was broadened to promote communication by including filmmakers from all countries. Through its most prominent members, the committee formalized exchanges and supported retrospectives of films that were no longer easily accessible. The films produced by Fernando Birri—including his work at the Documentary Film School of Santa Fé—began touring European and Latin American cities in 1980 (often accompanied by the filmmaker himself) after new copies were struck in Havana at the Cuban Film Institute.

In this period, the movement also set out to solidify its infrastructure. The International Festival of the New Latin American Cinema in Havana provided regular contacts and set the stage for the establishment of intercontinental organizations designed to support existing structures. The Federation of Alternative Distributors of Latin America and the Caribbean (FEDALC—Federación de Distribuidoras Alternativas de América Latina y el Caribe) was set up in 1985 in Havana during a meeting of distributors sponsored by the Havana festival. The objective of this group was to generate strategies for the circulation and development of cinematographic culture.

The Latin American Cinematographic Association (ACLA—Asociación Cinematográfica Latinoamericana) was formally set up in August of 1984 in Cartagena (Colombia) and ratified one month later in Madrid during the Second Meeting of Latin American Cinema, sponsored by the General Directory of Cinema of the Spanish Ministry of Culture. The document that established this organization was signed by the directors of government-funded film agencies from Argentina (Manuel Antín), Cuba (Jorge Fraga), Mexico (Alberto Isaac and Fernando Macotela), Brazil (Roberto Parreira), Colombia (Marino Tadeo Henao Ospinosa), Venezuela (Rodolfo Porro Aletti), and Panama (Pedro Rivera). The objective of this association, with headquarters in Bogotá (Colombia), was to create permanent conditions to facilitate and increase cooperative ventures for production, distribution, and exhibition of Latin American films.[48]

Simultaneously, the Foundation of the New Latin American Cinema was established in 1985 in Havana, as an extension of the Committee of Latin American Filmmakers. Presided over by Gabriel García Márquez, one of the first activities of this foundation was the publication of *Hojas del Cine,* a three-part collection of documents and manifestos. Its most ambitious undertaking was the establishment of the Film and Television School of the Three Worlds at San Antonio de los Baños near Havana in 1986. Initially directed by Fernando Birri and later headed by Orlando Senna (Brazil), this school was set up as a training place for young filmmakers from Asia, Africa, and Latin America.

In a sense, the institutionalization of the New Latin American Cinema brought a great deal of optimism, but, at the same time, the cinemas of Latin America were still susceptible to political and economic uncertainty. Thus, as B. Ruby Rich points out, by the late 1980s filmmakers faced a situation characterized by "local markets that can no longer return the investment necessary for late-1980s budgets, plans that require international stars and co-production money to get off the ground, movie theaters that are closing down by the hundreds as a combination of videocassette distribution and operating costs make them unprofitable."[49]

In this context, co-productions with Television Española provided the financial impetus, among others, to the series *Difficult Loves* (*Amores difíciles*), based on screenplays by Gabriel García Márquez, and films like *Barroco* (Paul Leduc, Mexico, 1989) and *Sandino* (Miguel Littín, Spain, 1990). Yet the conditions within which most of this production emerged were the result of more disturbing trends. To quote B. Ruby Rich again: "In tracing the kind of strategies that have become necessary in the wake of the declining film economies of Latin America and the loss of self-sufficiency they have brought about, I would describe as significant the recent alliance between a traditional, essentially conservative, form of authorship and a traditional, international form of co-production."[50]

Still, the New Cinema of Latin America was seen by some filmmakers as providing an aesthetic agenda capable of prevailing over infrastructural drawbacks. In 1988 Octavio Getino pointed out that transformative practices were those capable of "recuperating our legitimate right to cultural plurality" through "experiments by communities and individuals to express themselves in difference, according to their authentic needs and characteristics."[51] If emphasis on cultural diversity served—in the wake of redemocratization—to stress the transformative agency of the movement's cultural practices, there was evidence by the end of the 1980s that it was no longer business as usual for the New Latin American Cinema.

As in previous stages, national projects continued being incorporated into the movement. But this time, critics and academics played an important role. In the 1980s the national components of the New Latin American Cinema were being dynamically reevaluated through historical research. The archival activity undertaken in different countries, for instance, energized national cinemas' traditions while simultaneously increasing the awareness of regional connections and developmental similarities. National cinematheques located and restored films by directors such as José A. Ferreyra (Argentina), Humberto Mauro, Mario Peixoto and Carmen Santos (Brazil), and Fernando de Fuentes and Matilde Landeta (Mexico). This formidable enterprise was severely handicapped but not halted by the fires that destroyed the SODRE archives in Montevideo (late 1960s), the Cinematheque of São Paulo (1977), and the National Cinematheque of Mexico (1979). But a new generation of archivists, academics and critics with university training has begun to rewrite the histories of cinema in Latin America and of previously disparaged popular works.[52]

International festivals and exhibitions continued to play an important role in chronicling and sustaining the New Latin American Cinema. Major retrospectives of Latin American film were mounted in North America and Europe. "The Winds of Change" retrospective was organized by Helga Stephenson and Piers Handling at the Toronto Festival of Festivals (1986) and "Latin American Visions" was organized by Neighborhood Film and Video Project director Linda Blackaby with the assistance of Beatriz Viera at the International House in Philadelphia (1989–1990). In 1988–1989 Rosa Bosch mounted an unprecedented series of Latin American programs for the National Film Theater in London, and in 1987, 1990, and 1992, respectively, Paulo Antonio Paranagua coordinated major Brazilian, Cuban, and Mexican retrospectives at the Centre Georges Pompidou in Paris.[53]

While endorsing the infrastructural shifts in countries with major production capabilities, the New Latin American Cinema incorporated during this decade different strategies of social, cultural, and political organization. The movement facilitated the growth of cinematic practices empowered by Latin American culture, although they are situated outside its geographical boundaries. The integration of a cinema of social inquiry made by Chicano filmmakers in the United States and by filmmakers from Puerto Rico, for instance, reinstated debates on cultural dependence prevalent within the movement in its earliest years.[54]

The emergence of cinematic approaches that remain, as before, marginal to the mainstream agendas of national cinemas challenged (without necessarily endangering) the historical project of the New Latin American Cinema. If the processes of redemocratization in Argentina, Bolivia, Brazil, and Uruguay in the mid-1980s (and more recently in El Salvador and Chile) revived certain national cinematographies, these processes also contributed to the reemergence of practices organized around new social movements. The climate leading to the end of military rule allowed video collectives, for instance, to play an important role by creating alternative information networks or supporting groups, including women, to organize themselves outside the traditional venues for cultural and political action.[55]

In this period, women filmmakers and video collectives played a major role, and their work represented new challenges for the movement. The presence of María Luisa Bemberg (Argentina), Tizuka Yamasaki and Ana Carolina (Brazil), Marcela Fernández-Violante (Mexico), and Solveig Hoogesteijn and Fina Torres (Venezuela)—to name a few—within their respective national contexts signaled an important generational development. The practices of women's video collectives, like Group Cine-Mujer in Colombia, reflected former initiatives based on nonhierarchical modes of production and reception.[56] The incorporation of women's issues also opened the way for renewed representations of gender, challenging the deferred debates on the significance of feminism as a political practice within the New Latin American Cinema.

Thus a new generation of film and video-makers, particularly women, presented a substantial challenge to the movement because the agenda of this new generation has evolved at the margins of traditional politics and outside the anti-imperialist rhetoric of cultural nationalism of the 1960s. Through their films and videos, this generation addressed the relevance of the personal to relocate activism away and beyond the public space of partisan politics. As B. Ruby Rich points out, "In this new environment, a cinema which turns inward and which begins to enable viewers to construct an alternate relationship—not only with their government but with an authentic sense of self—is an indispensable element in the evolution of a new sociopolitical environment. Slogans, pamphlets, and organizing have been key to political change; character, identity, empathy, and, most importantly, a sense of personal agency, now are of equal importance to political evolution."[57]

Inasmuch as these new film and video practices have been inadequately programmed in the Havana festival, it seemed that the movement had chosen to sidestep some of the substantive implications of this ideological and rhetorical shift. During the 1987 Havana festival, as the New Latin American Cinema set out to celebrate the twentieth anniversary of the Viña del Mar festival, veteran filmmakers determined to promote the movement's historical status were faced with dissenting (and maybe more pragmatic) perspectives expressed by younger filmmakers.[58]

Still faced with self-questioning, and amid what Pat Aufderheide terms a "rhetorical and ideological crisis," many of the older film-makers were reluctant to respond to this challenge. Confronted with institutional and economic disruptions, and seeing the sociopolitical goals of the New Latin American Cinema jeopardized by the ever-recurring climates of crisis affecting the continent, practitioners reacted by neither rejecting its history nor its ideological agenda. Some filmmakers, like Paul Leduc, were willing to seek for new answers while maintaining the belief in a cinema capable of "affirming our culture and our language. Daring the encounter with our originality—and with reality, the profound relationship with what happens to us and what entertains, afflicts or liberates us."[59]

Although the heated debates left genuine (or perceived) concerns unresolved, the institutionalization issue was primarily addressed both in terms of generational and infrastructural differences. As Julianne Burton pointed out in a paper she read during the 1987 festival, filmmakers who had once produced at the margins were now making films from within mainstream cinematographic organizations. Arguing for the inevitability of this process, she also pointed out that a new generation was again working at the fringes of existing institutions, challenging the former opposition.[60]

The increase of co-productions (some envisaged as palliative solutions to decreased funding or shrinking audiences) reflected the financial and technological restructuring of film industries throughout the capitalist world. Yet the movement was being most affected by shifts in political perspectives and the broadening of audiovisual practices. If practitioners and supporters of the New Latin American Cinema may have felt that in the 1980s anything was possible, the new phase of continental solidarity (announced by Alfredo Guevara in 1979) eventually brought the realization, as Aufderheide writes, that "the groundwork laid in a more overtly political era made possible . . . institutionalization and production. However, it has not provided aesthetic or economic options for the future."[61]

Throughout this chapter I have argued for a historical approach to the New Latin American Cinema that relates its continental scope to nationally based initiatives—in other words, an approach that takes into account intersecting processes whereby the organizational fluidity of diverse national cinemas merges with a politically and culturally unified sense of purpose. Insofar as the movement's growth has been influenced by the institutions established to sustain its project, those institutions constitute—together with the autonomous developments of its national components—the network of structures and strategies that mediate Latin American cinematic practices.

Furthermore, the capacity of the movement to sustain itself (in spite of organizational and ideological realignments) suggests that the changes that were affecting the New Latin American Cinema in 1987, as Patricia Aufderheide writes, "mark the end of a historical process (and remind critics and theorists that it *was* a historical process). They also show the vitality and flexibility of cultural nationalism as a rhetorical strategy, and therefore to some degree an overarching way of understanding Latin American production as it changes in tenor and style."[62]

Creativity and Social Intervention

Auteur criticism, in its most widespread forms, has served to clarify the relationship between the personality and the work of a given director. The premises of auteur criticism evolved throughout the 1950s. Notwithstanding critiques which marginalized the author as creative subject in favor of theories of representation and signification, I would like to analyze the place that authorial considerations hold within the New Latin American Cinema.

The early stages of development of the New Latin American Cinema (preceding the first festival in Viña del Mar in 1967) coincided with the most productive period of European and North American auteur criticism. The distinctive features of the movement's productions, in particular because filmmakers were scriptwriters as well as producers, appeared to suit the critical views in François Truffaut's initial article on authorship in the cinema.[1] The films of Luis Buñuel (Mexico) and Leopoldo Torre Nilsson (Argentina), circulating throughout Europe and North America in the late 1950s and early 1960s, were evaluated exclusively in biographical and aesthetic terms.

But when a more diversified group of Latin American directors caught the attention of European critics, this approach proved less appropriate. These Latin American practitioners declared their sociopolitical intent, discouraging a method of appraisal exclusively based on aesthetics. During a film festival held in Mérida (Venezuela) in 1968, the Venezuelan critic Oswaldo Capriles pointed out that "in his contact with this New Latin American cinema, the film critic cannot forget that he confronts an emerging phenomenon. A new cinema: new in the means used by its directors, new in its practice, new because of the attitude of the young filmmakers, new in relation to the prevalent Latin American cinematographic production."[2]

Conventional forms of auteur criticism have centered on films and individual directors, on what Julianne Burton has called "discrete practices," overlooking all those other aspects of production that localize cinema as a "sociopolitical practice."[3] In other words, while European and North American auteur criticism weighted the value of art above sociological mediation, the New Latin American Cinema sought to reverse this traditional "segregation of labor." Latin American filmmakers contested the traditional premises of authorship and modified them to suit their own endeavor.

Authorship and Cultural Militancy

The oppositional strategies of the New Latin American Cinema were directed by the need to challenge the mainstream mechanisms of cinematographic production and reception. The political agenda of the movement underscored the pivotal role of social engagement over creativity and individual expression so that, from the outset, filmmakers clarified their own role as initiators of change and proposed modes of creative militancy that suited contemporary conditions. While filmmakers questioned the traditional ties between artist and society, the New Latin American Cinema armed itself with a new critical framework and found imaginative ways of shifting the agency of meaning away from the exclusive alliance of director and text. Through a revitalized understanding of human agency, the movement provided itself with a strong conceptual base from which it launched into a radical transformation of cinematic practices. The blueprint for the framework was sketched out in a series of critical texts and manifestos written by the filmmakers themselves. Although these texts were conceived to respond specifically to conditions affecting national cinematic practices, some of their premises were later incorporated into the continental agenda of the movement. In the opening section of *A Critical Revision of Brazilian Cinema*, for instance, written by Glauber Rocha in 1963, the earliest attempts by a Latin American filmmaker to place authorship into politics can be detected. In an attempt to redraw the terms of reference for the development of Brazilian cinema, Rocha appropriated the polemical article written by François Truffaut. However, he underscored the bonds between cultural practice and economic underdevelopment. As Julianne Burton has pointed out, "*La política de los autores* was more directly translated and translatable as a practical-strategical position (simultaneously a 'policy' and a 'politics')."[4]

The early acclaim gained by *cinema nôvo* films in Europe did not shield its filmmakers from debates raging at home. They found themselves actively engaged in formulating progressive policies aimed at the development of national culture. In his study of the Brazilian film industry, Randal Johnson has pointed out that in its early stages *cinema nôvo* evolved around debates "to create an authentic, national, critical consciousness of the country's underdevelopment and its causes."[5] The nationalist position taken by *cinema nôvo* eventually led to a tense, and sometimes contradictory, relationship between the filmmakers and the state, although both supported the need to establish mechanisms to sustain a national film production.

In order to extricate authorship from its purely aesthetic function, Rocha propelled this concept into cultural politics. Addressing style as an instance capable of exposing available production resources, he drew on the achievements of Italian neorealism and its relative autonomy from the institutions that controlled filmmaking in Italy during the war. Neorealism represented a useful model insofar as artisanal modes of production could guarantee the creative freedom that directors working in the industry could never enjoy. Therefore, Rocha praised the films of Humberto Mauro and Mario Peixoto (in the 1930s) and Nelson Pereira dos Santos (in the 1950s), endorsing them as historical models for an authentic Brazilian auteur cinema.

Although these films epitomized the marginality of artistic practice in underdeveloped countries, their authors embodied the vital connection between cultural politics and aesthetic innovation that *cinema nôvo* was seeking to activate. Rocha favored a politics of authorship that allowed him to probe the historical contradictions of Brazilian cinema, relocating its problematic in social relations rather than limiting authorship to expressive agency. In the midst of a highly volatile political situation that eventually led to the 1964 military coup, Rocha wrote that "the problems of our industry, in our contemporary historical period, are the same as those experienced by other productive sectors and by the working class in Brazil. . . . The sole task of Brazilian authors, if they are to subsist as a class, is to struggle against an industry before it consolidates altogether."[6]

Hence Rocha saw that a politics of authorship cannot be divorced from the dynamics of cultural struggle. He placed authorship at the center of an oppositional practice capable of contesting the thematics and politics of modernization and nationalization. The filmmaker wanted to ensure the survival of Brazilian cinema within the area of nationalist-cultural politics. One of the most remarkable aspects of *A Critical Revision of Brazilian Cinema* is Rocha's critical study of Brazilian filmmaking. He was particularly hostile toward directors, like Alberto Cavalcanti, who had attempted to develop cinematic production exclusively along industrial lines.[7] Therefore Rocha's attempt to validate an artisanal and collaborative mode of production was a means to resolve the historical contradictions of Brazilian cinema in the early 1960s.

Whereas traditional views on authorship validated individualism, the New Latin American Cinema has sought to transform authorship through the intersecting operations of aesthetics and politics, of creative process and social relations. The movement problematized the institutional framework of cinema, debating its social and cultural function. In critical terms the movement has never been an outright rejection of authorship but rather an acknowledgment of the author as only one instance within the diverse range of elements that mediate cinematographic practice and cultural production.

From that perspective, I would like to argue that authorship in the New Latin American Cinema has come to constitute a critical map operating across a variety of fields in a nonhierarchical manner. To "create a revolutionary cinema" was probably the most resolute slogan of the movement. It came to epitomize calls for a radical practice capable of breaking from dominant modes of filmmaking modeled on Hollywood cinema. Often misunderstood as a utopian and prescriptive formulation, the process of creating a revolutionary cinema was anchored in a joint engagement of subjective and collective positions.

Bearing on diverse mechanisms of intervention and fostering links between filmmaker and spectator, between ideology and social change, revolutionary cinema was conceived as always open, never complete. Therefore, authorship has played an important role in the development of the movement and has constituted an axiomatic center of its intervention in the social field. To the extent that the cinematic practices of the movement have attempted to disengage themselves from cumbersome notions of creativity, it might be useful to retrace this process in order to understand how the New Latin American Cinema has succeeded in this endeavor.

The Discovery of Self and Other: *The Brickmakers*

Although the New Latin American Cinema is primarily a continental project for the renewal of cinematic practices, it is arguable that discussions on particular issues (like authorship) have been generated from within regional and local experiences. From its earliest stages, filmmakers of the movement sought to operate in close contact with viewers. After the experiences of the Documentary Film School of Santa Fé in 1962, for instance, Fernando Birri stated that creative militancy required close ties with an audience, "or more precisely, [a] class of audience, in the economic and historical sense of the term—for whom we are making our films."[8] In "Cinema and Underdevelopment" Birri argued that cinema's revolutionary potential rests on the displacement of mechanisms that traditionally restricted its social function. He stressed that only a critical disclosure of social relations could account for those aspects of reality that have been systematically concealed by mainstream practices.

By the time "Cinema and Underdevelopment" was published, the politicized tendencies of Latin American documentarists were characterized by a search for a socially responsible cinematic model. As Julianne Burton remarked, "The common thread linking all these efforts is the will to 'de-alienate' alienated and alienating social relations, based on a dual recognition: that social change has its deepest roots in self-realisation, and that the creative process provides a quasi-utopian space in which more ideal social relations may develop."[9] Filmmakers developed a range of strategies to increase participatory mechanisms and transform patterns of authorship, not through their role as mediators of visual representation but primarily as participating members of society.[10]

Consequently, the Latin American documentary developed methodologies that emphasized the involvement of filmmakers, themselves social actors and actresses, as participants in the social process represented. In order to do so, filmmakers acknowledged that directorial intervention goes beyond personal investment. Although filmmakers control the technological means of cinema, they recognized that hierarchical modes of production were antithetical to the functional project of documentary.

In order to constitute an active and collective agency of authorship, documentary practitioners endorsed a notion of realism that was understood as a critical construct, a method of enquiry and a strategy of poetic representation.[11] They argued that cinematic realism was suited to challenge consensus and closure, and transform the cinema into an empowering instance of social action through oppositional strategies capable of integrating creativity into the struggle against underdevelopment.

This endorsement of cinematic realism was the result of the experiences that filmmakers themselves made as they came in contact with the reality of their respective countries. As Jorge Sanjinés wrote in 1971,

> . . . filmmakers from poorer countries, where poverty is the only constant fact of life, when they first removed the lens caps from

their cameras they saw only rags, garbage and dead children. They focused upon death, starvation and the suffering of the people. For years they had travelled those same streets without looking and the camera was like a magnifying glass through which they could see things honestly and objectively. Soon the question arose: What can we do? . . . A strong commitment emerged from this awareness. The overriding realization was that everyone was responsible and that this responsibility must be acted upon, for time was short. This same responsibility made it their obligation to search for explanations, which inevitably turned out to be political explanations. [12]

This commitment led to the development of strategies of production and exhibition simultaneously grounded in the need to clarify the social and aesthetic implications of documentary, its effect on the context within which it is produced and on the audiences to which it is directed.

The Brickmakers (Marta Rodríguez and Jorge Silva, Colombia, 1967–1972) originated from an academic research project on the social structure of class relations in the southern slums of Bogotá. As a student, Marta Rodríguez had been part of a group who worked with Camilo Torres, a sociologist and priest who in 1958 did research and set up cooperatives in Tunjuelito. After spending two years studying anthropology in France, she returned to Colombia in 1964 and pursued this research on the brickmakers of Tunjuelito as part of her doctoral thesis in sociology at the National University. In spite of the lack of support from the university, Marta Rodríguez decided to make a documentary about the brickmakers and secured the collaboration of Jorge Silva, a still photographer. [13]

In 1967, when they began working on the film, Camilo Torres had already been killed, but his research provided the methodology and political framework to understand how chronic underdevelopment promotes collective apathy and fragments social relations among the marginal sectors of society. [14] Camilo Torres's social analysis broke with the functional model prevalent in social sciences scholarship and advocated a new sociology capable of modifying its methods and theories to the Latin American context. He attacked what he called a "sociology of fear disguised as objectivity" because its methods proved unsatisfactory to resolve existing social issues. [15] The intense class polarization that characterized Colombian society in the mid-1960s required, according to Camilo Torres, that analytical tools be mobilized for change, and that the social scientists use their talent to overcome their class difference.

Between 1951 and 1964, the urban population in Colombia had doubled as a result of a massive influx into the cities. The political chaos that marked this period, known as *la violencia,* had an overwhelming effect on all aspects of social and economic life. The 1961 agrarian reform, funded by the Alliance for Progress, involved research and planning projects. Furthermore, 85 percent of the Columbian population was functionally illiterate. The majority of urban poor had to rely on the informal sector amid promises of financial prosperity for the middle class.

From this perspective, *The Brickmakers* was an attempt to set in motion a methodology of participatory observation and two-way communication to understand the conditions in Tunjuelito. As Julianne Burton has pointed out, the filmmakers proceeded by stages, and "the financial and technical limitations . . . turned to both political and artistic advantage."[16] Research in the field included explaining the intention of making a film on the oppressive dehumanization of the community. Marta Rodríguez and Jorge Silva spent six months in the brickmaking community before they even began shooting. Once the people recognized the importance of making a film, community cooperation was reinforced by solidarity and guaranteed participation during a five-year period.

As the filmmakers have explained, discussions allowed the community to become aware of its rights and its exploited condition. This awareness led to the eviction of the Castañeda family and the barring of the filmmakers from the site by the landowners.[17] The interviews and photographs provided a basic structure. After analyzing these materials, the filmmakers realized the film should be aimed primarily at working-class audiences and that a Marxist perspective was the most appropriate way of approaching the reality they confronted. Rodríguez and Silva, like other young filmmakers, were striving to use cinema in a political way, to break away from a filmmaking concept where the director structures the cinematic image according to preconceived ideas.

It might be useful to underline that these young filmmakers experimented with approaches which, according to Oscar Collazos, were aimed at "break[ing] abruptly and resolutely with the paralysis of 'good conscience'" within Colombian cinema.[18] From this perspective, *The Brickmakers* reflects a shift in the notion of didactic documentary. The filmmakers realized that the making of a film, rather than an end in itself, constitutes only a starting point, that the political work of the film begins with its audiences. As Rodríguez and Silva stated, they had the chance to let the community "teach us how to make a film."[19] Production ceases to be a matter of personal realization; it becomes a tool of class consciousness for the community and contributes to the discovery of self and other.

The Brickmakers articulates a variety of modes of sociopolitical representation that defy a linear and didactic reading. By blending distinct modes of empirical investigation (sociological analysis and historical materialism) and a variety of documentary devices (direct mode of address, observational and reconstruction sequences), Rodríguez and Silva constructed a complex perspective on the social and labor relations in the brickyards of Tunjuelito. The extensive use of nonsynchronous sound track—in part conditioned by limited technological resources—establishes, as Julianne Burton points out, a hierarchy of predominantly nonsynchronous voices.[20] Arranged over shots of soldiers and polling stations, an unidentified politician forecasts a hopeful future and Alfredo Castañeda explains his family's voting habits. In this pre-credit sequence, *The Brickmakers* moves beyond episodic particulars and places an electoral process basedon vague promises and perfunctory gestures within the military-political alliances that characterize Colombian politics. The credit sequence's graphics that mimic the urban landscape, the montage of still photographs of a religious ceremony over a presidential inauguration speech, and the observational shots of the Castañeda children working in the mud set up antinomic registers of social experience. Confirmed by the omniscient voice-over narration, the impoverished conditions under which the Tunjuelito community manufactures bricks invalidate the democratic modernity of state discourse.

Although the manufacture of bricks is structured according to its chronological stages—from digging up the clay to baking the bricks in a firing kiln—inserts and cutaways link the work environment with the communal aspects of family labor. In spite of the wretched images of urban misery, *The Brickmakers* never takes for granted the representation of exploitation. The radio soap opera, interrupted by commercials that intrude on the shots of the Castañedas, asserts their marginalization from a consumer society.[21]

The imaging system of the film, although based predominantly on expositional modes of documentary, displaces the descriptive options of cinematic realism. Poverty is presented within individual and collective manifestations of apathy. While insisting on private forms of violence (promiscuity, alcoholism, and domestic assault), *The Brickmakers* exposes other instances that legitimize its effects. The role played by religious belief is set up in the first communion and the funeral sequences. The mechanistic recitation of the seven sacraments and the ritualized dressing of Leonor Castañeda for her first communion ceremony are framed with the official images of state piety (a drawing of the Sacred Heart of Jesus and a photo of the Pope). The resignation preached by the unidentified voice of a priest over the forlorn burial ground reinforces the same kind of submissiveness that requires Alfredo to obey the landowner's orders.

The power of these socially coercive mechanisms is individualized through Maria's speech on her repeated pregnancies that includes the censoring comments of a doctor. Moreover, the representation of women in the film, particularly Leonor's, is given a metaphoric quality. The series of shots which show Leonor getting dressed for her first communion, as Julianne Burton points out, "coalesce into a kind of compelling refrain which directly challenges the passive voyeurism of the viewer and transports the film from the sociological register to the symbolic."[22]

The opening and closing quotations (taken from Karl Marx's *Capital* and Camilo Torres respectively) establish two distinctive modes of exposition. While the first authorizes a conceptual framework that structures the omniscient voice-over, the latter activates a functional discussion. This strategy refrains from providing easy solutions to the plight of the brickmakers. By abstaining from designating a political strategy, the film casts its resolution to the audience.

As Carlos Alvarez wrote in "For Colombia 1971: Militancy and the Cinema," documentary is "the necessary step towards a cinema of social observation and criticism, towards a militant political cinema, that actively intervenes in the development of a revolutionary conjuncture."[23] Given the economic and ideological structuring of class oppression, the production and distribution of *The Brickmakers* activated a process by which the Tunjuelito community was able to unmask the hidden mechanisms of its oppression. This awareness became a stepping-stone for concrete forms of social organization. As Marta Rodríguez explained in an interview, "Since (the film) was made, this brickmaking community has taken great strides in ideological awareness and political organization. They now have a union, for example, and the union has expressed interest in filming a kind of epilogue, which would show the level of organization they have achieved."[24]

Other unions made use of the film to encourage a dialogue among different labor groups. It is arguable that for students (the majority audience of alternative film distribution) the film unveiled the existence of a social subclass, subjected to feudallike conditions, that practically lives in those students' backyard. By promoting solidarity between progressive middle-class sectors and the working class, *The Brickmakers* might have contributed to reversing the endemic social indifference that blocked efforts to widen the social base of political resistance.[25]

The Authority of Daily Life: *Up to a Point*

To the extent that documentary practice in the New Latin American Cinema has provided the means to erase hierarchical modes of production, it is useful to examine how feature film production has tested participatory strategies of authorship. Tomás Gutierrez Alea, the Cuban filmmaker best known for *Memories of Underdevelopment* (1968), completed *Up to a Point* in 1983. His prestige as a director, both within and outside his country, has been the result of a distinguished career spanning over three decades.

Tempting as it might be to rank him as an "auteur," the well-deserved reputation of Tomás Gutierrez Alea furnishes only one critical key by which to approach his films. This director's work can equally be projected into a broadened perspective that establishes its simultaneous inscriptions within the institutional and aesthetic features of contemporary Cuban film.[26] Therefore, I will consider how the establishment of a state-funded agency has structured production strategies and how the changes in the aesthetic conceptualization of Cuban filmmaking have affected feature film.

Since 1959 the Cuban Film Institute, known by the acronym ICAIC (Instituto Cubano del Arte e Industria Cinematográficos), has controlled and coordinated all aspects of cinematographic practice: production, distribution, exhibition, promotion. Notwithstanding resource constraints, cinematic practices in Cuba have placed cinema at the center of change. Designed to have an impact on the social fabric, the cinema has sought—in the same way as other cultural practices—to play a critical role by favoring an organic alliance of art and politics, to encourage social awareness through collective and individual growth. This engagement of culture in the private and public spheres by means of participatory mechanisms has sought to modify power and social relations, to reverse the oppressive underdevelopment inherited by the revolutionary state.

The production of *Up to a Point* was preceded by the publication of a critical study written by Tomás Gutierrez Alea entitled *The Viewer's Dialectic* and followed by a structural reorganization within the Cuban Film Institute. As Julianne Burton has pointed out, the organizational structures and cultural strategies of the Cuban Film Institute have responded to the changing demands of the revolutionary process.[27] To the extent that the design of state agencies has been determined by periodical ideological realignments of state policy, these changes have also influenced the internal operations at the film institute. The making of *Up to a Point* coincides with one of these realignments. Given that the film deals (among other things) with filmmaking, that its narrative revolves around producing a script about *machismo* on the docks of Havana, I will argue that its institutional-aesthetic approach inserts itself in the changing paradigms of Cuban cinematic production.

The Cuban Film Institute has, at least once, been at the center of major ideological debates within the Cuban Revolution. As Michael Chanan has pointed out, "It developed and defended positions against both the sometimes near-hysterical attacks of liberals who feared the encroachment of the state, and the mechanical application of schemes from socialist realism on the part of more orthodox and traditional Marxists associated with the old guard of the prerevolutionary Communist Party."[28]

It was during one of those moments that Julio García Espinosa published "For an Imperfect Cinema." Writing in 1969, this filmmaker and co-founder of the Cuban Film Institute elaborated a complex argument about the role of art in a revolutionary society. By stating at the outset the problematic character of a cinema bent on demonstrating its technological and artistic excellence, he outlined the need to radicalize cinematic practice.[29] The circulation of "For an Imperfect Cinema" in Latin America was predominantly impeded by interpretations of it as a rejection of a technically proficient cinema, leading to a regrettable misreading of its conceptual merits. Therefore, I will insist on aspects that have so far been neglected.

In a letter written to a Chilean film magazine in 1971, García Espinosa insisted that "a new aesthetic cannot emerge if we do not contribute to the development of a new culture" and raised issues about cultural production.[30] Like Walter Benjamin and Bertold Brecht in the 1930s, García Espinosa sought to formulate a politics of culture that takes into account technological and social mediations as well as modes that favor the creative integration and collaboration of audiences. He wrote, "The task currently at hand is to find out if the conditions which will enable spectators to transform themselves into agents—not merely more active spectators, but genuine co-authors—are beginning to exist."[31]

By rejecting art as a disengaged practice, what he calls "*una actividad desinteresada*," García Espinosa acknowledged the interdependent nature of cultural processes, particularly in a context where intellectuals and artists have traditionally labored within contentious and minority positions. By reactivating the traditional convergence between European and Latin American avant-garde positions, García Espinosa (like Fernando Ezequiel Solanas and Octavio Getino earlier) asserted the need to reexamine the viability of such models for Cuban—and by extension, Latin American—filmmakers.

Instead of operating within a homogenized concept of cultural practice, "For an Imperfect Cinema" exposed the heterogeneous complexity of Latin American social formations, affirming that profound changes could result only after a deliberate challenge to institutional and class positions. Although limited by class origin (the middle-class extraction of Cuban and Latin American intellectuals), García Espinosa proposed at least one way in which creativity can engage itself in social processes. By transferring the individual agency of authorship to mechanisms encouraging cooperative models, he called for a new poetics, for an "imperfect cinema."[32]

The argument against closed forms of cinematic address emerged from the view that, as far as human agency structures social practices, a transformed creativity is bound to a change in social relations through the disinvestment of individualism. It is arguable that Cuban cinematic practices, although shaped by the structural coherence of the revolution, have had to discard patterns which were no longer adequate in order to revitalize its bearing on the social process.

Up to a Point emerges simultaneously from the relative stability of production methods and the changing demands made upon creative activity by the Cuban Revolution. By the time Tomás Gutierrez Alea made this film, the production structures of the Cuban Film Institute resembled only in spirit those which he had helped to set up in the early 1960s. Julianne Burton has identified four different stages in the organizational evolution of the Cuban Film Institute. The phase that stretched from 1975 to 1983 corresponds to the broad institutionalization in the wake of the resolutions taken during the first National Congress of the Cuban Communist Party in 1970. In this period, management operations became more complex and the administrative structure of the Cuban Film Institute was centralized to streamline its industrial base. "The formation of a National Ministry of Culture which incorporated ICAIC under [Alfredo] Guevara's continuing direction as one of its five vice-ministers," Burton states, "marked the symbolic loss of the privileged autonomy the Institute had enjoyed since its founding. Lest the motivations for the economic reorganization and redefinition of ICAIC appear to have come largely from outside the agency, it is important to note that these directives coincided with internal concerns to lower costs and increase productivity which date from the beginning of the decade."[33]

Co-productions with filmmakers from the New Latin American Cinema, for instance, increased in this period. Designed to take better advantage of the technical infrastructure and the human resources available, co-productions were also aimed at projecting the work of the Film Institute outside of Cuba. This strategy, however, entailed a marked decrease in feature films, and only ten fiction films were produced between 1976 and 1982. When Julio García Espinosa took over the ICAIC in 1982, Paulo Antonio Paranagua pointed out, "He intended to secure its continuity and renewal by promoting young directors" and to revitalize the "style and content" of Cuban cinema.[34]

Compared with *Memories of Underdevelopment*—still considered a major accomplishment of Cuban revolutionary cinema—very little has been written about *Up to a Point*. Although agreeing on its social relevance, Cuban critics found the film wanting. They remarked mostly on the thematic imbalance between the inquiry on *machismo* and the love story, an imbalance narrowing the film's concern to one of exploring "an ethical conflict that projects the artist's individual conscience into the field where his ideas have to contend with the social function of his work."[35]

This weakness of dramatic design was not limited to *Up to a Point*. It was recognized as a widespread problem of contemporary feature film. As a matter of fact, Gutierrez Alea himself stated in a seminar given during the 1982 International Festival of the New Latin American Cinema that issues of scriptwriting could not be resolved outside an overall strategy. He suggested a policy review that takes into account the need to increase production, diversify the thematic pool, and recognize the creative input of scriptwriters.[36]

This concern for the scriptwriter has to be understood in regard to the production methods that characterized the period from 1975 to 1983. While more scriptwriters were hired, their contribution was predominantly seen in terms of a much-needed training and a corrective for a production process predominantly centered on the director-scriptwriter. The methodology that guided the making of *Up to a Point* indicates to what extent Gutierrez Alea sought alternatives to unresolved procedural systems. In an interview he explained that shooting began with a provisional script, a kind of blueprint. Admitting the risks involved, Gutierrez Alea and his co-scriptwriter Juan Carlos Tabio, used an approach similar to documentary filmmaking whereby the result of research motivates narrative and formal choices.[37] This process set the stage for a complex interplay of documentary and fictional elements, a self-reflective quality that is rooted in the mode of production itself rather than in the film-within-a-film structure.

Up to a Point situates itself at the confluence of yet unsettled formal and thematic issues. While other Cuban films on the subject of women and *machismo* are important references, such as *Lucía* (Humberto Solas, 1968), *One Way or Another* (Sara Gómez, 1974), and *Portrait of Teresa* (Pastor Vega, 1979), *Up to a Point* localizes conflict by drawing attention to the intersecting operations of gender/class inequality. The formal shifts between the videotaped interviews and the love affair between the two main protagonists map out the conflictive field in which the scriptwriting and the romantic themes of the film converge.[38]

Up to a Point opens with videotape images of dockworkers talking about *machismo* and a film director, Arturo (Omar Valdés), explaining to a playwright, Oscar (Oscar Alvarez), the film script to be written. During the videotaping of a workers' assembly, Oscar is dazzled by the angry intervention of a female worker, Lina (Mirta Ibarra). He follows her and asks her to be the model for his female protagonist. The original intentions of the script Arturo wants to direct are threatened by Oscar's infatuation with Lina. The project finally falls through when both male characters are incapable of facing the discrepancies of preconceived ideals and when Lina leaves Havana.

The narrative logic of *Up to a Point* poses some interesting questions. Notwithstanding the early importance assigned to the videotaped statements, in other words, to what could be called its documentary element, the film's structure revolves around the unfolding of Oscar's relationship with Lina. It is as if the sociological purpose of the issues raised in the videotaped segments is progressively eclipsed by traditional melodramatic conventions. However, a close look at the patterning of these video materials within the narrative reveals the broader implications of this shift.

The personal remarks on *machismo* of the first three video clips are superseded by the collective voicing of labor concerns during the taping of an efficiency assembly in the next two clips, while the last two excerpts focus on individualized consciousness and critique. This repositioning of address—from private to public, from individual to communal—coincides with the dramatic illustration of Oscar's *machismo* and Arturo's inability to shed preconceived ideas. I would argue that the last two clips, viewed on a television monitor by each of the male characters, serve to recast the issues both are unwilling to confront. Notwithstanding the centrality of romance, the video interviews set the stage for a critique of gender and class relations, highlighting conflicts that the film-within-a-film is unable to resolve. Insofar as Oscar forces Lina's departure and Arturo realizes that he might not make the film he wanted, the last video interview propels reflection beyond the fictional characters. The simultaneous markings of closure—the worker's question "Are we finished?" and the off-screen reply—anticipate through an enunciatory shift Lina's resolve to maintain her autonomy.

In "For an Imperfect Cinema" Julio García Espinosa criticized the false consciousness of intellectuals when he asked, "Why does [the artist] pretend to consider himself a critic and conscience of society when . . . in a truly revolutionary society all of us—that is to say the people as a whole—should exercise those functions?"[39] In fact, *Up to a Point* exposes the dangers of just such false consciousness through the attitude personified by Arturo, his belief that he is capable of unmasking the remnants of insidious male-oriented behavior among the working class.

The sequence that follows a discussion in the dock cafeteria (after the fourth video clip) exposes Arturo's intransigence. In this sequence, he talks disparagingly to his wife Flora (Ana Viña) about the workers. He censures the workers for their impatience to resolve material difficulties and doubts Oscar's ability to deliver the agreed-upon script. From a strictly diegetical point of view, Arturo's false consciousness is framed against a backdrop of privacy. By establishing behavioral parallels between the couples—Arturo and Flora, Oscar and Marián, Oscar and Lina, Lina and Diego, Pedro and Marianela—the fictional exposition individualizes pervasive attitudes. While Flora justifies, in terms of men's self-doubts that come with age, Arturo's extramarital affairs with working-class women, Marián (Coralia Veloz) reproves Oscar's hypocritical behavior when he returns after spending the night, as she suspects, with Lina. While Lina forces Oscar to recognize her feelings as independent from the character he is constructing, she fails to stop Diego's (Rogelio Blaín) sexual demands; and Marianela's testimony for the video camera reveals her response to male perceptions about female permissiveness that she is unable to express in front of Pedro.

The film's textual complexity is activated by the way in which representation is engaged in the fluctuating boundaries of social interaction. In light of the recurring patterns that have marked the development of Cuban cinema since 1959, particularly its innovative blending of documentary and fictional elements, it is arguable that *Up to a Point* moves a step further by stressing the simultaneous convergence of aesthetically and socially informed representations. By prompting Lina's subjectivity, *Up to a Point* allows these systems to crack open; she not only takes exception to the absence of women within a crew making a film about *machismo* but challenges Oscar's continuous probing. By forcing Oscar to answer her questions, she refuses to be confined to the role of research object.

Furthermore, this dissent is enacted from within the instances that have traditionally restricted women's social role, thus reauthorizing subjectivity. Lina's struggle to maintain control over her life, in spite of Oscar's idealized love and Diego's rape, is framed in a recurrent musical motif. By moving from the interviews that establish the level of social awareness among dockworkers to a romantic Basque folk song, the post-credit sequence establishes antinomic poles of collective subjectivity. The lyrics of a song roll on the screen:

I could clip her wings if I liked.
Then she couldn't fly;
And she'd be mine.
But what I love is the bird.

This metaphorical intrusion that constructs woman as absence, in opposition to the testimonial figuration grounding men as presence, is blocked later in the film—at first when Oscar explains this folk song to Lina and she questions its meaning, then at the end when Lina's flight from male oppression is signaled by a birdlike image of an airplane taking off. This metaphor is once more rearticulated into the last shot of the film, the nondiegetic point-of-view shot of a gliding seagull given through Oscar's look, to symbolize his truncated desire to possess the love object.

There are two other songs used in the film. The first, sung by Pablito Milanés, is played over Lina's uneasy reactions before a furtive encounter in a hotel, and precedes her awareness of the vacuity of Oscar's infatuation. In this sequence the romantic lyrics that collapse woman into nature are disputed by Lina's discomfort as she plays with her drink. The other is performed by the group Irakere at an outdoor party attended by Lina and Oscar, and precedes her refusal to wait until he resolves the conflict with Marián. The bodily ease of the couples dancing to its rhythmic repetition fixes the double meaning of its untranslatable lyrics. "Mulata dejáte de atrevimiento" speaks not only of the impudence and boldness of black women but also of Lina's own impulsiveness and daring.

While Lina's contribution to the revolution is curtailed by the physical and material inadequacy of work on the docks, her capacity for safeguarding her independence hinges on her refusal to conform to imaging systems that inhibit gender relations. Thus the film sets up a forceful paradox between the romantic imaginary and social interaction as containing instances of female desire. From this perspective, her character acts out a subtle, yet powerful, resistance to *machismo*—that cultivated logic of "maleness" of which the male characters themselves are unaware.

By introducing Oscar and Marián as a successful playwright-actress couple at an opening performance of a Brechtian play, *Up to a Point* stresses the contradictory position of those who live in the limelight. Marián's banal wish to become a film actress so that she can attend international festivals and Arturo's idealized version of working-class reality that he wants to bring to the screen highlight the limits of their privileged role as performers and producers of revolutionary culture. By repositioning the workers at the end of the film, through the videotaped statement, *Up to a Point* stresses their role as initiators of a critical discourse that the fictional characters are unable to project into their script.

The film's refusal to solve the problems presented, to provide answers to the sociopolitical issues that affect gender and class relations in contemporary Cuba, is counterbalanced by the way in which *Up to a Point* activates a critical exchange between itself and the viewer. The convergence between the subjective and collective articulations of social experience is subtle yet extremely compelling. On the one hand, the social setting is constructed through careful attention to detail. *Up to a Point* localizes the mise en scène of its fictional characters in class-specific elements, each performing within contrasting imaging systems.

Insofar as the tight framing of the video interviews fixes the discursive, the particulars of Lina's one-room apartment are designed to refocus "dailyness" into the imaginary where gender conflict is played out. The close-up of the fork that Lina places on top of the cooking element before making love to Oscar, for instance, has an expressive force that an equivalent gesture—Marián turning off the light only to realize that Oscar is fast asleep—lacks. The same can be said about Oscar's awkward action to get a glass of water from the fridge in Lina's flat until she points out the lock that holds its door closed and Marián's quick reaction to prevent Oscar from using the broken patio chair in Arturo's house. By moving back and forth between the prosaic and the formalized presentation of experience, the mise en scène of *Up to a Point* allows the uneventful to gravitate toward the cinematic spectacle.[40]

At the same time, the fictional is projected back into everyday recognition. The mise en scène is conceived as a imaging system where social relations are reenacted, where the subjective meets the collective. The ocean view of Havana, for instance, confirms the urban topography of *Up to a Point*. The shots of the ferryboat that takes Lina to Casablanca and the car that Arturo drives on the Malecón (Havana's ocean-view boulevard) are part of the visual economy of Cuban filmmaking. At the same time, the open perspective from the streets of Lina's neighborhood and window is contrasted with visual containment of Oscar's townhouse and the enclosed streets of Havana. This geographical acknowledgment is reinforced by sociocultural formalities.

Oscar's swift exchanges with the waiter and the taxi driver at the hotel, for instance, abide to a standard protocol between customers and service workers. In the same way, Lina dashes Oscar's hopes to live with her in Havana with a candid question: "In this room, with me and my kid?" She concedes that cramped lodgings and romance are not only incompatible but affirms familiar complaints about habitational shortages. This is an irony that would not escape Cuban audiences familiar with the play *Se permuta*—*A House to Swap*—alluded to by the Brechtian play that Lina attends with Diego. This abundance of contextually specific inscriptions constructs a highly codified environment where documentary traces fortify the viewers' position. From this perspective, in *Up to a Point* cinematic expression ceases being a matter of personal realization and, as Julia Lesage suggests, "offer[s] viewers an aesthetic delight tied to effective conceptual discovery."[41]

The Collective and the Nation: *The Hour of the Furnaces*

The Hour of the Furnaces: Notes and Testimonies about Neocolonialism, violence, and liberation (1965–1968) has remained a landmark of documentary filmmaking and a point of reference for the New Latin American Cinema. Produced by Grupo Cine Liberación, made up of Fernando Ezequiel Solanas, Octavio Getino, Gerardo Vallejo, and others, this film is a polemical interpretation of Latin American and Argentine history. It was premiered at the International Festival of New Cinema in Pesaro (Italy) in 1968 and at the Latin American Documentary Festival held in Mérida (Venezuela), also in 1968. The Spanish-language title of the film—*La hora de los hornos*—alludes to the bonfires lit by native Indians on the Argentine shoreline which were seen by the arriving conquistadors and to the quotation taken by Ché Guevara from José Martí in his "Message to the Tricontinental Congress" in 1967: "It is the hour of the furnaces, and only light should be seen."[42]

In a very short time, this documentary became a paradigm for Third World filmmaking. Its production was only one aspect of a much broader project, an attempt to outline the organic links between theory and praxis. After a favorable reception of the film in Europe in 1968, Fernando Ezequiel Solanas and Octavio Getino drafted a manifesto designed to clarify what prompted the making of the film. "Towards a Third Cinema: Notes and Experiences for the Development of a Cinema of Liberation in the Third World" was widely circulated in the early 1970s. It furthered a revolutionary view of filmmaking and offered a blueprint for a critique of the instances that affect cinema in underdeveloped and neocolonial societies. The work of Grupo Cine Liberación was foremost an intervention in favor of a radicalized understanding of Argentine cinema insofar as the film and the manifesto exposed the inherent contradictions of national cultural practices and disputed the role of the intellectual as a political avant-garde.

Even from today's perspective, extensive clarifications are necessary to untangle the complex relationship between the film and its history. I want to argue that *The Hour of the Furnaces* is bound to processes that extend across a variety of registers, that its political agenda is affected by sociohistorical factors which in turn inform its reception and circulation. This film—as well as Solanas's subsequent film *The Sons of Fierro* (1973–1978)—operates within the ideological premises of the Peronist movement. The specificity of both films derives from a radical engagement with historical formations, as both are anchored in classic and polemical works that make up the conflictual axis of Argentine national identity.

To the extent that the work of Fernando Ezequiel Solanas is closely tied to unresolved national issues and to an oppositional mode of filmmaking, its placement within Argentine cinema remains problematic. Even today *The Hour of The Furnaces* discourages consensus. Nissa Torrents, for instance, questions its political agenda because it relies on discursive paradigms that have "been particularly harmful to Argentina, dividing the country and preventing the formulation of long-term political, social and cultural strategies."[43]

Argentina is one of the few Latin American countries that can claim an extensive cinematic history; paradoxically this history has remained one of the least studied components of the New Latin American Cinema.[44] While I do not intend to analyze the histories of Argentine film, it might be worthwhile to note that most have excluded, rather than included, oppositional practices. These histories have privileged either films or directors seen as having contributed to moulding an Argentine cinematic consciousness. Notwithstanding the fact that both *The Hour of the Furnaces* and *The Sons of Fierro* are based on literary works recognized as central to national identity, their contestational readings are unsuitable to the consensual arrangements that characterize discussions on national cinema. By drawing on *Facundo: Civilization or Barbarism*, a novel written by Domingo Faustino Sarmiento in 1854, Grupo Cine Liberación denounced, rather than endorsed, the mythologies of Argentine nationhood. The same can be said about the use that Solanas made of *Martin Fierro*, an epic poem written by José Hernández in 1872. Rather than reconstructing gaucho history, the filmmaker turned to contemporary working-class struggles to present a critical portrait of Peronism.

Therefore, it is useful to reexamine the three-pronged patterning of practices sketched out by Fernando Ezequiel Solanas and Octavio Getino in "Towards a Third Cinema." By positing the mutual interdependence of institutional structures and artistic formations, Grupo Cine Liberación launched a frontal attack on the controlling paradigm of national cinema. Their diagram of Argentine cinema is made up of the industrial cinema as the "first," auteur cinema as the "second," and militant cinema as the "third cinema." Within each one of these groupings, Solanas and Getino scrutinize the material, social, and cultural processes of filmmaking.

"Towards a Third Cinema" contains a strong endorsement of the "third cinema," a grouping of all the possible strategies capable of shifting aesthetics into the political arena and an unequivocal rejection of the industrial and auteur-oriented models. The challenge to the "second cinema," one of the modes of Argentine production in the early and mid-1960s, was based on the failure of filmmakers to secure a place within the existing structures. On the one hand, Solanas and Getino attacked the futility of a cultural struggle for self-expression and personal virtuosity amid the economic limitations inherent to Argentine cinema.[45] On the other hand, Solanas linked "auteur cinema" to the commodification of cultural practices, because it is a cinema that is "conditioned by consumer society and its political and economic structures," and therefore "perfectly capable of satisfying (its) needs and wishes."[46]

Notwithstanding this challenge to a traditionally accepted form of authorship, "Towards a Third Cinema" encouraged filmmakers to immerse themselves in every stage of cinematic production, including distribution and exhibition. Through the refusal of hierarchical models of creative labor, Solanas and Getino envisioned a practice that operates simultaneously within the imperatives of militancy and critical creativity, technological scarcity, and aesthetic inventiveness. Striving for a cinema that "dissolves aesthetics in the life of society"—knowledge into consciousness—they advocated a practice that values the collective over the individual, the "operative group" over the author.[47] Thus "third cinema" was based on a collective and nonhierarchical notion of authorship, requiring that the filmmaker act "with a radically new vision of the role of the producer, team-work, tools, details, etc. . . . His most valuable possessions are the tools of his trade. . . . The camera is the inexhaustible expropriator of image-weapons; the projector, a gun that can shoot 24 frames per second."[48]

The Hour of the Furnaces, which remains the referential point of Solanas's and Getino's concept of authorship, was the result of three years of work. Following extensive research, Grupo Cine Liberación interviewed 150 workers, intellectuals, and union leaders. The filmmakers traveled around the country and filmed in some of the most isolated and inhospitable regions of Argentina. In this period, the 200 hours of materials were studied, modified, and even partially discarded before assembly began. Ten different versions were made before final release. The editing process enabled a constructive structuring of the materials, whereby new ideas were developed and critical elements were tested. Grupo Cine Liberación undertook in this way to broaden the terms of reference of authorship. As Solanas remarked in 1969, "The editing was the synthesis of three years, of hundreds of people and a thousand ideas."[49] Furthermore, the filmmakers extended this concept into reception by defining *The Hour of the Furnaces* as a "film act." Its political potential could only be activated at the moment of exhibition when viewer participation "will always express in one way or another the historical situation in which it takes place."[50]

Therefore, I want to consider a model of authorship that acknowledges collective agency and enlists active modes of spectatorship. This distinctive patterning of authorship, which I will call collective, might be better understood through the actual conditions which generated *The Hour of the Furnaces*. In 1979 Octavio Getino remarked that "the practices of production and exhibition undertaken by the Grupo Cine Liberación were conditioned to the existence of a mounting mobilization and organization of popular forces prior to the cinematic-political practice itself."[51] The semi-insurrectional events that took place in the industrial cities of Córdoba and Rosario in 1969 were the culmination of a process that began a decade earlier. Between 1958 and 1965, Argentine left-wing politics was realigned by grassroots militancy.

While an increasingly radicalized student movement, motivated by the Cuban Revolution and the war in Vietnam, sought new strategies, working-class activism embarked on a struggle to replace the old-guard Peronists from the Central Trade Union. In this context, Solanas commented that "at the end of 1965 [when production began] we found ourselves dragged into the crises of the traditional left. That is the imperious necessity for the militant intelligentsia to root itself in Argentine reality and to contribute to the process of internal liberation of the movement of the masses."[52] As Robert Stam points out, *The Hour of the Furnaces* started as a short documentary on working-class struggles in Argentina but was transformed, after discussions with workers and political militants, into a monumental fresco of contemporary Argentine history and a testimony of the struggles against the military regime of Onganía.[53]

The Hour of the Furnaces is divided into three sections of unequal duration. Part I is entitled "Neocolonialism and Violence" (95 min.) and includes twelve segments with a prologue and an epilogue. Part II, "An Act of Liberation" (120 min.), is divided into two sections: "A Chronicle of Peronism (1944–1955)" and "Chronicle of Resistance." Part III is entitled "Violence and Liberation" (45 min.). The film has a total duration of 4 hours and 20 minutes, not including possible breaks for discussion set aside by programmers. Although it deploys some of the most traditional devices of documentary, like voice-over narration, found footage, and on-camera interviews, the film could well be approached as a documentary essay because it amalgamates a variety of audiovisual elements in order to elicit viewer investment. While its diegetic interruptions reroute what appears to be a purely didactic structure of documentary materials, its duration breaks with the protocol of cinematographic entertainment. It authorizes direct militant participation by making provisions for discussion. At the end of the film, members of the audience are addressed in the following terms: "The conclusions at which you may arrive as the real authors and protagonists of this history are important. The experiences and conclusions that we have assembled are of relative worth; they are to be used to the extent that they are useful to you, who are the present and future of liberation. . . . This is why the film stops here; it opens out to you so that you can continue it."[54]

The exposé of dependence and underdevelopment that forms the basis of Part I of *The Hour of the Furnaces* constructs an audiovisual critique of the neocolonial nature of Argentine political, social, and cultural relations. Contestational readings are produced, as Robert Stam explains, by compelling viewers to "take sides," to recognize themselves in or against the film's discourse.[55] Ranging from patriotic Argentine songs to international pop and dominated by the resonance of the *bombo*, the musical inscriptions of the film, along with its iconographic citations, which are taken from advertising, Western art, political films, newsreels—all provide a historically mediated space where the struggle for meaning is played out.[56]

The Hour of the Furnaces seeks an investment in conflicting instances of national consciousness. Segment 2 ("The Country"), for instance, begins like a traditional travelogue with a voice-over describing the geographic and economic makeup of a "country (that has been) many times renamed." By listing the designations used to define Argentina, the voice-over commentary suggests their conceptual frailty. Furthermore, the image track declares a class-based defiance of the commonplace exegesis of nationalism by interjecting close-ups of peasants looking directly into the camera.

This travelogue motif appears again in Segment 5 ("The Oligarchy"), which charts an ideological profile of the Argentine agribusiness aristocracy. Scenes of a cattle auction, a beach resort, and a vintage car parade, with the disembodied voices of the bourgeoisie rationalizing its class specificity, climax in a stylized exposé of decadence at the Recoleta cemetery.[57] Segment 7 ("The Political Violence") maps out marginalization and, like Segment 2, travels through a nationwide geography of oppression. While the voice-over comments on the effects of racism on Argentine consciousness, the musical citations expand its impact on class formations. The lyrics of "Sur," a tango composed by Homero Manzi, locate proletarian identity in the popular districts in Buenos Aires and confirm the territorial origin of Argentina's archetypal working-class expression. The *cumbia*, performed by a live orchestra in front of passive youths gathered at a dance hall, and the raspy-sounding lament sung by an old Indian man in a poverty-stricken *tolderia* express a loss of collective subjectivity. This survey-travelogue presentation has several purposes: it anchors subjectivity within the commonplace while challenging the meanings of "commonplace" through a shift of its fixed terms of reference.

It is from this perspective that the film challenges the classic antinomy of "civilization or barbarism" used by Domingo F. Sarmiento to describe the conflict between liberal positivism and conservative nationalism in the 1850s. Although individual segments appear to ratify its terms, *The Hour of the Furnaces* opens a space to ques-

tion them. For instance, the rhetorical motif used to explain Sarmiento's racist tenets of "barbarism" superimposes former—"Yesterday *gaucho, montonero,* riffraff"—and current—"today blackie,
trash, greaser"—devaluations of human worth. By stressing the historical ground of discursive utterances, *The Hour of the Furnaces*
collectivizes patterns of identity, what Robert Stam calls the "I-you
of *discours* rather than the he-she voyeurism of *histoire.*"[58]

This rhetorical pattern is used throughout the film and appears in
Segment 5 when the self-portrait of the oligarchy is briefly interrupted by images of police dispersing a demonstration in the Plaza
de Mayo. The cautious judgment on the governing military class—
through the question "Today's (soldiers) what do they know?"—is
given by a male voice following an admiring portrayal of yesterday's
cultured military elite. The changes in tone and vocalization alter
the omniscience of the voice-over narration, creating marked distinctions between a matter-of-fact neutrality and unrehearsed outbursts of irony and anger. The intertitles echo these distinctions
through their design and graphic structuring with words either ap-
pearing as classic quotations in the middle of the frame or moving
about, enlarging progressively and stretching the frame.[59]

Although each segment is a self-contained essay, its arguments
acquire a relational status within the body of the film, reconstructing their specific frame of reference. Part I of *The Hour of the Furnaces* exposes in an unequivocal manner the commodification of
culture, with its prepackaged desires. The slaughterhouse sequence
that constitutes the core of Segment 9 ("The Dependency"), for instance, makes use of slick advertising visuals to bring home the
nature of neocolonial relations to the pop-baroque strains of the
Swingle Singers.[60] While this segment serves to denounce the inequality of economic relations in Argentina, it carries on with the
class indictment of Segment 5. The civility of the entrepreneurial
class, following exposition of the methods by which it has built its
fortune—selective breeding of cattle and meat-packing—takes on
a different logic.

Thus *The Hour of the Furnaces* reconstructs the discursive axis
of Sarmiento's antinomy, anchoring the class origins of its terms of
reference.[61] The logic of capitalism, contained in Sarmiento's civiliz-
ing agenda, surfaces as the mainstay of oppressive class relations, as
a monstrous reality recast as a cultural practice. The collage that
closes Segment 12 ("The Ideological Struggle") juxtaposes the icons
of a consumer society (cars, fashions, movie stars, comic-book heroes) with images of the Vietnam War and the struggles for civil
rights. As rock and roll music is replaced by the sounds of gunfire,

the banality of consumerism is displaced by political upheaval and violence.

Although *The Hour of the Furnaces* is predominantly an exposé of the impact of underdevelopment and neocolonialism on Argentina, the goals of the film are formulated within a broader historical agenda. While most of the visual material in the three parts of the film relates directly to a nationalist project for liberation, the inclusion of Third World images projects the film into an internationalist context. The recurring references to Frantz Fanon, Ho-Chi-Minh, Aimé Césaire, Karl Marx, and Jean-Paul Sartre (alongside Ché Guevara, Juan Domingo Perón, Juan José Hernández Arregui, and José de San Martin) expand a strictly regional point of view. But the Third World citations are also used to redirect already established arguments.

The brief call for solidarity, for instance, that follows the visual montage of struggles in Africa, Latin America, and Asia at the beginning of Part II—notwithstanding its historically dated role—inverts the antithetic purpose of the collage that ends Segment 12 in Part I. The voice-over commentary, quotes, intertitles, archival and found footage, and music serve to expand the territory of the film's problematic. The "third cinema," as Fernando Ezequiel Solanas and Octavio Getino have pointed out, seeks new ways of expression and encourages the viewer to revise the evidence presented.

The struggle for meaning in *The Hour of the Furnaces* is "a war between two cultures—one that enjoys all the official advantages, the means of distribution, and the other that must invent its possibilities of development."[62] It is from this perspective that the issue of collective authorship can be considered. Insofar as familiar images and sounds are consistently subject to review, their function is regulated by discursive rather than aesthetic formations. By stressing the capacity of images and sounds to mean a number of things in different contexts, *The Hour of the Furnaces* places political address simultaneously inside the film and outside—in other words, in the conditions in which it is viewed.

A similar argument can be made in regard to *The Sons of Fierro*, a film that reappropriates a literary classic in order to reclaim the contested history of Peronist struggles. In doing so, the film ventures from the formative period of Argentine nationhood into the political chaos that led to the "dirty war." Through a critical representation of populism, it takes a critical view of national mythologies.

Martin Fierro was written to celebrate the rebellious saga of the gaucho and his struggle against the destructive efforts by the government in Buenos Aires to colonize the pampas.[63] Although *The Sons of Fierro* is based on Hernández's poem, it disengages itself from the literary source and seeks to map out the dialectics of national consciousness. The film is divided, like the poem, into three sections—"The Departure," "The Desert," and "The Return"—promoting affiliations to Juan Domingo Perón's departure in 1955, his exile and return in 1973. To the characters of the poem (Martin Fierro and his three sons, Picardia, Cruz, and Vizcacha) Solanas added new ones (Pardal, Angelito, "El Negro," Esteban, Alma, Teresa and Elvira, and others that represent the army, the police, the factory boss, the union leader, the torturer).

The film is characterized by an imaginative blending of representational forms that range from documentary realism to epic spectacle. It juxtaposes different historical periods, combining well-known episodes of the poem and direct allusions to events that marked Argentina from 1955 to 1973.[64] It narrates twenty years of Peronist resistance—without overlooking the ambiguity of its victories and reversals—and fosters historical readings that are not necessarily linked to an explicit chronology. The narrative design of the film is enhanced by popular musical forms that echo the patterns of the *payada* and the *milonga*.[65] The epic and operatic structure of *The Sons of Fierro* is grounded in popular music and theater, historically dated cinematic techniques, and generic codifications. The strategies of the film are put to the service of a subjective and communal identity offering the possibility of renegotiating the representational paradigms of nationhood.

Whereas the poem places class as the founding principle of the national consolidation, Solanas's film positions Peronism as a fragmented and unfinished revolutionary agenda. As Paulo-Antonio Paranagua pointed out in 1978, "The Argentine viewer will not discover, but recognize" the historical inscriptions of a film that "transforms the scattered versions of contemporary history shared by certain popular sectors into a poem, a myth, a legend."[66] By imaging history through the prism of myth, *The Sons of Fierro* engages with popular memory at a critical level and seeks out elements that constitute the metaphorical underpinning of collective identity.

The film stands at the crossroads of a practice that attempts to fuse the ideological resolve of Peronist politics and the expressive creativity of the cinematic spectacle. I would argue that this process represents, precisely, the revolutionary inventiveness of the film. While it rescues, through its literary form, the oral tradition of the Argentine gaucho, *The Sons of Fierro* breaks away from historical accuracy and projects popular memory into the expressive arsenal of cinema. The voice-over narration and the interior monologues mimic the stanzas of *Martin Fierro* that Argentine schoolchildren recite by heart to provide a collective space of recognition.

To the extent that *The Hour of the Furnaces* presented Peronism as a resisting alternative, it was ranked as a revolutionary film. In spite of Solanas's standing, the exhibition of *The Sons of Fierro* was restricted by the deep-rooted mistrust for Peronism outside Argentina. The power struggle that began in 1974, and involved both right-wing—personified by Isabel Perón and López Rega—and left-wing groups, discredited the movement. Although the film approaches the opposing reformulations of Peronist symbology by its competing factions in a critical manner, this critique remained unrecognized even after the overthrow of the Peronist government in 1976.[67]

The ambivalent responses to the films of Grupo Cine Liberación and Fernando Ezequiel Solanas make sense in the framework of culturally and historically mediated views on Argentine cinema. The concepts mapped in "Towards a Third Cinema," including the three-pronged classification of cinematic practices, obviously challenged the controlling model of national cinema. However, as Ana López has pointed out, the making of *The Hour of the Furnaces*, and later *The Sons of Fierro*, coincides with one of the less homogeneous periods of Argentine production.[68] By questioning the industrial model and the author's cinema, Solanas and Getino were attacking a homogeneity which was no longer readily apparent in the development of Argentine cinema.

To the extent that Peronism has haunted contemporary history, that its bearing on the social and political agenda of the country has been highly contested, *The Hour of the Furnaces* and *The Sons of Fierro* dispute the paradigms that control national cinema. The ideological project of these filmmakers, with its extended notion of authorship, challenges the weakness of consensual cinematic practices and brings to the foreground the antagonistic inflections that have pitched nationalist populism against bourgeois liberalism since 1956.

Hence, and as suggested by the films studied in this chapter, the New Latin American Cinema has attempted to disassociate authorship from individual agency. Either by rearranging the customary verticality of the production process (*The Brickmakers*) or encouraging viewer input at the moment of reception (*The Hour of the Furnaces*), filmmakers have seen themselves as partners in—rather than sole initiators of—a critical dialogue. This transfer to collective agency has been enacted through an unequivocally militant aesthetic, and in films that question conventional patterns of gender relations (*Up to a Point*) and subvert historical—and even partisan—interpretations of class struggle (*The Sons of Fierro*). What is ultimately at stake here is not an ideal model of authorship—either as an individual expression or as a collective mode of reception—but rather the production and circulation of a critical agency whereby existing social relations can be transformed.

Gendered Identities and Femininity

In the last two decades, as more women began making films, their presence within the New Latin American Cinema has offered new challenges. Women are developing audiovisual practices which question conventional perspectives on women and men. Like women artists, writers, and artisans who have promoted women's issues, female filmmakers and scriptwriters have attempted to make gender central to social change. This project coincides with overall transformations in the nature of political activism in Latin America and with the emergence of women's movements throughout the region.

Although women are still underrepresented within the New Latin American Cinema, their practices represent a broad challenge to a movement that has generally overlooked women's issues. In terms of representation, the films of the movement have perpetuated if not explicitly endorsed traditional images of women. By underscoring class as the primary instance of social relations, the films of the New Latin American Cinema have rarely taken into account gender-specific forms of social and political oppression. The emergence of a new generation of women film- and video-makers in the last decade is only a first step in the attempt to integrate women's concerns into the movement.

To assess the impact that women film- and video-makers, as cultural and political activists, have had on the New Latin American Cinema requires consideration of the characteristics of their participation. Through their practices they have begun deconstructing the ideologies that sustain gender inequality, bringing a much-needed awareness of women's issues into the movement. These women film- and video-makers are responding to the challenging prospect of expressing themselves as Latin Americans and as women by espousing—consciously or not—the goals of feminism.

As activist Estela Suárez writes, "During the last decade the number of women in Latin America and the Caribbean who declare themselves as feminists has grown visibly and at a dizzying pace. The result has been, in diverse forms and spaces and from multiple points of action, the development of a highly pluralistic feminist movement of great potential."[1] From this perspective, it seems fitting not to overlook feminist approaches to film and representation. Therefore, this chapter seeks to validate the usefulness of a feminist critical stance to understand how women filmmakers are developing new strategies for the representation of gender within the New Latin American Cinema.

Women Filmmakers and Representations of Gender

The international symposium "Women and the Audiovisual World," held during the 1986 Festival of the New Latin American Cinema in Havana was a first attempt to integrate women. The following year an important retrospective of films made by Latin American women was one of the festival's special programs. Films by Matilde Landeta (Mexico), Margot Benacerraf (Venezuela), Nieves Yancovic (Chile), Gabriela Samper (Colombia), and Nora de Izcue (Peru)—all pioneers of the medium in their own countries—were shown. Filmmakers who worked in the 1940s, 1950s, and 1960s were then rediscovered.[2] As Julianne Burton states, women in different countries "have discovered that they are not the first, and have begun the difficult but exhilarating task of rescuing their foremothers from oblivion."[3]

Cocina de Imágenes: The First Festival of Film and Video Made by Latin American and Caribbean Women, organized in Mexico City by Angeles Necoechea and Julia Barco in October 1987, was a unique event. The congenial atmosphere of this festival allowed for informal exchanges among producers, distributors and programmers, critics and scholars. About one hundred women from Latin America, North America, and Europe attended this event and discussed a variety of concerns—in particular, the accessibility, effectiveness, and circulation of women's films and videos in Latin America. Participants also had the opportunity to discover the contemporary tendencies of women's cinema in the region.

Women's creativity in Latin America has been framed within a broad political perspective that takes different forms. The cinemas of Latin American women are characterized by an heterogeneity of modes of production and reception according to diverse national, institutional, and personal contexts and ideological objectives. The interconnection between audiovisual production, cultural activism, and feminist political militancy has been a mutually energizing experience for women. It has permitted women of different social

backgrounds to come together and to attempt to negotiate sometimes incompatible perspectives on women's histories.

Since the early 1970s women have organized themselves around a
wide variety of organizations.[4] Latin American women—even if not
always calling themselves feminists—have had to contend with historical forms of exclusion and have struggled to participate in public
life. As Marjorie Agosin points out, "Women have participated in
the fight against the politics of terror from a new and different perspective, developing metaphors and symbols that have already come
to form part of a collective female political ideology."[5]

The contemporary practices of women film- and video-makers in
Latin America are informed by these public struggles. But these
practices also involve an activity that, as Julia Lesage points out,
"often derives from an analysis of the ideological constraints inherent in traditional cultural structures and institutions."[6] The imaging of women's stories has involved mainstream strategies and
avant-garde experimentation, independent and collective modes of
production. Through formally innovative approaches to documentary and fiction, makers of films and videos have given a new form
to the daily struggles of women, their will to speak up against oppression and break the silence that has marginalized them.

The distinctive aspects of Latin American women's cinemas have
yet to be investigated. But rather than examining in detail the variety of women's audiovisual production in the region, I want to identify how women have confronted the representations that oppress
and stifle women's creativity. In keeping with a feminist approach, I
will examine the means by which filmmakers are reshaping notions
of social and gendered experience, history, and memory within the
New Latin American Cinema.[7]

To identify new territories of feminist creativity is an enterprise
that extends beyond naming. Rephrasing B. Ruby Rich, it involves
opening the way for new critical possibilities.[8] In Latin America
film- and video-makers have struggled to open a public space for
gendered expression, in other words for an expression that is both
generated in and informed by the experience of women. They have
sought to control the creative process and redefine discursive
boundaries. It might be appropriate to place feminist cultural politics within an alternative modernism that entails, in Jean Franco's
words, "a struggle over meanings and the history of meanings, histories that have been acquired and stored within unofficial institutions."[9] The contemporary modernist tendencies of women's filmmaking in Latin America are an echo of previously charted
territories.

The creative struggle of women to transform the patterns that have excluded them from full participation in social change has a long history in Latin America. In the period that extends from the 1910s to the 1950s, for instance, feminist-oriented interventions in the field of literature incorporated a "perception of the inadequacies of the traditional places from which [women] were allowed to speak and act and [a] search for strategies that would relieve them of the burden of patriarchal tradition and fulfil the need for reform."[10] More recently, and as Marjorie Agosín states, female writers and artists are "address[ing] the triple issues of sex, patriarchy, and the militaristic society that engenders violence."[11] The street performances of Lotty Rosenfeld (Chile), the novels of Cristina Peri Rossi (Uruguay), the poetry of Alaide Foppa (Guatemala), or the testimonials of Domitila Barrios de Chungara (Bolivia) have subverted accepted aesthetic standards to claim a public space for issues previously relegated to the private sphere.

Thus, it is possible to see women's cinema from the perspective of a revitalized quest for female empowerment. In addition, the project of women film- and video-makers to authorize gender may be seen as part of a far-reaching goal to contest the predominantly male canon of the New Latin American Cinema. As María Luisa Bemberg points out, "What I envisioned when I started making films was to change the uninteresting image of women in film. Latin American film in regards to women is either pitiful or dreadfully rhetorical. But if women begin to speak about themselves, men will become aware that they are insensitive and prejudiced toward women and may begin reassessing their views."[12]

The study of gender within the New Latin American Cinema is foremost a feminist intervention that attempts to go beyond the mere consideration of the place of women in representation. A feminist intervention, as Griselda Pollock suggests, "demands recognition of gender power relations, making visible the mechanisms of male power, the social construction of sexual difference and the role of cultural representations in that construction."[13] Moreover, and with the increase of films made by women within the New Latin American Cinema, a feminist intervention serves to explore the political pertinence of practices that are engaged in concrete ways with historically and culturally specific forms of gender representation.

In this chapter, I have chosen to deal with four films, each rejecting social realism in favor of modernist strategies, to evaluate the impact of address on sexual difference and on the social constructions of identity. In the context of a movement that has sought to contest or invert assumptions about existing social relations, new ways of seeing and speaking about identity—without overlooking gender and sexual difference—have the potential of displacing, questioning, or transforming the discourses that have excluded women and limited their participation in social change.

_____

Machismo and Gender: *A Man, When He Is a Man*

The documentary *A Man, When He Is a Man* was shot in Costa Rica and produced in Europe by Valeria Sarmiento, an exiled Chilean filmmaker who lives in France. The film offers a very personal view of gender relations in Latin American cultures, attempting to approach the complexity of *machismo* through a variety of textual and representational systems and mobilizing strategies that encompass both the direct address and observational conventions of documentary and the historically codified elements of Latin American popular culture.

Like Marilú Mallet and Angelina Vásquez, Valeria Sarmiento belongs to a generation of women who began making films in the early 1970s during the socialist government of Salvador Allende but were forced to pursue their careers in exile. Sarmiento trained as an editor with Carlos Piaggio, an Argentine who worked on numerous features and documentaries produced during the Popular Unity period. Her only project as a director remained incomplete. While most filmmakers were documenting the sociopolitical chaos in the wake of the 1973 military coup, Sarmiento made a film, entitled *Color-Tainted Dreams (Un sueño como de colores)*, on the strippers in a popular cabaret. After moving to Paris in 1974, she worked as an editor on the films of her husband Raúl Ruiz and other directors.

Her working and marital partnership with Ruiz prevented Sarmiento from receiving funds from French film agencies, while his projects were subsidized and he was eventually recognized as a leading avant-garde filmmaker. She was forced to seek financial support in Spain, Belgium, and Germany for the short features and documentaries she directed between 1976 and 1982. She also faced other problems. *People from Everywhere, People from Nowhere* (1979), for instance, staged the fragmented life of immigrants in the suburbs of Paris in imaginative ways. But the experimental mode of the film displeased the Belgian funding agency. As a result, this film had a very limited distribution.

This was not the case of *A Man, When He Is a Man*. Produced by German television, it was shot in Costa Rica by a crew made up entirely of Chileans living in Europe and then edited in Paris in 1982. This film was positively received and allowed Sarmiento to produce a feature film based on a novel by Corín Tellado—the most famous Spanish-language writer of women's romance—entitled *Our Marriage* (*Notre mariage*, France, 1984).[14] More recently she shot in Chile a second feature: *Amelia López O'Neill* (Chile/Switzerland and France, 1990).

A Man, When He Is a Man works through the gendered character of individual and collective forms of social conduct and unveils the forms of behavior that have entrenched the myth of sexual mastery of Latin males.[15] Interviews with males of all ages alternate with folk dances, *mariachi* bands, film clips, coming-out parties, and weddings. The cockiness of urban middle- and working-class men is contrasted with the commodification and rituals of romance and the troublesome silence or voiced complicity of women.[16] As the film-maker has stated, "After seeing *A Man, When He Is a Man*, no one can fail to recognize that this is an everyday phenomenon. The small details that keep accumulating form a threatening whole."[17]

A Man, When He Is a Man represents *machismo* through naturalized, yet competing, productions of meaning. Costa Rican middle-class and urban boys and men speak directly to the camera about their obsessive maneuvers to seduce women. The pranks of schoolboys, the etiquette of adolescent dating, sexual stamina, and the sublimated (sometimes violent) passion of married men are punctuated by observational sequences. These sequences show the rituals that boys and men, girls and women enact throughout their lives. The popular songs and clips from Mexican films provide an ironic counterpoint to the dominant male voices questioning the naturalized authority of *machismo*.

My reading of this film is designed to seek out and reconstitute points of tension. Moreover, I want to consider the transgressive impact of deconstructive strategies on the naturalized imagery of Latin American romanticism entrenched in mundane social events and popular representations. One of the most important features of this film is the stress on spectatorship as a negotiating process. In fact, the juxtaposition of interviews, images from everyday life, and musical sequences questions spontaneous and repressed understandings of sexuality and desire. The film promotes a critical distance and confronts the viewer with the least gratifying images of Latin America.[18]

The film's narrative development complies with a biologically accepted chronological order. By marking childhood, adolescence, and maturation, it follows human stages of socialization and provides a fictional cohesion to what Jean Franco calls the "plotting of women into gender roles."[19] The addition of musical sequences interferes with this cohesion and rearranges the film's exposition. The musical performances disrupt the sequential ordering and interfere with common-sense linearity. The songs and film clips are used as an ironic commentary in *A Man, When He Is a Man*, undermining the logic of maleness. By alternating popular romantic archetypes with the interviews of middle-class urban men of different ages, the film throws the Latin codes of romance into disarray.

The performances of serenading musicians and *mariachis* of well-known romantic ballads and country-western songs locate the music circulated by Mexican cinema in the 1940s and 1950s in a "timeless zone," as "nondiscursive pauses . . . and nonverbal spaces [that] offer a challenge to linearity."[20] This modernist device connects the music with its historical sources by conjuring the figure of the *charro* as the prototype of the Latin male. The film clips that are interspersed among the interviews show Jorge Negrete, who was (with Luis Aguilar and Jorge Infante) probably Latin America's most mythic and popular male star.[21]

The observational sequences that echo the fanciful rituals of courtship function in a similar way. However, because they reconstruct the private and public articulations of femininity, these sequences place romance back into the social. A serenade, for instance, is preceded by a sequence in a bar where the musicians ready themselves by rehearsing and donning their distinctive dress, and followed by a wedding ceremony. The association between the lyrics of the ballad and the marriage vows, as Julia Lesage suggests, "uncovers the lies and self-deception (that is, the fiction) of the people filmed in an everyday milieu."[22]

Certain of these observational sequences are also designed to deconstruct the organic links between socialization and representation. The pre-credit sequence, for example, projects social roles into folklore and mocks at the same time the charm of traditional dances. This sequence moves from a shot of monkeys playing in a tree to shots on a cattle farm that reveal the traditional division of labor among peasants. The men herd cattle and oversee the mating of bulls while the women wash clothes by a river. Through montage the film unsettles the evocative value of rural imagery. A folkloric dance is performed for the camera in front of an affluent-looking hacienda. Its choreography mimics the gestures of the preceding shots that show cowboys taming horses and displaying them performing an Andalusian trot.

Later in the film, in an interview with the filmmaker, a polygamous taxi driver states, "My wife says I am a good stud [in Spanish, *semental*] when we have sex." He hastens to illuminate the culturally specific meaning of the word *semental* as a bull used exclusively for breeding because it can mate up to ten times a day and is very much in demand for export. At this point, the deceptive primitivism of the pre-credit sequence is cracked open. Social representations are transferred into common speech through metaphor. The connections between male potency and animal endurance, mating stamina and exportable resources, male vanity and national eminence, authorize an ideology of maleness that circulates across a network of discourses.

Although class is not an obvious element in the film, the observational and interview sequences are placed in a lower-middle-class urban setting. The montage of the taxi driver's interview, for example, establishes that he supports three wives who all value him as a dutiful husband and father. His promiscuity depends on the car he uses to provide for each family. The social conventions that turn a blind eye on male self-indulgence are framed by a middle-class ethic of rectitude and generosity. Later in the film an elderly pharmacist explains kindness and good taste as ideal female values, and he expounds upon his single daughter, the ideal auditor for his cello playing, as a model companion.

The casual, amused, and amusing tone is the most valuable asset of *A Man, When He Is a Man*. By relying on music and humor, the film draws the spectator into the concealed violence of *machismo*. The interviews move from candid statements to somber concluding confessions by two men serving prison terms for having murdered their wives.[23] The contrast between lust and brutality discloses the hideous underside of *machismo* after having mapped its innocuous manifestations. Rather than leading the spectator through ready-made assumptions about gender and romance, the film allows viewers to reject the social complicity that makes male behavior toward women acceptable in Latin American cultures.

The gaps between desire and experience, between subjectivity and social norms, are made visible in *A Man, When He Is a Man*. The film's codification leans toward a surplus of meaning and lends ambivalence to the text, ruling out the possibility of a common and uniform position for the viewers. This excess forces a negotiation between subjective and discursive boundaries, or what feminism recognizes as an investment of the personal in the political.

The tropical landscape, the attire of flamboyant performers, and the clichéd lyrics of the songs in *A Man, When He Is a Man* expose the social environment of *machismo*. The film scrutinizes the Costa Rican topography and acknowledges its perverse erotic charge to deconstruct the performances and expressions of urban musical styles. In the performance sequences involving *serenateros* or *mariachis* (obviously staged for the camera), as Julia Lesage points out, "artifice marks the visual background, exaggerated costumes, and most of the musical interludes."[24] By urbanizing the cowboy code of the *mariachi*, the film expands a geographic setting for romance and the commodification of popular culture.

In one of the performance sequences a *mariachi* group sings a *ranchera* made famous by Pedro Vargas and entitled "The King." The melodramatic lyrics are characteristic of Mexican *rancheras:*

> The day I'll die,
> you'll cry, you'll cry.
> I do as I please
> and my word is the law.
> I have no throne or queen
> and none to understand
> but I'll always be the king.[25]

The musicians that surround the lead singer, the falsetto cries that punctuate the lagging drawl, and the mixture of violins, guitars, and trumpets all epitomize Latin American folklore. The cross-cultural effectiveness of this performance hinges on highly codified images.[26] The camera pans through an overgrown garden that echoes the theatrical costumes of the musicians. In a sense, the tropical setting detaches the music from its social context.

However, this bold insistence on landscape undoubtedly represents the filmmaker's own fascination with the tropics, which (as a Chilean) she shares with Europeans and North Americans. The tropics embody the exotic Other to her own Andean-based culture, the site where its erotic excess is enacted. *A Man, When He Is a Man* unveils the exotic imagery that is tied to *machismo.* Moreover, it suggests a complementary system of meaning that brings to mind the pervasive attraction that the tropics hold in the collective imaginary of the north.

While this film admits a critique of a social formation, it nevertheless draws upon a pleasurable acknowledgment of popular songs that are still well liked, particularly by urban working- and middle-class men and women in most Latin American countries. Therefore, I want to suggest that the critique of gender relations in *A Man, When He Is a Man* is located in pleasures, as Julianne Burton argues, that are "ethnic, community, class, national, or gender-based," in "the discovery and expression of previously unrepresented or underrepresented aspects of the 'self' as social and cultural being."[27]

The pleasures reproduced by the film admit a critical detachment and also contest, through the film's representational and exposi- tional excess, the gratifying symbols of romance that constitute a collective imaginary. To the extent that *machismo* is sanctioned in discourse and mediated by representation, it is an issue that Latin American women cannot afford to ignore. The expositional and for- mal characteristics of *A Man, When He Is a Man* suggest the com- plexity of *machismo*. At the same time, the film indicates the cru- cial role that *machismo* plays in the construction of social and subjective identities. Its gendered perspective charts social experi- ence and, even though the film foregrounds recognizable elements of romance, the modernist stance promotes a critical distance.

Experiences of Femininity: *Mujer transparente*

This composite film, released in 1990, represents a marked shift in Cuban filmmaking. *Mujer transparente* (*Transparent Woman*) in- tegrates five dramatic shorts, each produced by a different team un- der the direction of Hector Veitía, Mayra Segura, Mayra Vilasís, Mario Crespo, and Ana Rodríguez.[28] Most of the producers, direc- tors, scriptwriters, cinematographers, editors, and musicians on each crew belong to the new generation of Cuban filmmakers. All had previously made documentaries or served as assistants in fea- ture films.

Mujer transparente is one of the films to come out of the three Creative Groups set up in 1987 at the Cuban Film Institute (ICAIC). It confronts women's issues in a manner not previously done by Cu- ban cinema. Notwithstanding the compilation format, this film presents a compelling portrait of Cuban women. Each short film constructs—through its main character—the struggle that women wage to express themselves. The film was coordinated by Humberto Solás, who, as director of the group, has encouraged projects address- ing socially sensitive issues.[29]

Humberto Solás points out that "in order to be consistent with the fact that we live in a revolutionary country," filmmakers de- cided that "cinema must also be revolutionary, starting from its very foundations, its material base and the structure of its organisation. We concluded that the only way to achieve such a qualitative leap and to respond to that concern for coherence, was to decentralise the film industry, to arrange things in such a way that no bureau- cratic agency was in a position to sit [in] judgement over our work."[30]

Therefore, *Mujer transparente* needs to be considered from the perspective of important changes within Cuban cinema that affected its institutional and aesthetic growth. On the one hand, the Creative Groups were set up when filmmakers were frustrated by the bureaucratic process. As Manuel Perez explains, "I see the creation of the Groups as an experiment . . . that attempts to encourage the freedom and responsibility of the filmmakers [so that] their autonomy grows in the stages [of production that were previously] assessed and approved at the management level."[31] On the other hand, *Mujer transparente* reveals a shift within the thematic and formal concerns of Cuban cinema. Its critical treatment of gender, in particular, reformulates subjectivity by representing inner rather than social articulations through the predominance of voice-over narrations in all but one of the short films.

Isabel (directed by Hector Veitía and co-scripted with Tina León) deals with a middle-aged woman (Isabel Moreno) who is promoted to a managerial position. This first short traces the slow awakening of female consciousness and the struggle against ingrained forms of behavior. Isabel revolts against the insensitivity of her husband Luis (Manuel Porto) and her grown-up children. The character's thoughts and desires are articulated through a voice-over that expresses her own limitations and those of others. As she wonders "Why can't I ever say no?" she also sees her co-workers as "people [who] don't dare to do anything by themselves. How can they be so stupid?" and Luis as "a good husband [who] treats me like his mother." Here the voice-over has a reflective quality. In other instances, it comments on daily routines and foreshadows conflict. Its humor stems from vernacular idioms and images such as "I should stop being the Joan of Arc in the family." Always questioning, the voice-over exposes the confining and contradictory workings of subjectivity.

Isabel defines herself as "a melodramatic mother who awakens gasping for air." The persistent references to melodrama, either as representation or fictional mode, articulate the deep-felt ambivalence of her emotions. While she recognizes her penchant to "take things too seriously," she realizes that "my kids don't take me seriously because I turn everything into a melodrama." Melodrama permeates the daily life and consciousness of the character. The soundtrack of a television soap opera, for instance, is inserted over an image of Isabel ironing clothes. But Isabel is aware of its triviality. In a shot that shows her walking on the beach, she wishes to live a fantasy and "to say abracadabra and start all over again." Yet she wonders "if illusions are enough to make you happy." Melodrama's excess is equally resistance when she leaves the house at the end of the short. Over a shot of Isabel in a park, she says, "I want to do something drastic, like running away with a young boy, a tattooed stevedore or a Martian."

To shed her ambivalent self-image Isabel adopts "a plan harder than the Party's platform; chapter one: rectification." This plan involves changes in her physical appearance and behavior.[32] When Luis fails to notice her new haircut and excuses himself for not realizing how uncaring he is, Isabel decides in advance: "If he asks me to make him coffee, I'll tell him to go to hell." The character's growth at work is contrasted to her domestic stagnation. By showing Isabel cheerful and surrounded by her co-workers or angry and detached from her family, the film questions public images of women's achievements. Moreover, the film highlights private images of success. Isabel's salary increase, for instance, means that she can buy herself some new clothes. When Luis overlooks her new shoes displayed on the bed by sitting on them, Isabel thinks, "If he only knew that those shoes belong to a head of section." The irony of her voice is complemented by an almost farcical close-up of Luis' backside as he lets himself drop on the bed.

Although the short film centers on Isabel, her relationship with Luis—and with her grown children—serves to contrast her self-probing actions with the others' insensitive self-assurance. Not only does Luis neglect to ask about her work, he rebuts her thoughtful insights into managerial protocol. Her daughter deflates Isabel's concern by saying "What is wrong with life?" and, to her request for consideration, her son says "Don't get tragic." Isabel's story is developed in a linear manner by announcing closure, but ends without resolving her frustration. The final shot of Isabel in the park is set to a popular song entitled "The Tunnel," which tells about young women eager to take a ride in a car that once stalled in a dark tunnel. With its lively rhythm, repetitions, and sexual innuendo, the song is misleading. It links Isabel to a world of sexual fantasy, not unlike the one she imagines in her anger. If melodrama is presented as a fiction where private emotions are given free rein, the tunnel metaphor also indicates the implausibility of a happy ending.

Adriana (directed and scripted by Mayra Segura) enters into the fantasy world of an older woman (Veronica Lynn). The imaginative treatment of image and sound contrasts fantasy and solitude. Shot in a single setting, this short film recreates the haunting power of memory. The opening tracking shot, for instance, fragments rather than describes the space inhabited by the character. The muted colors are barely brightened by streaks of light, and the incessant sound of a radio tuned to an all-day news station insinuates bleakness.

Adriana withdraws from the drudgery of daily life and escapes into a world of hallucination. She dresses in fine lace and enters, through her reflected image in a mirror, a party where she approaches a young man and begins dancing with him. An off-screen voice beckons "Look at me" over a frontal close up of her face. The vision is disrupted by female voices, and at the end by a doorbell. Insinuating a past of frustrated desires, the voices enquire ("What are you doing?") or reprove ("Look at yourself"), thus breaking Adriana's fantasy.

The sole dramatic element is provided by a request to repair the telephone. Adriana tells an operator that she is calling from the street and suggests the same young man be sent over. When he arrives, Adriana watches him through the keyhole, but a voice scolds "Don't go, I don't like you looking out." The last shot shifts the point of view out onto the street, where the repairman is leaving. Through mirror images, eerie voices, and weary gestures, Mayra Segura recreates the archetypal old lady whose existence sways between madness and boredom and who needs to imagine she is still desirable.

Julia (directed and scripted by Mayra Vilasís) stages a woman's recollections of a failed marriage and her subsequent divorce. This short film intercuts Julia (Mirta Ibarra) performing everyday gestures with images of her past. Julia's voice-over punctuates two different sets of images. One is made up of shots that show her arriving home, taking a shower, serving herself a drink, lying in bed, and so on. And the other set shows her with a young man or her former husband, or her husband with his young lover.

The narrative establishes the flashback structure with the opening shot that overlaps Julia's arrival home with an off-screen dialogue between a quarreling couple and the sound of a car leaving. While Julia enters the darkened apartment, her figure partially concealed by the slotted shadow cast by the Venetian blinds, her voice-over narration begins. She likens divorce to a boxing match that "is won by knockout, abandonment, or lassitude." This metaphor is taken up in the last shot when her husband enters the apartment. As Julia turns on the ceiling light and faces him standing by the door, the mise-en-scène mimics a boxing ring. Julia's closing words are "A good fighter never gives up."

By stressing metaphor and displacing meaning from the daily routines acted out by the character, *Julia* imagines subjectivity as an embattled space. Julia's recollections are set against the backdrop of her failed marriage and her ambivalence toward divorce. The extramarital affair of her husband with a philosophy student and her own with another young student provide a contrast between her husband's emotional numbness and her intimate joys and desires. Julia compares the indifferent silence of her husband to her own sexual gratification. Moreover, the use of metaphor—unlike in the first short of *Mujer transparente*—has an introspective quality. When Julia asks "Why do women have an atavistic memory of men?" and compares marriage to a tattoo, she connects her desire to the indelible marks of the past. She admits a gendered penchant for melodrama but—unlike Isabel—invalidates its excessive pathos through self-assurance. "With time," she reflects, "I have lost fear of loneliness," and just before her husband enters, she wishes that "maybe we could be friends, just friends."

The husband's return to Havana after a year's sojourn in the provinces is announced by recurring shots of a white car that Julia sees on the street during an evening rendezvous with her lover. Hence, the character's recall is patterned by association. For example, when Julia combs her wet hair the film cuts to the same gesture performed by the young lover. Or when Julia pours herself a drink, this action is duplicated in the next shot where—sitting on her husband's lap—she recalls the painful decision to defer pregnancy.

The visual economy of *Julia* is designed to emphasize privacy as the space in which interiority is given full expression. The character's intense questioning of past and present plays itself out in a darkened apartment. The silence of the evening is disrupted only by ordinary noises coming from the street or the sounds of Julia's actions. In this way, and without distracting from Julia's inward journey, Mayra Vilasís has explored the courageous resolve of a divorced woman. She presents an affirmative image of retrospection and, despite its ambivalent ending, an empowering portrait of femininity.

Zoé (directed by Mario Crespo and scripted by Osvaldo Sánchez and Carlos Celdrán) contrasts the nonconformist life of a young artist (Leonor Arocha) with that of a student leader (Leonardo Armas) sent to investigate her absences from the university. The filmmaker chose a single setting to observe gender and social differences and to draw an imaginative portrait of marginality. The garage-cum-artist studio where Zoé lives is a refuge, a shrine where accepted rules are ignored. From the haunting self-portraits to the wrecked furniture, the unlighted penumbra reflects dissent driven underground by established mores. The expressionist mise-en-scène, where even the most predictable shots are composed in a painterly manner, reveals an alternative aesthetic option. Mario Crespo visualizes a world alien to Cuban cinema that demands to be noticed.

Zoé's punky image—her hair, bleached white and cropped, and

her angular body—is the antithesis of the athletic physique of the young man she ironically calls "Battleship Potemkin." She is introspective and oblivious to other people's feelings. Her anarchism offends his righteousness, although both have made opportunistic choices. She has exchanged university admission for a garage apartment; he has accepted an art history scholarship to be able to live in Havana. In fact, Zoé's behavior challenges the principles he represents. At first awkward, yet concerned, he remains baffled by her nihilism and is unable to control the situation.

Zoé, unlike the other shorts of *Mujer transparente*, does not use a voice-over narration. The character's inner thoughts are revealed through a cassette recording that "Battleship Potemkin" plays after she has left the screen to wash his stained pants. Zoé talks about her indifference ("I am turning cold like a stone") and solitude ("To be different is terrible"); she confesses that she is deceitful but asserts that "the others are like leeches" and "I don't want to do what others demand."

The clash between their different lifestyles and antagonistic views is presented in real time and over a single evening. If night offers excitement because it belongs—in Zoé's words—to "crazy people like me," day is colorless and suits him, "the most boring student leader in the world." Daybreak brings an end to the brief closeness of lovemaking. Unwilling to conform, Zoé practically throws him out. As in *Julia*, the blinding light that streams into the garage accents her desire to remain the way she is.

Laura (directed and scripted by Ana Rodríguez) explores a woman's uncertain emotions toward a female friend returning to Cuba for a visit. By intercutting images of adolescence with shots of Laura (Selma Soreghi) waiting in a hotel lobby, this short film sets up a dialectical space for memory and reality. In comparison with the other shorts, subjectivity is inserted into the collective but retains its gendered point of view through Laura's voice-over. The opening line—"Who are you, Polly Magoo?" over a black and white photograph of young women in miniskirts—sets off Laura's interior journey. Although this question remains unanswered, it sets up a poignant portrait of female bonding between the bespectacled, introverted Laura, the ugly duckling, and the enigmatic and flamboyant Ana. Still photographs and stock footage from Octavio Cortazar's *Varadero 70* provide a historical background to this friendship, which was interrupted by Ana's departure for the United States. With their cocky and audacious representation of youth, these images express the nostalgia and the sense of loss experienced by Laura.

Ana Rodríguez has directed the most obviously political short film of *Mujer transparente*. By using found images, including film clips and newsreels, she has given a documentary context to the character's introspection. These images inject the social into the personal and contrast the estrangement of people in the hotel lobby to Laura's and Ana's friendship. The group compositions express a sense of community that is lacking in the hotel sequences. The camera centers on the anonymous crowd around the bar, reception desk, and elevators while the soundtrack offers a bitter critique of the distortions of tourist privileges. In fact, Laura's meeting with Ana is shown through an image of the past as the only site where intimate contact is possible.

Laura voices her hostility toward people she encounters in the lobby. Of the desk personnel, she asks, "Why do [they] treat those of us who stayed [in Cuba] with such contempt?" and about an acquaintance, "What is this whore doing here? I'd better say hello."[33] Moreover, she resents public gestures and accepted ideas about those who left the country. Over footage of rallies that preceded the massive departures from Mariel, Laura says, "You cannot see in black and white the most concrete feelings." An imagined exchange liberates this critique from its individual implications. Although Laura's question ("Who are you now?") to Ana remains unanswered, Ana's voice is briefly inserted. Laura, as if replying to Ana's only letter, says, "I could not help you, you were far away. I lost you and you lost yourself." By switching between first and second person, *Laura* opens a dialogue between the Cubans who emigrated and those who stayed. It contests irreconcilable differences that have marked the society.

This short film engages subjectivity as representation. At the opening of the film, Laura says, "I look at myself in those photos, and I don't recognize myself." But it is actually the spectator who is looking at the pictures. Therefore, I would like to argue that *Laura* articulates misrecognition as a collective—rather than individual— symptom. Ana Rodríguez has constructed a fiction that is both public and private. It is as if the filmmaker has demanded that Cuban viewers go beyond the character and into themselves, to reply to Laura's question "Who are you, Polly Magoo?" By plotting the private as public, this last short of *Mujer transparente* disturbs the tendency in Cuban cinema to disregard gender as a valid perspective from which to approach broad social issues.

The strength of this film resides in the nonessentialist treatment of femininity. As a result, it achieves an interesting balance between recognizable aspects of private and social life. In *Mujer transparente*, femininity is always contradictory. Contextualized by generation, social background, and personal history, female experience and introspection are set against a stifling social background. And as the quote from the Family Code inserted in the opening credits suggests, the equality of women dictated by the 1978 constitution has yet to be realized. The perspectives brought to the film by Hector Veitía, Mayra Segura, Mayra Vilasís, Mario Crespo, and Ana Rodríguez might be a first attempt to liberate the imaginative and critical power of women's desire in Cuban cinema.

Reviewing Women's History: *Camila*

Women filmmakers have taken on the challenge to review stories of individual, historical women. *Camila* (1984) and recently *I, the Worst of Them All* (1990) are both unusual in scope and perspective. Both films were directed by María Luisa Bemberg and produced by Lita Stantic (for GEA Cinematográfica S.R.L.). The first deals with Camila O'Gorman, an upper-class Argentine girl who fell in love with a priest and was executed by government order in 1848. The second deals with Sor Juana Inés de la Cruz (1651–1695), the Mexican nun and woman of letters who was forced by the Church to relinquish writing and her library. Bemberg has brought women's history into the mainstream by endowing her films with a contemporary perspective.

As B. Ruby Rich points out, "Bemberg's brilliance lies in her exploration of women in her society as the site of a continuing battle between repression and liberation. [Her] perception of the link between sexuality and political control is acute."[34] I will discuss *Camila* insofar as it draws on conventional genres—historical reconstruction and melodrama—to interpret the life and times of Camila O'Gorman.

The film was co-produced with Spain (Impala S.A.) and filmed in Argentina following the election that returned the government to civilians. Its high production values give it a sense of historical authenticity that is both attractive and pleasing to the viewer. Its exhibition in Argentina was very successful; competing with twenty-five other national productions released in 1984, it was the first Argentine film to dominate box office ratings.[35] From an international perspective, this film was the first Argentine film to receive an Oscar nomination.[36]

Most films made that year dealt with contemporary themes. Bemberg took a risk by bringing to the screen a passionate drama set in a still-controversial period of Argentine history. The love story of

Camila O'Gorman and Ladislao Gutierrez, their escape and execution, is restored to history without deflecting its heart-rending impact. *Camila* endows romance with a political dimension. The filmmaker took care to extend the traditional generic mode through elements of class privilege, honor, and authority. The film is based on an episode that has figured prominently in the historical accounts of Juan Manuel de Rosas's rule (1829–1852). This event has been described as "the most singular exercise of power in the whole regime."[37] It came to epitomize the terror and anarchy that dominated the postindependence period and undoubtedly has contemporary resonances. As Bemberg herself pointed out, the film places human rights in a gender-specific context.[38]

While portraying historical forms of women's oppression, the film also subscribes to the mythical aspects of the initial anecdote. Representation is organized around desire as a liberating element in order to restore Camila O'Gorman's story into women's history. The film opens up suggestive spaces of resistance to patriarchal domination. As Bemberg has said, "I think of it initially as interesting for *women* to see the workings of an outraged person becoming outrageous. Because an outrageous [woman] has a kind of defiance that makes [her] free and unafraid of what others might say."[39]

What I would like to argue is that the film attempts to retain a critical outlook. In a sense, the film connects the historical and legendary aspects, and joins distinct representational modes. On the one hand, it constructs the social, religious, and political framework of Camila's story. It suggests, as Jean Franco points out, that "religion, nationalism and finally modernization . . . constitute the broad master narratives and symbolic systems that not only cemented society but plotted women differentially into the social text."[40]

On the other hand, *Camila* also submits to the pathos of melodrama and the refinement of historical reconstruction in order to reorganize the implications of this story. Although the film's dramatic closure retains elements of the original anecdote, it is equally inflected by the surrounding myth. The affective impact of the final prison sequences channels outrage, and the closing image of the two dead lovers in a coffin (with the voice-over's repetition of their last conversation) reinstates the story of Camila O'Gorman into legend.

Camila uses excess in a selective way. As Bemberg has pointed out, "Melodrama is a very tricky genre, because at any minute it can turn into something sentimental, which I detest. So I had all those little tricks, such as the handkerchief, the gold coin, the priest who is sick with love, and the thunder when God gets angry. They're all like winks at the audience."[41] The style of the film directs viewer expectations, including those about destiny and pathos, to accommodate a wider range of meanings.

Excess fissures the spectacular mode. By introducing gender-specific issues into the portrait of an era characterized by its repressiveness, the romantic mannerisms of melodrama are weakened. The film's imaging pattern avoids sweeping camera movements. It eludes the pageantry that characterizes historical films. *Camila* makes use of soft-focus photography, but its function is not purely decorative. This technical device is predictably deployed to set up mood but also as a counterpoint to the stifling moralism of the period. It simulates and secures meanings in historically codified symbols.

The predominance of earth tones, instead of stressing refinement and patrician elegance, serves to construct a world where terror overshadows pleasure. Red details on clothing and furnishings refer to the symbology imposed by Rosas. In a society where loyalty was to be shown by the color of blood, uniformity becomes a style.[42] At the same time, this uniformity furthers ironical readings. The soldiers who execute Camila and Ladislao, for instance, are decked out in the federalist manner. A tracking shot that reveals the aged and young faces and their rural origins also stresses the crudity of their military outfits. Their drab red *chiripás* (chaps), caps, and ponchos undermine their authority.

The story of the film begins with Camila as a girl and the return of her grandmother, called La Perinchona (Mona Maris), to the O'Gorman *estancia* after a long exile in Brazil. Her well-publicized liaison with the viceroy, Santiago de Liniers, is a source of shame for her son Adolfo (Hector Alterio). The date 1847 introduces the family some years later in their Buenos Aires house. At a birthday party Camila (Susu Pecoraro) is playing blindman's bluff when she meets a young priest, Ladislao Gutierrez (Imanol Arias), who has just arrived from Tucumán and will become her confessor.

Their fascination for each other is established against household habits and religious ceremonies. Incidents involving the mother, Misia Joaquina (Elena Tasisto) and sisters, the black nanny, Rita, and the grandmother, as well as the father and the brother, Eduardo, develop Camila's ambiguous compliance to family rules. Ladislao's interaction places him within the traditions of his ecclesiastic role. In a reversal of roles, and when Camila decides to satisfy her passion, she runs away with him to Goya, a small town in the province of Corrientes. They become teachers under assumed names. At a social gathering, they are discovered by a local priest, Father Gannon, and apprehended. Taken to the garrison of Santos Lugares, they await their execution, despite efforts by an officer to save Camila, who is pregnant. The film ends with the execution of the lovers.

The narrative revolves around configurations of obedience, conformity, and subservience. Hence the fixation on daily routines that express the incidence of private behavior on the social fabric. Tradition is preserved by lineage and doctrine; it is enacted in the household and the Church. The couple's initial compliance with custom, for instance, is set within social and religious precepts that regulate individual and collective needs. Camila consents to rules set by Adolfo, and Ladislao seeks the sanction of his fatherly superior.

But as their passion unfolds in the privacy of religious observances, their attraction transcends the physical barriers that separate them. Between Camila's first encounter with Ladislao, who has taken the place of her usual confessor, to her admission of love, the lattice of the confessional acts as a visual allegory of desire. Camila's face is invisible when she reveals her rebellious temperament. But when she begins confessing her bodily sensations, Camila's eyes and lips become the optical focus. The shift to visible sexuality insinuates the releasing of carnal emotions. It underscores the ambiguous function of the confessional. The place of devotion becomes the site of libidinous subjectivity.

The film patterns identification on instances of resistance that deauthorize the historical patterns of power. Point of view in the credit sequence (as in most of the film) revolves around the female characters and empowers their perspective. Camila and her mother Joaquina, in particular, are independent and compassionate. As the family melodrama plays itself out, their self-possession is contrasted with the unyielding behavior of Adolfo. Insofar as male attitudes are located within honor and class privilege, they serve to connect private and public forms of power.

Male characters, with the exception of Ladislao, become agents of repression. Their role is to enforce the law. In the sequence where Adolfo justifies marriage to Camila, for instance, he says that it is necessary for the family and the country because "it is order." When Adolfo resumes the conversation, he asks, "Where were we?" His wife Joaquina answers, "Marriage is like a country; the best jail is the one you don't see." Faced with two choices (marriage or convent), Camila opts for neither and for both.

Camila's elopement with Ladislao Gutierrez is a crime in a society organized around the allegiance to family, church, and state. The red badges that everyone (including priests) wears to show support for Juan Manuel de Rosas, the governor of Buenos Aires, epitomize this alliance. Hence the place Rosas occupies in the film. Hero of the patrician landowning class and the *gauchos*, he is invoked only by name (like God). His portraits appear constantly—in homes, in churches, or on badges, a perverse reminder of pervasive power. The sequence that confirms the execution order is composed of two shots: the delivery of a letter and a drawing of Rosas.

Conversely, Rosas speaks through others when the archbishop reads his ordinance to the parishioners or through the grotesque heads of his victims. Rosas's decree to punish the couple is communicated through his clerical and civilian advisors.[43] In his house Adolfo O'Gorman personifies the absent father of the nation; he defends law and order even if it involves sacrificing his daughter to the state's ideals. After his daughter's elopement, Adolfo urges the state to punish the sacrilegious liaison. Equating her treachery with his mother's, he refuses to intercede on her behalf.

The film's visual economy gives prominence to details that become retrospectively significant. The post-credit sequence shows the whole household (including the black slaves) performing the weekly bath. Camila herself is nowhere to be seen. Later she is found in the attic by her brother Eduardo. The sudden appearance of Adolfo foils her wish to save a litter of newborn kittens. The drowning of the kittens by the father prefigures Camila's execution, thus cementing the film's resolution.

The paternal wrath against the kittens also serves to equate free sexuality as a threat that interferes with orderly reproduction. The banishment of La Perinchona to the turret of the *estancia* plays a similar role. She is chastised for her past behavior and isolated from the household. Although her punishment is moderate compared with Camila's, she is brought back from her exile in Brazil as a state prisoner. The young Eduardo remarks on the military escort and inquires if his grandmother is a spy.

In the scene with her grandmother, Camila reads the viceroy's passionate love letters. Encouraging her grandmother to share her memories, she takes the place of a faithful maid and companion. Camila becomes an accomplice of memory when La Perinchona's fragile mind recalls the details of an amorous episode. The minuet between the two women is interrupted by Adolfo, who orders his daughter out. Once again Camila's nurturing inclinations are thwarted by authority.

In an environment where pervasive cruelty dominates, gallant gestures act as a protest against patrician power. It is interesting that Camila's decision to satisfy her desire is set in the context of her grandmother's death. During the wake she leaves a rose on the casket before going to Ladislao. The white rose, like the red shawls over her mourning dress in the belfry sequence, signals transgression as well as the impossibility of romance. Camila can resort to neither exile nor madness; her fate and desire are linked to death.

I find the film's construction of femininity very intriguing. It assigns power to male characters and subservience to female characters, but lack of restraint and indiscretion are consistently feminized. Ladislao's character is contrasted to the other males in such a way that his self-flagellation is fixed in mystic experience rather than in the logic of austerity. The feminization of this character is achieved through the symptoms attributed to love sickness. When Camila attempts to soothe Ladislao's fever-induced delirium, she is frightened by his body's erotic responses and runs away. By merging religious fervor and irrational sexuality in Ladislao, *Camila* seeks to free masculinity from its traditional role.

The sequences bracketing the grandmother's wake contest the repressive atmosphere of the period. From Camila's disclosure of her passion in the confessional to her elopement, the camera is put at the service of desire. Its voyeurism contrasts with the blindness that Karen Jaehne identifies as a guiding metaphor of the film.[44] In the same way, the scenes in Camila's room (with her sisters and the black nanny, Rita) play upon feminine expression and affective gestures. When her sister Clara announces her engagement, Camila imagines herself free to chose a husband. By shifting from male control to fantasy, the film sets up an interesting tension between its ironic and realist mode.

One of the sequences in Goya illustrates how this tension operates. From the door of their cottage, Camila and Ladislao observe a religious procession. Lighting gives the cortege a ghostly appearance. Once the people have passed, the couple go inside and make love on the same table where Ladislao had been writing. This sequence sets up Ladislao's dilemma without overlooking its religious and moral backdrop. The couple seeks God's sanction amid signs of divine anger. This segment links spirituality (as a communal ritual) and sensuality (as a tangible experience). But the fragility of this connection is brought to a dramatic climax in the thunderstorm. The fury of nature epitomizes sacred and secular wrath and the couple's surrender to its power.

Camila's terrifying memories of childhood are set in contrasting shots whereby violence is either suggested or shown. The murder of Mariano, the bookstore owner and Camila's friend, is established through a disturbing commotion outside her window. She ultimately confronts these fears in the next shot with the sight of Mariano's head stuck on the church gate. This macabre apparition is later associated with a steer's head in the shot that follows Camila's escape with Ladislao. Their passionate lovemaking, intercut with the coach speeding away from Buenos Aires, is abruptly broken by a soft-focus shot of Adolfo (in full *gaucho* regalia) watching over a slaughtered animal.[45]

By connecting the terror of Rosas that dominated the period 1839–1842 to the livestock that shaped Argentina's economy, *Camila* draws on meanings perversely codified by history. The period's popular mythology is filled with *gaucho* violence and national sovereignty. The classic antinomy of "civilization or barbarism" places an emblematic burden on Rosas's obsession with throat-cutting. This obsession becomes an agency of state terrorism, the symbol of the moral degeneration of tyranny. The film predictably invokes this antinomy in a sequence in which a lawyer reads from an editorial written by a prominent Unitarian exile and opposer of Rosas. The letter of Domingo F. Sarmiento from Santiago (Chile) condemns the state that allows a debauched priest to seduce a well-to-do girl and demands punishment.

By invoking Sarmiento, the promoter of civilization against barbarism, the film extends its critique of authoritarianism to the ideological struggles that shaped Argentine nationhood in the postindependence period. In other words, it provides a space for the divergent meanings assigned to patriotism. What is interesting from this perspective is that, even among Rosas's leading opponents, his infamy breeds sexual perversion. Only punishment for the transgressors can cleanse the nation.

As Doris Sommer suggests, the Latin American romance novels of the period stand as metaphors for national emancipation. In regard to José Mármol's *Amalia* (1851) she states, "We should ask whether the perverse society under Rosas could be the background for ideal relationships."[46] *Camila* makes love incompatible with state formation. Instead of being a founding principle that reinforces harmony, love serves to reveal the nation's violent origins. The film refuses to construct a gendered allegory of the past precisely because of the perverse character of Camila's punishment. The death sentence exposes the antagonism between sexuality and law within a patriarchal society. In this way the film interferes with the coherence—that is, the promise of reconciliation—of romance literature.[47]

Although Camila O'Gorman's story had important repercussions at the time, it was not consigned to literature.[48] I would like to argue that *Camila* attempts to fill this void but gives the romance a contemporary design. By pointing at the transgressive power of love, the film destabilizes the idealized mythology of romance. The erotic charge of the love sequences between Camila and Ladislao validates pleasure. It liberates women's sexuality from its reproductive role within master narratives.

The pregnancy of Camila, for instance, acquires a certain emotional poignancy at the end of the film. But, as in the true story, it is not enough to save her. Rather than endowing motherhood with its redeeming function, *Camila* dissociates femininity from salvation. Neither religion nor law can shield the characters from their fate, and their destiny is determined, in Sommer's words, by "the polarized gender roles of the populist political imagination we have inherited."[49]

The film establishes a distinct tension between its historical and contemporary designs. It relies on the empowering possibilities of outrage, and promotes affective and political modes of identification. Even though it reconstructs the past, *Camila* maintains a gendered perspective. Its visual economy promotes connections between subjective and collective forms of expression in order to disenfranchise the monopoly of patriarchal power. The film's confident appropriation of historical and generic conventions liberates gender from traditional models. From this perspective, it serves a double purpose. *Camila* reconstructs the legend of Camila O'Gorman, yet imagines the past through an alternative and women-centered vision.

Identity and Representation: *Frida: Naturaleza viva*

Frida: Naturaleza viva (Paul Leduc, 1984) is a formally innovative film about the Mexican painter Frida Kahlo. It takes a political approach to the issues of representation and cultural identity specific to the New Latin American Cinema. This film contests the contemporary readings that have confined Kahlo's exotic femininity to the solitude of otherness by making new connections between history and myth. The film was produced independently by Manuel Barbachano Ponce, a veteran producer of Mexican cinema whose name is linked to Luis Buñuel (*Los olvidados*, 1958; *The Exterminating Angel*, 1962) and Jaime Humberto Hermosillo (*María de mi corazón*, 1982; *Doña Herlinda and Her Son*, 1984). Shot by Angel Goded in 16mm and then blown up to 35mm, the film is characterized by a highly decorative mise-en-scène and a camera that glides through elaborate sets, a preference for sparse dialogue, and a skillful use of period music.

The film profited from a renewed national and international interest in Frida Kahlo. Its release followed the publication of biographies written by Haydén Herrera in the United States and Raquel Tibol in Mexico, major exhibitions in New York, Washington, and London, and several documentary films such as *Frida and Tina* (Laura Mulvey and Peter Wollen).[50] The early documentary film *Frida Kahlo*, directed by Marcela Fernández Violante in 1971, is also worth mentioning. Without a doubt, the rediscovery of Frida Kahlo is bound to the feminist concerns in her paintings.

But the contemporary recognition of Frida Kahlo's art has been a mixed blessing. For instance, as Joan Borsa points out, fashion spreads have featured models "mimicking, fetishizing and eroticizing the Frida look of pain, the Kahlo look of integrity, and the Frida Kahlo look of Mexican peasant."[51] Art historians Oriana Baddeley and Valerie Fraser have written that "the emphasis given in her work to the body, to personal emotion and motherhood" and to images that "represent an archetypal image of woman as victim" has disregarded the articulation of Frida Kahlo's art within the subjective and collective distinctiveness of Mexican culture.[52]

I would like to argue that *Frida: Naturaleza viva* attempts to reverse this tendency. The film encourages culturally inscribed convergences between the personal and collective subjectivities that construct Mexico's fragmentary entry into modernity. Therefore, I will discuss two segments at the beginning of the film, one structured around images of the tramway accident and the other evoking the theme of courtship. Both consider key events in Frida Kahlo's biography and illustrate how the film detaches private memories to then reinsert them into public memory.

The title of Paul Leduc's film—*Frida: Naturaleza viva*—plays on the Spanish term for still life, which is *naturaleza muerta* and literally translates as "dead nature." The director has credited Ofelia Medina, who bears a remarkable likeness to the artist, for activating the film's production. In an interview with Denis West, he admitted, "Nobody would set out to do a film on Frida—who painted so many self-portraits and was so present in her own work—without counting on the services of an actress who resembled the painter."[53]

Therefore, it is necessary to distinguish between Frida Kahlo's biography, the historical narratives of her life including her self-portraits, and her representation on film—that is, between Paul Leduc's construction of a historical persona and Ofelia Medina's performance. Moreover, this distinction also implies the need to take gendered authorship into account. Frida Kahlo's art is the result of a distinctive outlook on the feminine, but the filmic reconstruction of her life remains ambivalently attached to the artist's mythical status.

Frida Kahlo's life is the stuff of legend. She was born in 1907 but claimed 1910, the year that marked the beginning of the Mexican Revolution, as the date of her birth. She was married twice to artist Diego Rivera. Her life was marked by polio, abortions, and miscarriages. A tramway accident, in which her uterus was pierced and her spine broken, led eventually to the amputation of a leg. She was bisexual and an exotic beauty, a communist and a rebel. She was the subject and object of her own art. Since 1958, her house in Coyoacan has been the Frida Kahlo Museum, a perfect setting for a movie.

Set within and against the legend of Frida Kahlo, and structured around the recurring image of Frida lying on her deathbed, the film circumvents the traditional linearity of the artist biofilm yet reconstructs well-known anecdotes. By rejecting conventional realism, the filmmaker has in a sense found a filmic equivalent to the modernism of Frida Kahlo's art. The camera movement and mise-en-scène give body to Frida's memories, and the imaged recollections present her as the controlling agency of representation and self-representation. Frida's memories are divided into eight filmic segments, each one evolving around a thematic axis. Each segment functions as a biographical indicator and promotes parallels between preceding ones and sometimes prefigures others. The organization of sequences within each segment sets up parallels that ultimately play themselves out in the body of the film.

The tramway and courtship segments at the beginning of the film offer an interconnecting perspective of Frida's private and public history. The private stream is made up of scenes that show Frida as a young girl—at a window, at a night vigil for the dead, being brought home after the accident and being photographed by her father—and as an adult courted by Diego (Diego Gurrola)—in the bathroom, her studio, and a public building where he paints a mural. The public stream is guided by two predominantly musical sequences that contrast an onlooking and a participant Frida. From a purely iconographic perspective, these sequences echo traditional images of Mexico. By locating Frida within the rituals of the Night of the Dead and the pro-Zapatista rallies of the revolution, the film secures a cultural and political bonding with social traditions and national history.

The play with mirrors, the choreography set up by tracking shots, and the use of songs promote a variety of associative connections. The tramway segment, like the other seven segments, begins in Frida's bedroom. A long tracking shot unveils a multitude of objects (including photographs) and Frida lying on her deathbed, her face reflected in a small mirror. While these recurring shots serve to punctuate Frida's recall, their still-life quality has a pictorial function. The arrangement of these shots recalls the artist's paintings and shifts meaning away from the decorative into the emblematic. The open knife stuck into a half-sliced papaya, for instance, is simultaneously a citation and a metaphorical engagement with Frida Kahlo's recurrent imagery of the body.

The dislocated composition of Frida's stream of consciousness accentuates suspension and deferral. The narrative of the accident is halted by Diego's first appearance in the film; the narrative of the romance is temporarily delayed by "The Two Fridas," one of the best-known self-portraits of Frida Kahlo, painted in 1939, and the introduction of her father Guillermo (Claudio Brook). The entry of the painting into the film is provoked by Frida. The alternate panning over the two seated figures is structured by a shot-countershot accompanied by the screeching sounds of a wheelchair.

This classic device asserts Frida's look. As she pauses on the medallion holding a childhood photograph of Diego Rivera, the sequence is interrupted by a black screen imitating the shutter of a camera that initiates the romance narrative of the courtship segment. Thus the viewer's glance moves away from the medallion to the stopwatch held by the father in the next shot. Furthermore, the shot-countershot connects the viewer's glance to the sister Cristina (Cecilia Toussaint), who observes the father taking a photograph of the young Frida.

By linking Frida's sister and husband, the editing anticipates the betrayal theme of "The Two Fridas." Haydén Herrera has related this painting to Frida Kahlo's separation from Diego Rivera, providing the following interpretation of the two figures sitting side by side on a bench, their hands joined: "The Frida Diego no longer loves wears a white Victorian dress; the other wears a Tehuana skirt and blouse, and her face is perhaps just a shade darker than that of her more Spanish companion. . . . Both Fridas have their hearts exposed. . . . The unloved Frida's lace bodice is torn to reveal her breast and her broken heart. The other Frida's heart is whole. Each Frida has one hand placed near her sexual organs. The unloved woman holds surgical pincers, the Tehuana Frida a miniature portrait of Diego Rivera as a child . . . ."[54]

The integration of the painting in the film, particularly through the editing strategy of this segment's opening, also submits to nostalgia. The medallion of Diego Rivera as a child in the painting prompts an image of Frida's own childhood. In the sequence where Guillermo is taking a photograph of Frida, the young woman's self-possessed gaze mimics the mature self-portraits of Frida Kahlo. Frida glances at the camera when her German-speaking father gently coaxes her to hold her pose. Whereas Guillermo asks her to be attentive to the shutter, in Kahlo's self-portraiture, her rigid posture and intense gaze assert her own power, demanding the viewer to stop and take notice of her fragmented subjectivity.

Rather than interpreting Frida Kahlo's life exclusively in terms of the placement of the paintings within her biography, the film spreads her work across a variety of psychological and historical registers. At the same time, as Joan and Denis West suggest, "our impressions of Frida Kahlo are formed as if we were examining a series of her self-portraits hung side by side in a gallery."[55] The iconographic engagement between Frida Kahlo's art and her cinematographic biography is an excursion into multiple subjectivities or, as Jean Franco sees it, into "the split [that] made it impossible for Frida to recognize herself as a unitary subject."[56]

By making Frida an activating agent of memory, the film emphasizes the fragmented mix-and-match strategies of memory. The consistent use of mirrors is a visual and narrative motif that regulates the unfolding of Frida Kahlo's cinematic biography. In the recurring shots of Frida's deathbed, as already mentioned, a small hand-mirror reflects her image, binding the viewer's look with Frida's cinematic gaze and with the inner Frida Kahlo, the portrait painter. This voyeuristic pattern is taken up in a multiplicity of ways. While it echoes the technique of self-portraiture, it also provides a cinematically codified bridge between the attempt to represent Frida and the power of self-representation.

As its title suggests, *Frida: Naturaleza viva* struggles to animate the inertness of a "still life" and to distance itself from the hieratic immobility of Frida Kahlo's self-portraits. As Paul Leduc points out, "Frida was closed up in her body, in her house, in her studio. In the midst of all these *noises* of her time (the politics, the demonstrations, in which she also took part), there was her expressive silence. Of images."[57]

Nonetheless, the film neglects to show Frida painting because Paul Leduc's mise-en-scène is so deeply attached to Frida Kahlo's art. With the exception of the shot in which she handpaints a plaster corset, Frida is presented as a spectator of her own work. It is arguable that by making Frida a consumer, rather than a producer, the film remains attached to archetypes of female passivity. Although constantly in the foreground, Frida's remarkable activity is sus-

pended in time, and commodified particularly by the intertitle epilogue which begins the film. This ambivalent treatment of the artist
as a cultural icon remains problematic in spite of Paul Leduc's de-
constructionist approach to Frida Kahlo's biography.[58]

This ambivalence is equally obvious in other aspects of the film.
As much as *Frida: Naturaleza viva* journeys through the emotional
and physical memories of Frida, its representation of the artist's public life is anchored in the iconography of the Mexican Revolution.
The changing perspectives of Frida's politics are signaled by the recurrent presence of Emiliano Zapata, Leon Trotsky, and Joseph Sta-
lin and allusions to the Spanish war, the bombing of Hiroshima, and
the U.S. intervention in Guatemala. Photographs and drawings of
historical figures are prominently placed in the film, and newsreels
and newspaper headings are interjected in Frida's public stream of
memory. They serve as historical markers and foreground the syncretic nationalism of the 1930s and 1940s that dominated Frida's
lifetime. This syncretic sense of nationhood, grounded in the
achievements and disappointments of the Mexican Revolution, and
the cultural struggles for self-definition led to important remappings
of the country's *mestizo* origins that are capable of disputing populist idealizations of history or cosmopolitan fantasies of modernity.
Thus, historical imagery in *Frida: naturaleza viva* underlines, yet
contests, what Gerald Martin aptly describes as "the sense of isolation and abandonment of Europeanized minds in Mestizo bodies,
the sense of living nowhere and of living outside of history."[59]

From an aesthetic point of view the film foregrounds its affiliation
with the images that have codified national identity, most particularly in the postrevolutionary period. Hence the representational
richness of the film, its use of citation that endorses *mexicanidad*.
Frida: Naturaleza viva blends luxury and asceticism. It combines
subtropical and monochromatic colors, epigrammatic dialogue, and
entire songs. The fixation with whimsical details and iconographic
fancy is central to the film's self-conscious imagery because it serves
to locate nationality and identity.

The calculated sense of the baroque in the mise-en-scène formal-
izes the multiple sources that make up the Latin American imagination. Once again the filmmaker has chosen to draw attention to
the pictorial characteristics of Frida Kahlo's work. As Laura Mulvey
and Peter Wollen have pointed out, "The style and iconography [of
Frida Kahlo's paintings] is that of popular baroque, in which inten-
sity of expression is given precedence over beauty and dignity, and
like most popular forms there is an archaic, almost medieval aspect

to the representation, a love of minute detail, a disparity between foreground and background setting, a disregard for proportion and perspective."[60]

The endorsement of popular religious iconography, particularly its *mestizo* roots, suits the film because it captures the exoticism of the period. The composition of the tramway and courtship segments blends popular and official art. Dried flowers and photographs of Zapatista soldiers that adorn the caskets as well as the wooden instruments that accompany the somber ballad of the Night of the Dead scene belong to the indigenous and populist elements of Mexican revolutionary mythology. The high-angle shot of the Zapatista rally recalls the grouplike compositions in Diego Rivera's murals, especially those in which Frida Kahlo appears alongside other political figures.

In the same way, the blend of popular musical forms of Mexico (*corridos*, ballads, and folklore) and Europe (opera and *zarzuela*)—including period songs—accommodates the syncretic character of Latin American cultures. In the courtship segment, Frida's and Diego's romance is framed by music. One sequence uses a romantic duet, orchestrated to the Saint-Saens opera *Samson and Delila* playing in the background while the next incorporates a popular love ballad. These sequences suggest associations between Frida's private and Diego's public art, between the refined European and popular Mexican music, emphasizing Frida's shifting sense of identity. Further into the film, songs stress the rural and urban, racial and class-bound roots of Mexican music.

The boldness and the ultrafemininity of Frida Kahlo's dress blend with the hedonism of the mise-en-scène. Costume frames Ofelia Medina's characterization of Frida (her filmic identity) and dialectically joins the "two Fridas"—the actress and the historical figure. It gives form to private and public elements of subjectivity because it refers to Ofelia Medina's performance as Frida and to Frida Kahlo's paintings. Its value within the film fuses two distinct representational systems. Costume and dress are simultaneously spectacle and citation. The combination of Indian and Spanish motifs in the colors and textures of dress and jewelry reflects a self-conscious affirmation of a *mestizo* identity. The anecdote that Frida Kahlo borrowed clothes from her maids to wear at her wedding in 1929 suggests a dual articulation of class and ethnicity. To the extent that the film frames Frida's social engagement with the Zapatista peasant movement, the Tehuana dress acquires a programmatic value. It refers to the class struggles that permeated the period. This costume also in-

sinuates a specifically Mexican rearrangement of regional indigenous and European cosmopolitan elements characteristic of Mexican cultural practices in the 1930s and 1940s.

But as Laura Mulvey and Peter Wollen suggest, "The ornament [of
Frida Kahlo's dress] borders on fetishism, as does all masquerade, but
the imaginary look is that of self-regard, therefore a feminine, non-
male and narcissistic look."[61] Frida Kahlo, like other Latin American artists and intellectuals of the period, resisted the European-
centered surrealism with its hijacking of the unexpected and the
primitive. She transformed herself from an *objet trouvé* into a *sujet
trouvé* that exults in and bluffs the exotic. Frida Kahlo's art, its emphasis on syncretic subjectivity, embodies a distinctly Latin American way to affirm cultural identity. In this context *Frida: Naturaleza viva* acknowledges the role of deconstructive and multifaceted
strategies in aesthetic production and self-representation.

To the extent that Paul Leduc has sought to free Frida Kahlo from
the solitude of her inward-looking art, the political project of *Frida:
Naturaleza viva* hinges on its potential to reinsert art into history.
The back and forth movement between historical iconography and
cinematic mise-en-scène is designed, in my view, to contribute to
the rewriting of women's history in Mexico and Latin America. It
grapples to free Frida Kahlo from the solitude of her inward-looking
art and from the figurative body of her paintings. With its refusal to
conform to linearity and its distinctive emphasis on the poetics of
realism, it relocates Frida at the center of the Mexican.

In spite of the obvious modernist tendencies of the New Cinema
of Latin America, very little has been written about its relevance for
women's filmmaking. Through the films examined in this chapter,
I have sought to identify how modernist strategies contribute to reimagine the place of women in society. As Janet Wolff argues, the
"destabilizing strategies [of modernism] have the ability to disrupt
and interrogate the prevailing modes of viewing and reading, and
hence to expose the ideological character of representation, and put
into question what has hitherto been taken for granted."[62]

Moreover, these films call attention to female agency in the re-
imagining of gendered subjectivities by focusing on the romantic
ideals that regulate gender relations (*A Man, When He Is a Man*) and
the liberating power of female introspection (*Mujer transparente*),
sexuality (*Camila*), and creative expression (*Frida: naturaleza viva*).
These films have introduced a much-needed feminist perspective
into the New Cinema of Latin America and contested the exclusion
of gender issues from the struggles for social change.

Popular Memory and the Power of Address

The politics of the New Latin American Cinema cannot be divorced from considerations regarding social class. The movement has furthered alternatives to traditional modes of individual and collective participation. Aesthetic strategies have been mobilized to foster active readings and promote exchange. In this way, the movement has sought to contribute in a dynamic way to social change. Through an oppositional notion of popular cinema, the movement has explored marginalized aspects of social experience with the goal of empowering groups excluded from official representations.

With the purpose of altering existing social relations and eliminating the gap between the artist as producer and the viewer as consumer, Latin American filmmakers have integrated popular forms at all levels of creative practice. In "For an Imperfect Cinema" Julio García Espinosa has remarked that "popular art has always been created by the least learned sector of society, yet this 'uncultured' sector has managed to conserve profoundly cultured characteristics of art. One of the most important of these is the fact that the creators are at the same time the spectators and vice versa."[1]

Popular forms have been understood as hybrid and syncretic expressions that are the result of the historical and cultural transformation of the social fabric of Latin American countries. To the extent that these forms have often occupied a marginal position in the history of culture, they have been seen as having the potential of contesting mass commodification. Therefore, the New Cinema of Latin America has developed a notion of popular cinema that subverts populist and folkloric appropriations of the popular. The movement has simultaneously explored traditional and avant-garde expressions of popular culture, its historical memory, and its power as an agent of social change.

The concept of the popular has a complex history in Latin America and has been associated concurrently with folklore and mass culture. Since it subsumes positions that are specific to culture, history, and nationality, the popular is also organically linked to notions of tradition and modernity. Rather than defining what is popular culture, it might be more useful, as William Rowe and Vivian Schelling propose, to regard "popular culture not as a given view of the world but as a space or series of spaces where popular subjects, as distinct from members of ruling groups, are formed."[2]

Popular Cinema and Social Class

The cultural lives of the popular classes in Latin America have been shaped by ruptures and continuities. From the time of the Spanish and Portuguese conquests to the 1940s, as Rowe and Schelling point out, "certain conditions, such as the mixing of European and native American elements, have continued through the whole period; some features, such as magical rather than rationalist ways of thinking and seeing, have remained fairly constant over the long term."[3] Although much of popular culture in Latin America tends to be seen in terms of premodern and atavistic memories of the region's past, the history of popular culture has at many stages converged with the history of nation-states.

It was mainly in the period beginning in the 1820s with independence and ending in the 1940s with technological and industrial modernization that the cultures of popular classes either merged with or broke with national histories and with modernity. To quote Rowe and Schelling again: "The discontinuities [of popular cultural forms] include changes in communication media (newspapers, radio), social revolutions, industrialization and population migrations; the main break, which includes all these, has been the effect of modernization."[4]

Discourses on state formation and national identity have been based on social, economic, and cultural factors that promote— rather than slow down—progress. While the emerging middle-class sectors have been primarily addressed as agents of modernization, popular sectors have often been seen as obstacles for development. To coax popular classes (in other words, peasants, workers, and groups marginalized because of their ethnic and class origins) into the mainstream has been considered crucial and inevitable for the elimination of underdevelopment and the consolidation of national projects.

From this perspective, it is understandable that the concept of the popular in Latin America has fulfilled complementary ideological functions. The selective integration of popular elements through folklore, for instance, has served to identify what elements can be preserved and safeguarded as part of a national heritage. As Jean Franco writes, "Cultural nationalism usually relied on a stereotyped and static view of popular culture and thus masked the process of transformation which was eliminating the very basis of this culture in rural societies."[5] In this way, opposing visions and disparate experiences of popular culture have been merged into national identity. To the extent that popular culture has intersected with populism, nationalist ideologies have appropriated populist forms to compensate for elements excluded because they are perceived as threatening to national consolidation.

The history of Latin America's indigenous peoples, for instance, has been seen as either an obstacle to development or a nostalgic reminder of the past. For instance, in Argentina indigenous peoples have been eliminated from the official histories. Not only were indigenous peoples physically decimated during the military campaigns that started in 1875 to secure fertile lands for capitalist expansion, but they were replaced by the *gaucho* as the figure and voice of Argentine popular culture.[6] In contrast, during the 1920s indigenist ideologies suited the nationalist aspirations of countries such as Mexico, Peru, and Bolivia with important native populations. Marginal expressions—originally excluded—were reinserted into collective representation and designated integral to popular culture.

Moreover, the debates on popular culture have taken place predominantly in relation to urbanized forms contingent on technology and mass circulation, such as literature, visual arts, music, and cinema. In this sense, mass culture has often tended to be seen as a site where popular culture is submerged by uniformity. This view does not take into account the social, political, and cultural context in which specific forms of mass culture have been introduced. The overwhelming popularity of mass culture is believed to be capable of corrupting what is perceived as genuine within the predominantly rural cultures of Latin America.

In contrast, progressive approaches to popular culture have valorized the potential of popular culture to alter either fixed notions of folklore or the commodifying tendencies of mass culture. The class- and ethnicity-based sources of popular culture have served to contest homogeneous and uniform representations of nationhood and to reject the nationalist-populist outlooks that see in popular culture a search for authenticity or a return to original sources. In Latin America traditional and modern forms of representation intermingle, and artisanal and industrial modes of production coexist. While popular culture is not the same as mass culture, mass culture has affected popular culture and vice versa.

The cultural history of the continent offers an impressive range of expressions and representations that reflect the encounter between precapitalist and capitalist forms of cultural exchange. In addition, Latin America has produced distinctive forms of popular culture that, while originating in the past, have been transformed by mechanical reproduction. Examples of this complex dialectic can be found in religious and secular festivals (the carnival in Bolivia and the Conquest plays in Guatemala), handicrafts and dance (the patchwork *arpilleras* in Chile and the samba in Brazil), and poetry and music (the *payadas* in Argentina and Uruguay and the *corridos* of Mexico)—to name a few.

Latin American intellectuals have taken a political position toward marginalized groups whose histories and representations they see informing collective identity. They have engaged with the issue of popular culture in a mobilizing and self-questioning manner. Rather than endorsing popular traditions in an unproblematic way, they have deconstructed and reconstructed their subversive power. José Carlos Mariátegui (*Seven Interpretative Essays on Peruvian Reality*, 1928), Octavio Paz (*The Labyrinth of Solitude*, 1950), and Eduardo Galeano (*The Open Veins of Latin America*, 1971), for instance, have explored the processes by which class-based ideologies regulate nationality and erase social conflict. They have discussed how, as Homi K. Bhabha points out, "the historical necessity of the idea of nation conflicts with the contingent and arbitrary signs and symbols that signify the affective life of the national culture."[7]

Moreover, and insofar as nationality has been the point of departure of representation, the reimaging of popular culture has involved new approaches to inequality and oppression, to historically shared patterns of exclusion or inclusion that are distinctive to each country. A striking element in the definitions of popular culture is the permanence of the concept of people, not as a sociological category but, in Guy Brett's words, as "a creative force, a popular or vernacular culture which has been constantly re-inventing itself through the centuries of conquest, colonialism, immigration and partial modernization."[8]

Therefore, popular culture is linked to class in the same way as class serves as a reference for nationhood. In the 1960s, for instance, the New Latin American Cinema advocated new approaches to popular culture through a renewed perspective on rural and working-class issues. Filmmakers sought out popular expressions that had been ignored in mainstream representations and adopted modes of production and reception as an alternative to the commodifying tendencies of mass culture.

Popular cinema assumed a variety of forms, according to regional traditions and national characteristics. As part of a project of national liberation, it proposed to reflect the shortcomings of underdevelopment and class marginality. As Jorge Sanjinés wrote in 1972, "Revolutionary art will always be distinguished by what it shows of a people's way of being, and of the spirit of popular cultures which embraces whole communities of people, with their own particular ways of thinking, of conceiving reality and of loving life. . . . By observing and incorporating popular culture we will be able to develop fully the language of liberating art."[9]

To create a popular cinema entailed an innovative aesthetic generated by collective traditions and representations imbedded in the history of Latin American peoples. The traditions were understood, in the words of Ernesto Laclau, as "the residue of a unique and irreducible historical experience [that] constitute[s] a more solid and durable structure of meanings than the social structure itself."[10] Therefore, a search for a popular cinema entailed the release of popular creativity through and by the expressive agency of the underprivileged and disempowered sectors of society. As Fernando Ezequiel Solanas and Octavio Getino wrote in 1968, "The social layers which have made the greatest contribution to the building of a national culture (understood as an impulse towards decolonisation) have not been precisely the enlightened elites but rather the most exploited and uncivilised sectors."[11]

Filmmakers of the New Latin American Cinema looked beyond the predominantly urban paradigms of cinematic representation through a radical critique of imperialism and cultural dependence. They placed cinema at the service of class struggle and decolonization. Popular cinema was seen as a weapon against social alienation. In 1962 Fernando Birri wrote, "The cinema of our countries shares the same general characteristics of this superstructure, of this kind of society, and presents us with a false image of both society and our people. Indeed, it presents no real image of our people at all, but conceals them. So the first positive step is to provide such an image."[12]

Notwithstanding the populist slogans that characterize the writings of Latin American filmmakers in the 1960s, the concept of a popular—and revolutionary—cinema involved formal but also political choices. For filmmakers, mostly from the urban middle class, the concept of a popular cinema presented a challenge. Although initially filmmakers subscribed—consciously or not—to ingrained class prejudices toward rural expressions and working-class struggles, they finally took a stance against nationalist ideologies and promises of modernity. They placed their creative militancy at the service of groups most affected by underdevelopment and denounced development policies that maintained—rather than rectified—existing social inequalities.

"The artist who finds himself at the centre of a conflict between two parallel and co-existent cultures," as Jorge Sanjinés has pointed out, "cannot be partial to either one if he proposes to express and deepen reality, not only because he is profoundly affected by both but also because he knows that from their conjunction and synthesis a new culture will be created."[13] From this perspective, the concept of popular cinema takes on an ideological dimension. It implies a critical attitude toward social relations and empowers the popular imaginary.

Filmmakers worked with technologically sophisticated tools, sometimes in regions without the most elemental amenities of progress (like electricity), and sought to reconcile incongruous development with the resourcefulness of social traditions. As a result, the New Latin American Cinema developed ingenious ways to overcome the limiting effects of underdevelopment. The collage techniques that characterized Cuban documentary in the 1960s, for instance, were determined by scarce resources. However, filmmakers transformed the found footage, graphics, and music into a dynamic audiovisual landscape reflecting the revolutionary energy of the country.[14] Similarly, the experimental strategies of Brazilian filmmakers in the early 1970s were described as an "aesthetics of garbage" that, as Joao Luiz Viera and Robert Stam state, "expressed an aggressive sense of marginality, of surviving within scarcity, condemned to recycle the materials of dominant culture."[15]

As filmmakers turned to the history of Latin American peoples, they felt compelled to understand, as Sanjinés wrote, that "our people's past belongs to us and determines what we are; it is our revolutionary duty to understand it, to free it from lies, and, essentially, to develop it starting with the salvage and elaboration of knowledge and techniques forgotten because of the pressures exerted by a colonizing policy which had that as its objective."[16]

Filmmakers also reconstructed popular history. They sought to give expression to a past scarred by violence but filled with promises of a better future. By recognizing that the systematic destruction of popular memory, either by physical repression or social assimilation, has been instrumental to class domination, filmmakers also saw in historical memory a living expression of resistance and revolution. Memory becomes in this way a resource to contest official histories and a site where an alternative future can be imagined.

Given the predominance of national experiences within the New Latin American Cinema, popular cinema is linked to distinctive political, social, and cultural settings. Therefore, any attempt to approach popular cinema as a uniform aesthetic is doomed to failure. This popular cinema, despite its differences in emphasis, is inflected by class and location, by history and memory. But filmmakers from different countries have produced a popular cinema capable of communicating to audiences in other countries in Latin America.

To the extent that the impact of certain films has spilled over their national borders, popular cinema has converged with the revolutionary agenda of the New Latin American Cinema. Because the movement has sought to empower—in spite of the essentialist tendencies of most of its manifestos—experiences that are generated within given conditions, it has accommodated rather than restricted national differences. Therefore, popular cinema is basically an oppositional mode of filmmaking—rather than an historically sanctioned practice—that seeks to produce oppositional meanings and underscore the resisting power of popular culture.

Social Inquiry and *Los inundados*

Los inundados (*Flooded Out*, 1962) was the second film produced by Fernando Birri and the students of the Documentary Film School of Santa Fé. This film takes up within a fictional framework the social issues first examined in the documentary *Tire dié* (*Throw Me a Dime*, 1956). Both Birri and the school have figured prominently within the movement.[17] I am less interested in Birri's historical profile than with the development of a popular cinema in Latin America. I want to investigate how the objectives of this popular cinema, which emerged at the geographical and institutional margins of Argentine cinema, were later integrated into the agenda of the New Latin American Cinema.

Birri's project materialized in the Sociology Department of the Universidad Nacional del Litoral in Santa Fé. Birri found there a favorable environment to develop a pedagogical and cinematographic experiment based on field surveys, on what he called photo-documentaries. These were basically slide-tape shows made with still cameras and magnetic sound recorders. Given the sparse resources available, production was envisaged as a step-by-step process. Formal questions were gradually resolved. The photo-documentaries dealt with social and regional issues. Out of all the slide-tape shows, only the survey on children that beg along the railroad line was turned into a film, entitled *Tire dié*.[18]

Birri envisaged audiovisual production as a method of research and a creative apprenticeship. This method represented, from a strictly biographical point of view, a break with Birri's own film training. He had studied at the prestigious Centro Sperimentale de la Cinematografia in Rome after having worked at the Argentina Sono Film Studios in Buenos Aires.[19] Upon the return to his home province of Santa Fé, Birri adapted the lessons learned from the Italian school of neorealism to a politically motivated approach to social reality.

In spite of infrastructural limitations, Birri developed a new concept for documentary filmmaking. He stated that the aim of documentary was "to confront reality with a camera and to document it," to use documentary as a tool in "the awakening of the consciousness of reality."[20] It might be useful to clarify that Birri advocated a socially expressive cinema capable of deconstructing, and not simply registering, reality. Although stimulated by John Grierson's ideas about social documentary, he added a critical outlook that equated knowledge with consciousness.

An overview of the cultural politics that Birri began advocating in the mid-1950s can be found in "Cinema and Underdevelopment." Written in 1962, this text contains a polemical evaluation of commercial production and art cinema in Argentina. In it Birri criticized mainstream genres, such as the tango film of the 1930s and the social melodrama of the 1940s, that depended on audience approval and commercial success.[21] He questioned the predominantly urban tenets of Argentine cinema and the historical silencing of regional perspectives, and he called for a practice that responds to conjunctural realities rather than historical models.

Birri advocated an alternative cinema that engages filmmakers and spectators critically in regard to underdevelopment. Amid the rhetoric of economic growth and progress that dominated the Frondizi government, the filmmaker chose to show the reality "that remains unable to surface, subject to claims about its metamorphosis and destruction, but that is there and stays there."[22] The project for a popular cinema was intended, in Birri's own words, "to conjure away any fetishes which may make this proposal seem utopian" through a political agenda.[23] He called for "a realist, critical and popular cinema" capable of "affirm[ing] the positive values in our societies: the people's values. Their reserves of strength, their labours, their joys, their struggles, their dreams."[24]

Los inundados reroutes the generic sources of popular cinema in Argentina. Its affiliation with picaresque comedy is inspired by Italian neorealism. The film breaks away from the existential modernity that characterized the art films of the *nueva ola*. Moreover, the method of production of this film—its participatory and interactive approach to social enquiry—sets it apart from models sanctioned by the Institute of National Cinematography (Instituto Nacional de Cinematografía—INC).

It is useful to recall some of the details about the making and reception of *Los inundados* since the film has only recently been recirculated. Based on a short story of the same name written by Mateo Booz, the script was written by Fernando Birri and Jorge Alberto Ferrando. The photo-documentaries and the film *Tire dié* were used as background material for the script. Financial backing was provided by the Universidad Nacional del Litoral through a production company—Productora América Nuestra—set up by Birri with Edgardo Pallero and David Cwilich acting as executive producers.

The preparation stage involved location scouting. Urban and rural sets were chosen. They included the streets and houses of Centenario, the shores of the Salado River, and the train stations and farms along the route to the Chaco. Semiprofessional and amateur performers were invited to audition, together with ordinary people. The cast was made up of people who had experience in radio and theater, in regional circus ensembles and local musical establishments, or simply tended small plots or held regular jobs.

During the production, Birri was forced to adopt the filmmaking standards of Argentine cinema. In a 1979 interview with Julianne Burton, he explained that credit guidelines of the INC required that professionals affiliated with the Union of the Argentine Film Industry (Sindicato de la Industria Cinematográfica Argentina—SICA) be hired. Nevertheless, Birri insisted that each technician be teamed up with two assistant apprentices from the Documentary Film School. "In this sense," he said, "in spite of participating in the industrial structure, [the film] marginalized the traditional working methods of the industry . . . to transform itself into a film-school."[25]

Los inundados was shot over a period of six months (from December 1960 to May 1961) by a mixed crew of seventy-five professionals and students. Although the film relies heavily on the protocol of documentary (natural locations and social protagonists), production was organized around the principles of fictional filmmaking. Given the involvement of the community in the production, individual requirements such as child care and transportation were taken into account. The crew had to accommodate job and school schedules. Standard problems and the unforeseen flood that destroyed the cottages built on the river were solved, thanks to collective solidarity.

The film opened in Santa Fé on November 30, 1961. The opening was, in the words of Manuel Horacio Giménez, "a real popular party, where the audience stormed the cinema and punctuated the screening with spirited calls and applause while groups of people who could not enter set up an impromptu show of music, song and recitation."[26] *Los inundados* was shown in Buenos Aires for four weeks. Birri, Pallero, and others organized publicity and promotion. Birri recalls, "In the lobby of the theatre we improvised a rural scene. We brought a bit of the lowlands—the mud, the bugs—to the centre of the city. We brought a cage with a female monkey. The 'heart of the city' viewed all of this with distrust and a great deal of resistance."[27] The film was later invited to European festivals, such as Karlovy Vary and Venice in 1962. The Opera Prima award of Venice was received with disbelief by the INC commission that had refused to select the film for the Cannes Film Festival.[28]

Birri's attempt to conciliate alternative and marginal models of filmmaking eventually proved disastrous, hence the critique in "Cinema and Underdevelopment." The distribution of *Los inundados* was inadequate. The exhibitor tried to replace the film, arguing low box-office receipts.[29] Moreover, the relatively high budget of the film limited its prospect to recuperate costs, and the adoption of the 35mm professional gage narrowed its circulation to mainstream cinemas. As a result, the film practically disappeared from circulation for more than a decade.

Los inundados is set in the lowlands of Santa Fé. It follows the misadventures of Dolorcito Gaitán, his family, and neighbors who are forced to evacuate their shacks on the flooded river banks. Their attempts to carry on with daily life are frustrated by indifferent politicians and bureaucrats. Only an unforeseen train trip to the northern part of the province breaks the dreariness. Finally, Dolorcito and his family return to rebuild their home on the river bank. In spite of the wretched fate of its characters, the film highlights individual and collective tenacity.

Two parallel comments by Dolorcito bracket the film. In the prologue, and over a darkened screen, he says, "When this film ends, I, almost all of us, will return to the flooding lowlands, to the mud, where they found us to make this film."[30] The return home and to normality is summarized in his final comment. Dolorcito says, "That was really some life; when will it flood again?" These comments are not only self-reflexive but serve to emphasize the inevitability of cinematic closure.

The drama of *Los inundados* centers on the resolution of the Gaitáns' forced displacement. But the film also provides a rhetorical space that is reflective and ironic. The mode of address allows the characters to dispute their social marginality. To the apathy of city officials, they respond with an equal dose of nonchalance. Dolorcito's refusals to accept job offers, for instance, are expressed by either disdain or malice. He tells an official: "Today it won't be possible; besides, we are flooded out" or pretends he is deaf. During an electoral rally, Don Orellana (the ragpicker) and his wife make malicious comments about the candidates' promises. And when Dolorcito and his friends meet the designated mayor, he says, "What a fine government we will have." As B. Ruby Rich points out, "The family and the community of squatters as a whole reveal powers of invention, analysis and strategy that counterpoint the myopic stupidity of the bourgeoisie and the mendacity of politicians."[31]

The use of irony is traditional in picaresque narratives. *Los inundados* lampoons social relations and, in keeping with the strategies of Italian neorealism, sheds light on the characters and their environment. Sarcasm is used in a critical manner, and collective solidarity is placed within culturally specific forms. Behavioral tics, such as Dolorcito's relaxed manner or his wife's angry outbursts, stress their individuality but also what in Argentina passes as provincialism. These tics also serve as a contrast to the resigned behavior of other neighbors salvaging their belongings from the rising water.

In the first part, the film shows the events that follow the flood. Farcical elements are inserted in what are basically documentary sequences. From the sequence that shows the flooded community welcoming the firefighters to the forceful eviction of the families from the wagons parked in the train terminal, humor is used as a dramatic digression. This digression unsettles the exposition and draws attention to individual characters. In the scene in which Dolorcito is pulled onto the truck that takes people into town, for instance, slapstick serves empathy.

Comedy is also used to show the absurd situation of the evacuated neighbors, including the Gaitán family. The community is involved in a necessary, yet futile, exercise to secure provisory shelter. Moreover, the digressions serve to intensify the dramatic plight of the community. Even in situations that involve secondary characters, humor is used to expose the fragility of class position. When Don

Canuda—an old attorney approached by Dolorcito—tries to prevent the police from evicting the neighbors, for instance, he pulls out a law book. The humor of this sequence is tempered by the indifference of the police. The rickety figure and the bombastic recitation contradict Don Canuda's self-image and social rank.

In contrast to the humorous empathy that individualizes the community of squatters, *Los inundados* emphasizes anonymity when it shows the city people. Even in the sequence in which students are raising money for the squatters, the group's lack of identity is reflected by the ease of its movement among the crowd. In a similar way, local politicians and city officials remain nameless. Their actions, even if sympathetic to the squatters' dilemma, remain significantly attached to class positions.

The soundtrack of the film is also used to underscore varying levels of social location. The community's emotional attachment to the river, for instance, is conveyed in the folk ballad sung during a party in the squatters' camp. The lyrics speak of the Paraná River, whose "water floods everything, and takes everything away," and of the "day I'll return to set up my shack in Santa Fé." The saturating effect of sound in the city sequences emphasizes a vitality that proves oppressive to the squatters. When the neighbors go to town, for instance, they are caught in the deafening sound of loudspeakers. An extreme long shot reveals the mayhem that follows a near-collision between two cars that advertise air-conditioned homes and solicit votes for local candidates.

The accordion music that accompanies the opening shots and the tango that ends the film have two distinctive functions. On the one hand, these tunes express communal solidarity in the face of impending dislocation and hopeful renewal. On the other hand, these tunes stress the community's origins as being both rural and urban. In fact, *Los inundados* continuously emphasizes the peripheral location of the river-bank people. The film moves between rural settings, such as the party in the camp by the train yard, and urban situations, such as the electoral campaign. As pointed out above, the neighbors' expeditions into town reflect their unease and awkward relationship to the city.

Moreover, the rendezvous between Pilar (Dolorcito's eldest daughter) and Raúl takes place somewhere between the river and the train yard. The mise-en-scène of these sequences underscores tension. Although their romance is not adequately resolved, it reveals gender and social differences. Raúl's aggressive behavior and dress, for instance, brands him in Pilar's eyes as a *compadrito*—an urban con-artist. Pilar might reprove but remains attached to him. In the same way, the neighbors reproach the foreign origins of a drunk man everyone calls "the Chilean." During the party in the camp, they intervene to stop a fight for the sake of communal harmony.

Once the family finds itself wandering from town to town, the emotional center of the film shifts. The drama is now set in the cramped quarters of a boxcar, and the narrative point of view is reversed. In the early sequences, the fate of the Gaitán family is connected to that of their neighbors. In the train sequences, the narrative stresses introspection. The characters' address is directed toward the passing landscape. They discover the countryside. From inside the wagons, the children and their parents observe wheat fields filled with combines and grasslands occupied by birds. They greet laborers, migrant workers, and villagers along the route.

During the unscheduled trip north, the implausibility of a happy end is anticipated through the contrast between urban apathy and rural solidarity. The last dialogue between Dolorcito and Ottima is marked by double entendres. It inflects their happiness to go home with a mixture of hope and critical awareness. Pilar's wish at the sight of the Southern Cross has come true, but with it the realization that, as Dolorcito says, "Don Orellana was right; all the Argentines are the same, but some think that we are stupid. Things can't go on like this."

Although *Los inundados* highlights the rural origins of popular culture, its textual strategies empower the address and expressivity of popular culture. The use of the vernacular regionalizes speech and locates its class origins. The use of popular expressions also serves to question meaning. For instance, Dolorcito often refers to himself as an *otario*—a distinctly Argentine word that means dumb, foolish, or silly. When Dolorcito protests the way he is treated by the railroad personnel, he says, "The dispatcher takes me like baggage from one place to the other as if I were *un otario.*" He is speaking not only about indifference but also about class prejudice.

By shifting identification toward the squatters on the Salado River, the film gives voice to a marginal community. But as B. Ruby Rich points out, in *Los inundados*, "these people, the 'oppressed', are granted their own subjectivity . . . their own sense of identity, their own consciousness, their own emotional life, their own *joie de vivre*. Even their own solutions."[32] The reflective and ironic tone of Dolorcito's comments, for instance, is not necessarily predetermined by destiny. Given that the river floods periodically, Dolorcito's remarks have a critical function.

The renewal of the community rebuilding the shacks is a signal of its resolve. Rather than stressing concrete solutions, the film uses

a fictional format as a means to empower social and cultural consciousness. The squatters' responses to a predictable natural disaster
are localized through geography and class. Thus Fernando Birri has
imagined the vital links between solidarity and survival. Through
the characters of Dolorcito, Ottima, Pilar, Don Orellana, Don Canuda, Raúl, and the other neighbors, the filmmaker has drawn attention to those aspects that constitute the affective life of popular
culture.

The *Sertao* and *Cinema Nôvo: The Guns*

The Guns (*Os Fuzis*, 1964), directed by Mozambican-born filmmaker Ruy Guerra, is one of several *cinema nôvo* films that deal
with drought, poverty, and mysticism in the Brazilian Northeast.
Unlike *Barren Lives* (*Vidas secas*, Nelson Pereira dos Santos, 1963)
and *Black God and White Devil* (*Deus e o Diabo na Terra do Sol*,
Glauber Rocha, 1964), *The Guns* provides a critical perspective on
religious belief and violence. It deconstructs historically fixed meanings—in other words, the representations and discourses through
which the Northeast has been interpreted.

Ruy Guerra had attempted to produce *The Guns* in 1958. The
screenplay was originally set in Greece and told the story of soldiers
who are brought into a village to defend a community threatened by
a pack of wolves. But Greek censors denied Guerra permission to
shoot. When the film was finally produced in 1964, Ruy Guerra
adapted the screenplay to Brazil and added culturally specific elements. Before shooting *The Guns*, Ruy Guerra had already established himself in Brazil with a short film (*O Cavalo de Oxumaré*,
1961) and a long feature (*Os Cafajastes*, 1962).[33]

The Guns is set in 1963. Its plot is organized around two stories.
In the first, hungry and landless peasants follow a mystic and a sacred ox in the *sertao*.[34] They pray for the rain that will end the
drought. The animal is finally sacrificed and its meat eaten by the
people. In the second, five soldiers arrive in a small town to guard a
storehouse. A restless soldier shoots a goatherder, and the sergeant
accuses the migrants of the murder. A truck driver tries to stop the
food from being moved out, but is killed by the soldiers.

As Randal Johnson explains, this film "is constructed through the
use of discontinuity, through the stretching of conventions of time
and space, and through a deliberate breakdown of genres, modes of
representation, and modes of discourse."[35] Ruy Guerra takes an innovative approach toward the oppressive and alienating realities of

the Northeast. He draws on historical and contemporary representations of the region that have been circulated through a variety of texts. They include literary chronicles (Euclides da Cunha's *Rebellion in the Backlands*, 1902), novels (Rachel de Queirós's *The Years Fifteen*, 1930, and Graciliano Ramos's *Barren Lives*, 1938), contemporary essays (Rui Facó's *Cangaçeiros and Fanatics: Origins and Struggles*, 1963), poetry (Joao Guimaraes Rosa's *Life and Death of Severino*, 1954–1955), and oral folklore collected in the *folhetos do cordel*.

The *Guns* deconstructs the sociological, ethnographic, and aesthetic codes that have served to portray the *sertao*—its drought, hunger, mysticism, and violence. The themes of this film also serve to draw attention to the discourses that have limited the self-representation of the people of the backlands. Therefore, the film takes into account popular culture as an expressive agency. As Anne Marie Gill states, "The representation of the *sertao* (in *The Guns*) as a geographic, historical, and cultural formation is accomplished through the deployment of codes that have their origins in this intertext . . . that immediately calls up roughly 60 years of interrelated discourses."[36] I want to argue that Ruy Guerra's film can be approached through this intertext. By appropriating this intertext, the film promotes dialectical readings of the region's history.

The film is made up of two distinct narrative blocks. One is constituted by the procession of peasants, the other by incidents triggered after the arrival of a contingent of soldiers in a small town. These two blocks are alternated throughout the film but do not converge into a single narrative. By overlapping these two stories, *The Guns* establishes a dialectic between powerlessness and alienation, revolt and apathy. However, the violent history of the backlands is never dramatically resolved. The decentered construction of the film, as Roberto Schwarz points out, "mark[s] the discontinuity between the two worlds. It serves as a critique of moralism since it accentuates both moral responsibility and its insufficiency. The important link, in this case, is in the very absence of a direct link."[37]

The black and white photography by Ricardo Aronovich, the haunting score by Moacir Santos, and the agile editing by Ruy Guerra are crucial to the film's dramatic construction. The mise-en-scène of *The Guns* is designed to take advantage of every element. In spite of the arbitrary juxtaposition of shots, signification is gradually expanded. The film appears at first to depend on the contrast between the two narrative blocks. However, this initial focus is destabilized. As the stories of the peasants and the soldiers develop, the film's structure becomes more complex. Narrative coherence is produced, as Michel Ciment argues, by "letting a network of meanings gradually come to the surface."[38]

The haunting quality of the images is the result of visual composition that produces tension between foreground and background. The almost classic use of depth of field draws attention to the movement and gestures of the characters. The film choreographs the lethargic mysticism of the Northeast through a combination of close-ups and long shots that place the landless peasants in the parched landscape. In the same way, camera angles and camera movement reveal the asymmetric power relations in the town. The mise-en-scène of *The Guns*, in spite of its realist codes, constructs highly expressive images of landscape and people. It conveys the desolate beauty of a region where torrential rains leave deep scars in the soil, where drought forces people to take to the road in search of food, and where the presence of people is not the trace of life but of death.[39]

In the sequences involving the soldiers, visual composition and choreography suggest that the soldiers—either as individuals or as a group—have a threatening, yet fascinating, effect on the townspeople. The arrival of the contingent, for instance, is given through a high-angle shot from a half-opened window. The townspeople are shown looking out of windows and then standing at street level. Close-up and low-angle shots of the soldiers' feet and guns emphasize a fragmentary and faceless authority. But, as Roberto Schwarz states, "seen from below [the soldiers] represent authority, but from above they are 'the people.'"[40] In a second set of close-up shots, the individual soldiers are introduced. After Mario (Nelson Xavier)— and through noticeable directional shifts—"301" (Ivan Candido) and the sergeant (Leonidas Bayer), and Pedro (Paulo César Pereiro) and Zé (Hugo Carvana) are presented in sequence.

Moreover, the use of sound reinforces rather than dramatizes the action. In the sequence that I have just described, the shots of the soldiers are accompanied by the metallic grating of a musical instrument. From an emotional point of view, the sound intensifies the soldiers' anxiety. At the same time, this sound originates in the preceding sequence, in which an old woman talks about a fire that blinded her and killed her great-grandchildren. By connecting the arrival of the soldiers to the story of the old woman, sound insinuates complex links between the unfolding narrative and the historical memory of the Northeast.

This pattern is set up from the beginning of the film. In the opening shots, for instance, the disembodied voice of the mystic has a haunting effect that never allows the images to become ethnographic. The *beato*'s sermon, combined with foreboding images, signals the entry into a topographical abyss. A blinding sun fills a dark screen that slowly becomes almost white. Shots of thorny *caatinga* bushes, lizards, and bleached remains of animals are intercut with shots of a white ox. The yearning for redemption expressed by the sermon is merged with the primitive landscape. Moreover, the *beato*'s deranged lucidity is fixed into history. With its hallucinatory pitch, the voice mimics that of Antonio Maciel (the Conselheiro), the messiah of Canudos whose voice terrified the people who heard him preach.[41]

While the messianic movements of the *sertao* have been traditionally described as futile forms of popular resistance, mysticism has been the archetypal representation of social alienation and not the result of chronic hunger. The opening sequence of *The Guns* places hunger and religious fervor within history. The cracks in the scorched soil lacerate the earth and the twisted tree branches disfigure the skyline, suggesting that the markings of history on the landscape are a permanent and material reminder of the past. Rather than concealing the traces of history, the dry climate of the *sertao* has preserved the memory of hunger and death. The landscape is a lasting reminder that can be reread by other generations.

The aural codes of this sequence echo the processes by which popular memory is transmitted. The *beato*'s sermon translates the memory of Canudos through the imaginative universe of allegory. The melodic recitation of the sermon also evokes the performances and public readings of oral literary expressions like *literatura de cordel* (string literature). This literary mode is distinct to the Northeast of Brazil: it has circulated either in spoken or written form (*folhetos*), disseminating the stories of the legendary heroes and heroines of the backlands.[42] In this way, *The Guns* draws attention to popular culture as a formal system and as vehicle to retell the region's history of violence.

Moreover, the stories told by old people to the camera connect the two narrative poles of the film. This layering of oral histories provides a chronological bridge between 1963 (the date on the credits) and collective and historical intertext that informs the film. Through these testimonies, the *sertanejos* reclaim their historical voice. The old man talks about peasants following a sacred man and an ox in the desert. His story is told throughout the film, and it provides a historical framework to the landless peasants' march. It functions as a commentary but also explains the religious and social motivations that have driven people across the inhospitable region in search for salvation.

The old woman who tells about the fire that blinded her recalls the day that Getulio Vargas committed suicide in the Catete Palace in Rio de Janeiro in 1954.[43] This account stresses the role that *literatura de cordel* has played in the preservation of popular memory in the Northeast and, as Anne Marie Gill points out, "dispel[s] any notion of the historical discourses originating in the Republic as isolated from those developing in the *sertao*."[44] Another old man evokes the arrival of 1,200 soldiers, the campaign organized by Carlos Machado de Bittencourt and the massacre at Canudos in 1896. He reappears at the end of the film to eulogize the twenty men who died in the final battle.

The mise-en-scène of these sequences places the testimonies in neutral settings—neither in the desert nor in the village—as if to underline their mythic origins. But the formal composition of these sequences resembles the protocol of documentary filmmaking and stresses that oral narratives are neither history nor myth but both. The direct mode of address authorizes the testimony of protagonist-witnesses and their role as oral mediators of historical narratives. In addition, the documentary strategy fractures the chronological space and draws attention to a temporal logic that operates simultaneously outside and inside the narrative movement of the film.

In *The Guns* time is constructed not only in terms of dramatic effect. Long sequence shots develop according to a dynamic that is both internal and external to the action. When Mario sees Luiza (Maria Gladys) on the street, for instance, a group of women praying is seen circling the church. This small procession disrupts his attempts to approach her. But at the same time, the back and forth movement of the group mimics Mario's awkward courtship. The ritualistic composition of each shot is heightened by Mario's almost aggressive acknowledgment of the procession and by the pervasive sound of the prayers. The tension of this sequence comes from the way in which the filmmaker presents class and gender difference. In fact, Mario's affair with Luiza climaxes in a possession/rape sequence where, in Randal Johnson's description, "the camera pushes Luiza and Mario along, precedes them, circles them until it finally loses its orientation and turns sideways and upside down, thus reflecting the characters' disorientation."[45]

The mise-en-scène of *The Guns* illustrates and expresses the rhythm of the *sertao*, and consequently time is drawn out only to be interrupted by sudden bursts of action. The tavern sequence in which the soldiers demonstrate their weapons to the townspeople, for instance, begins very slowly. Pedro walks around explaining the functioning of the rifle. Close-ups of the observing audience serve to present the passivity of the people and the boredom of the soldiers. The entrance—acknowledged only by Mario—of Gaúcho (Atila Lorio) and a group of *vaqueiros* provides a brief digression from what is basically a show of authority. But when Pedro defies Gaúcho to assemble the cocking device of the rifle, the camera focuses on their gestures. Gaúcho rebuffs Pedro's question ("Where did you learn this?"), and the answer comes through the nervous laughter of Mario.

While stressing that authority comes from ownership of guns, the film also establishes the ambivalent power invested in the soldiers. Although Vicente Pereira (Rui Polonah), the store owner, is assured that the food will be protected, the sergeant is unable to avoid conflict among his soldiers. His promise to Pereira that "if necessary the region will be riddled with bullets" is kept. But the bullets are meant for an ex-soldier and trucker, Gaúcho, who steals the gun from Zé and tries to stop a truck loaded with food from leaving town.

The sequence of Gaúcho's death is the dramatic climax of *The Guns*. It begins in the tavern where Gaúcho taunts Zé while the trucks are being loaded outside. A young peasant carrying the dead body of a child walks in. Gaúcho screams at him ("He was starving to death and you didn't do anything") and then at Zé ("There is no food and you're taking the food away"). Gaúcho then grabs the soldier's gun and shoots at the windshield of the truck. From this moment on, the contained animosity between Gaúcho and the soldiers explodes. The initial sounds of barking dogs and the deep breathing of the fleeing soldiers give way first to a tense silence, then to the burst of gunshots. The sequence ends with Zé screaming and Mario sobbing over the dead body of his friend.

Gaúcho is a man from the South, and as a migrant he is both landless and a foreigner. It is his action that triggers the violence, but it is also through him that class enters the film. His character establishes the ambiguous class position of the soldiers. Although they represent order, the soldiers are agents rather than protagonists of their own history. They mistrust the people, and their fear makes them even more hostile. When Pedro accidentally shoots a goatherd and the sergeant has to decide what to tell the people, for instance, the soldiers' actions are vicious and ruthless. While one of them extracts the bullet from the man's body, the others are seen eating their food, more concerned about their assignment than about the morality of their action.

With the predictable explosion of violence, and through the role assigned to Gaúcho, Ruy Guerra has allowed Mario to be the only character who reaches some level of individual consciousness. In an earlier part of the film, Mario visits Luiza and tells her about an armed action in which three men—who "really thought the property was theirs"—were killed and a fellow soldier was wounded. This sequence follows a bet between Pedro and Zé that results in the death of the goatherd. Mario's comment ("We shouldn't have done so much killing") expresses his awareness of the futility of violence. After the death of Gaúcho, Mario changes his uniform for a white shirt, and later when the soldiers march out of town, he is the only one who turns back to look at the camera.[46]

This close-up of Mario's face is followed by a white screen and a fade into the landscape of the desert. On the urging of the *beato*, the skinny ox that has led the procession of the landless peasants is sacrificed. In an ironic turn of fate, the animal's no longer sacred flesh is consumed by the starving people. As Anne Marie Gill suggests, the last shot, a close-up of the ox's head, "leaves the spectator to construct an historical discourse which will go beyond the alienation represented in the film."[47] *The Guns* explores social relations by placing individual and collective forms of power and powerlessness in a dialectical relationship. The patient gestures of a peasant carving an edible root out of the parched desert soil, for instance, are contrasted with the passive grief of the father who requests an empty crate in which to bury his dead child.

It is useful to point out that *The Guns* was produced in a period characterized by intense debates on underdevelopment. Between 1955 and 1964, the regimes of Presidents Juscelino Kubitschek and Joao Goulart set in place a series of nationalist policies to encourage economic and industrial growth.[48] These policies were conceived at the Higher Institute of Brazilian Studies (Instituto Superior de Estudios Brasileiros—ISEB), founded in 1955. Its members formulated an influential dichotomy that, as Randal Johnson states, "conceived the major contradiction of Brazilian society as being not capital versus labour, but rather the 'nation' (that which is authentic) versus the 'anti-nation' (that which is alienated from the 'nation's' true historical being)."[49]

The ideological split implied by this dichotomy furthered the marginalization of the Northeast. Josué de Castro points out that in 1964 ". . . with the exception of the feudal oligarchy, [Brazilians] have agreed to recognize that the conditions of the Northeast derive from an economic system."[50] Therefore, some intellectuals and activists like Josué de Castro set out to draw attention to the drought and hunger as an effect rather than the cause of underdevelopment.

This project not only involved an understanding of the social, economic, and political roots of underdevelopment. It was also inspired by the representations through which the Northeast told its own history.

In this context, the filmmakers of the *cinema nôvo*, and especially Ruy Guerra, sought to engage critically with the reality of the region. The so-called *sertao* cycle sought to probe into the roots of underdevelopment by merging history and mythology, class struggle and popular culture. While *Barren Lives* (Nelson Pereira dos Santos)—a critical adaptation of the homonymous novel by Graciliano Ramos—desentimentalizes the plight of the *sertanejos, Black God and White Devil* (Glauber Rocha) explores the historical consciousness of the Northeast by integrating popular culture.[51]

In a sense, *The Guns* goes beyond the project of these two films. It takes a dispassionate look at mysticism and hunger and (rather than drawing a picture of misery) invites a reflection informed by history and politics. By alternating two stories, this film takes a critical stand. It also considers the social and religious forces that have driven the people of the *sertao* into passivity. Moreover, it dissects the complex dialectic of class and power. In this way, Ruy Guerra's film constructs the dynamics of misery and suffering that have muffled class struggle in the Northeast.

Popular Memory and *The Courage of the People*

The Courage of the People (*El coraje del pueblo,* 1971), produced by Jorge Sanjinés and the Ukamau Group of Bolivia, is considered one of the most important films of the New Latin American Cinema. The film is a reconstruction of a massacre of miners in the town of Siglo XX on the night of June 24, 1967. In collaboration with some of the survivors of this event, the filmmakers document one of the most repressive actions taken by the Bolivian government against its people, and in the process they produce what eventually became a model of revolutionary and popular cinema. Through its participatory mode of production, the film demonstrated the bearing of collective memory on the notion of popular cinema.

In a text written in the mid-1970s Jorge Sanjinés reiterated the urgency of leaving aside traditional assumptions about political filmmaking. In "Problems of Form and Content in Revolutionary Cinema" he wrote: "If the self-proclaimed revolutionary artist continues to believe in his or her right to create without reference to anyone else, and to think that what counts is the release of his/her own 'private demons', with no concern for intelligibility, then s/he is locating her/himself clearly within the key ideological postulates of bourgeois art. Opportunism begins by lying to yourself."[52]

The Ukamau Group, made up of Jorge Sanjinés, Oscar Soria, Antonio Equino, Ricardo Rada, and Alberto Villapando, produced three long feature films in Bolivia: *Ukamau* (1966), *The Blood of the Condor* (1969), and *The Courage of the People* (1971). The international awards conferred to the three films gave Bolivian cinema a profile it had never had. At the same time, the experiences of making these films prompted Jorge Sanjinés to promote his ideas about popular cinema. To discuss *The Courage of the People,* it is useful first to look at the circumstances that led Jorge Sanjinés and the Ukamau Group to develop a participatory and collective concept of filmmaking and reception.

The production of the first two films of the group—*Ukamau* and *The Blood of the Condor*—was in a sense a process of political apprenticeship. The making of *The Roads of Death* (never completed) and *The Courage of the People* was an opportunity to reverse the ideological and formal weakness of the earlier films. For *The Blood of the Condor,* Sanjinés writes, "we still chose shots according to our own personal taste, without taking into account their communicability or cultural overtones. . . . In certain scenes we put the emphasis entirely on sound, without paying attention to the needs of the spectators, for whom we claimed we were making the film. They needed the images, and complained later when the film was shown to them."[53]

Having exhibited *Ukamau* and *The Blood of the Condor* among mostly peasant- and working-class audiences, Jorge Sanjinés and the Ukamau Group came to realize that subject matter alone could not ensure the political validity of cinema. The filmmakers began then to redefine the relationship between production and reception, formal strategies and creative motivations. In writings and interviews, Sanjinés insisted on a concept of filmmaking capable of acknowledging "the needs of both the participating spectator and the people as protagonist" and resolving in satisfactory ways the issue of accessibility.[54]

In his first feature film Sanjinés dramatized the appalling conditions of Bolivia's indigenous population. *Ukamau* deals with the rape of an Indian woman by a métis and her husband's revenge. In spite of its political perspective on violence and exploitation, the film reinforces the mythical fatalism attributed to indigenous cultures. Through its predominantly ethnographic approach, *Ukamau* remains attached to a poetic realism that stresses timelessness and universality. In the second feature the filmmaker tried to avoid the shortcomings of the first by addressing specific social and political issues. *The Blood of the Condor* dramatizes the reaction of a community against the forced sterilization of its women.

The script was written by Oscar Soria. The film was entirely shot in Kaata (400 kilometers from La Paz) after problems that arose between the filmmakers and the villagers were resolved.[55] The main characters were played by Benedicta Huanca, Vicente Verneros—both miners from Huanuni—and Marcelino Yanahuaya—the communal leader of Kaata. When the film was released, the obvious similarity between the Progress Corps—which runs a sterilization clinic in the film—and the Peace Corps led to a protest by the U.S. Embassy. The censor's office of the municipal council of La Paz gave in to embassy pressures, but widespread reaction forced the lifting of the ban. By 1971 the Bolivian government had ordered the expulsion of the Peace Corps.

The Blood of the Condor intercuts Paulina's (Benedicta Huanca) trip to the city to seek help from her brother-in-law Sixto (Vicente Verneros) with her account of the events that led to the shooting of her husband Ignacio (Marcelino Yanahuaya). Sanjinés subsequently criticized this flashback structure because it confused the indigenous spectators to whom the film was directed. Nonetheless, the flashbacks serve to locate the characters within a specific social and ethnic context that allows for parallels between rural and urban episodes and provides a comprehensive portrayal of indigenous experience in Bolivia.[56] Moreover, the outcome of the film (Sixto's return to the community after Ignacio's death) is strengthened by connections between the village and city sequences.

The film begins in the village, and, following the shooting of Ignacio, the story is told by Paulina. The village sequences stress the collective and locate social and ethnic identity as a living experience rather than an archaic leftover of the past. When Ignacio and Paulina visit the *yatiri* who will perform a traditional ceremony, for instance, the mise-en-scène highlights the prophetic power of the coca leaves.[57] The camera seeks out gestures and meanings acknowledging the ritual's significance for the community. The poetic resonances of this scene accent solidarity and respect for the soothsayer's decision.

In the city sequences, the observing camera isolates Paulina and Sixto, exposing a harsh and racist environment that silences and renders the Indian powerless. The scenes in the hospital and in the country club, for instance, reinforce the characters' resignation and their inability to act. The mise-en-scène underscores marginality and discrimination. However, when Sixto returns to the village in the final scene of the film, his Indian dress signals a return to a cultural community. The empowering effect of this image is heightened by the shot of raised guns that places resistance in the context of insurrection. As Roque Dalton pointed out, *The Blood of the Condor* "is more than just a film. [It] is a cinematic-revolutionary event that poses profound and burning problems of living Latin American reality, but also adheres to . . . the revolutionary potential in the indigenous sectors of our countries, constituent parts (since they are made of peasants) of the main force of the continent's national revolutions."[58]

In spite of the political impact of the film, the Ukamau Group changed their approach to filmmaking. As Sanjinés writes, "The human and political experiences of the people are moving, vital, creative forces. The level of political consciousness of the Bolivian miners, for example, is so high that the possibilities for their participation are immeasurable."[59] Therefore, the filmmakers began looking for a way to make a cinema through which the people could relay their own history. It was no longer a matter of filming according to a preconceived plan, but to let the protagonists enact their own experiences.[60]

In 1970, after the negatives of *The Roads of Death* were damaged in a German laboratory, Sanjinés withdrew his share from Sociedad Ukamau Limitada—the company set up for *The Blood of the Condor*—and began working on a new film. *The Courage of the People* was co-produced by the Ukamau Group—now the name of a production company—and by RAI-TV for the series "Latin America as Seen by Its Filmmakers." Walter Achugar, a Uruguayan who had distributed *The Blood of the Condor*, and Edgardo Pallero, an Argentine executive producer of *Los inundados*, made the production arrangements. Sanjinés asked two of his former collaborators to become partners in his new company: Oscar Soria, who had written *La sangre de San Juan* (a chronicle of the massacre that took place in Siglo XX in 1967), as a scriptwriter and Antonio Equino as director of photography.

The group adopted a horizontal rather than vertical method of production. Some of the miners who had survived the massacre participated in the making of *The Courage of the People*, both to perform and advise the crew. Sanjinés discarded the traditional working methods of fictional filmmaking such as nonchronological shooting, extensive blocking and close-ups. Alfonso Gumucio Dagrón, who worked as producer in *Get Out of Here!* (1976), which was shot in Ecuador between 1973 and 1975, comments that Sanjinés's "reliance on the long take avoids having to interrupt the historical actors when they are involved in redramatizing their own experience. . . . To direct historical actors as one would direct professional or conventional actors is to de-naturalize them, to block all that their memory might spontaneously offer."[61]

From this perspective, the filmmakers sought to stress the resisting function of collective address that characterizes the orally transmitted narratives of Andean cultures. As Rowe and Schelling suggest, orality is the instance through which "native knowledge has been preserved, often in disguised or semi-clandestine ways."[62] *The Courage of the People* also stresses the primacy of ritual and performance aspects of orality to reactivate the past. Therefore, techniques used for the shooting of the film were designed to reflect the manner in which members of the traditional communities can access the past and participate in its reenactment.

The film was shot in the actual places where the historical event occurred. In this way, the setting—like the oral narrative—becomes, in the words of Rowe and Schelling, "a site for storing and processing memory."[63] In order to maintain an emotional and expressive authenticity, the film did not include (as did the previous films) professional actors or members of the crew. While performers in *The Blood of the Condor* had to memorize and repeat the script without any changes, Sanjinés explains that in *The Courage of the People* the "dialogues from reconstructed situations were recorded on the spot. They were discussed there, on the very site of the historical event, with the actual participants in the event."[64]

The postproduction of *The Courage of the People* was done in Europe. This stage of the film coincided with the military coup of Colonel Hugo Banzer and the overthrow of General Juan José Torres, who had enabled the organization of a People's Assembly of workers, miners, and students. The events in Bolivia forced Sanjinés to remain in Europe and inhibited the initial circulation of the film. Although the film received an award from OCIC (Oficina Católica Internacional del Cine) in 1972, as Walter Achugar explains, it "caused great consternation within the ranks of RAI, which cut certain sections and delayed the film's international release and distribution for years."[65] In 1974, when *The Courage of the People* began circulating in Europe and North America, it was celebrated as an accomplishment of revolutionary cinema.

The new Bolivian regime issued a ban on the film, and Antonio Equino was briefly imprisoned in 1973 when police discovered that he had a print. However, the Ukamau Group distributed the film in Peru, Ecuador, and Colombia between 1971 and 1979. Jorge Sanjinés estimates that 40,000 workers saw the film in Quito, while 340,000 workers, peasants, and students in various regions of Ecuador saw all the other films made by the group.[66] In spite of having exhibition rights for Bolivia, the Ukamau Group was unable to show the film until 1979, when the Cinemateca Boliviana in La Paz organized a Sanjinés retrospective. At that point, the filmmaker and some of his collaborators returned to the country after a long exile. The showing of *The Courage of the People* in Bolivia triggered intense debates on its ideological agenda in spite of its international and Latin American reputation. Moreover, three weeks after its première, the film was withdrawn from exhibition. The censor's office banned the film at the demand of the Bolivian army and, in particular, General Ramón Azero, named in the film as co-author of a massacre of miners.[67] Even after sixteen years, the Bolivian army felt threatened by a film that records one of their most infamous actions.

Although *The Courage of the People* reconstructs a massacre ordered by the regime of René Barrientos in 1967, the credit sequence shows a similar event that took place in 1942 involving miners and families from Cataví. The film opens in the *altiplano* (the mountainous region of Bolivia). By alternating long shots of the landscape and close-ups of waiting soldiers, the film builds to an emotional climax as a crowd of children, women and men led by Maria Barzola advances.[68] The sequence ends with a high-angle shot of bodies piled in a common grave and the sound of drums.

By placing the event in the actual location where it happened, the film's reconstruction connects the performers with a historical landscape. Thus the people of the mining cooperative of Villa Imperial and the workers of Siglo XX are introduced not only as players in a film but as subjects of history. About the opening sequence Jorge Sanjinés writes: "What we saw on the editing table convinced us that we were treading solid ground. Those images had not been conjured up by some scriptwriter. They had not been set up or invented by a director. . . . No, these were images created—or rather remembered—by the people. They were situations created on the spot by people who, amid the turbulence and the explosions, were reliving their past. An incredible capacity for expression had developed among those who collectively reenacted the massacre."[69]

The shot of the victims of Cataví initiates a montage of still photographs with printed intertitles that identifies those responsible for the 1942 massacre and other military actions in the mining region.[70] In this way, *The Courage of the People* not only establishes a historical context but makes mine owners, military officials, presidents, and union leaders accountable for the brutal murder of Bolivian miners and their families. A voice-over narration, over shots of

Siglo XX, addresses the appalling conditions that have existed in the mining towns. The voice-over names the people who will act in the film and who will represent those who were killed in 1967.

The voice of Domitila Barrios de Chungara introduces herself over shots in her house. She talks about her father's support when she wanted to go to school and how she organized the Housewives' Committee in Siglo XX. The film then shows her with other women protesting the shortage of food at the company store, persuading the miners to support the demands of the women, and disputing the arguments of the mines' representatives during a hunger strike.[71] Over the shots of workers in the mines, a second character introduces himself. Fernando Vallejo talks about the hardship he endured in his childhood. He is then shown in the office demanding the whereabouts of people who have been arrested, after being picked up at night and tortured, and dumped from a truck into a ditch.

The voice-over of Felicidad Coca, walking in the market, recounts how her husband, Rosendo García Maisman, had gone to Santa Cruz and how he died on the night of June 24, 1967, defending the radio transmitter of the mine. In the sequence that follows, a man talks to the workers in the mine about the need to support the guerrillas led by Ché Guevara. The next two segments are introduced by Simon Reinaga, a miner who was doing his military service with the Rangers, commanded by Colonel Villapando, and Eusebio Gironda Cabrera, a student who went to Siglo XX to organize the Ampliado Nacional Minero (plenary meeting) planned for June 25.

In this way, the stories of some of the survivors introduce the events that led to the 1967 massacre. As Ana López points out, *The Courage of the People* "functions both as a historical reconstruction of a crucial event in the history of the Bolivian class struggle and as a documentary of one community's collective remembering and recreation of that event."[72] The collective recreation of a historical event is thus set in motion by personal stories. Each character represents herself or himself, but also categorizes particular forms of solidarity, experience, and memory. While Eusebio Gironda Cabrera's story reveals the extent of the military occupation in the region, Simon Reinaga's account particularizes the dilemma of individual soldiers. As the latter explains why he refused to shoot at the miners, the first substantiates another instance of class solidarity through the soldier charged with controlling access to the region.

The events that took place on the night of June 24 are given without the mediation of a historical protagonist. This part of the film begins with a village party, which is traditionally the way in which miners celebrate the feast of St. John. Shots of the soldiers descend-

ing from railway cars at the Cancañiri station are intercut with images of miners singing around bonfires. The filmmakers' refusal to
light the night gives meaning to the murderous violence released by
the army. At dawn the sound of the mine's siren gives way to the
sirens of ambulances driving the wounded to a hospital. Here again
the camera conveys the confusion, horror, and grief of the people of
Siglo XX. An extreme long shot of a rock pile shows a group of miners who, armed with dynamite sticks, try to prevent a summary execution. Although one is killed by an airplane flying over the village,
the others escape. The last shot of this sequence shows Domitila
Barrios de Chungara being arrested and taken away from the village
in an army truck.

Accompanying the shots of the cemetery is a voice-over that
names some of the people who died as well as those responsible
for the massacre (as in the beginning of the film). *The Courage of
the People* ends where it started. A large group of people advance
toward the camera carrying flags. Combative, yet jubilant, this shot
expresses the tenacious history of miners' struggles. The reappear-
ance of the miners on the horizon of the *altiplano* implies promise. This closing shot celebrates a historical capacity to turn defeat
into hope.

The political impact of this film comes from a conscious attempt
to rethink historical reconstruction. Sanjinés and the Ukamau Group,
as Ana López points out, sought "to develop a form of filmmaking
as self-conscious historiography, as the inscription of a history in
the present."[73] The epic quality of this film comes from an approach
to narrative construction that is both conventional and innovative.
The documentary protocol of the film, for instance, is designed to
further a sense of location that spills over into the fictional. Even
the systematic intercutting, used to construct emotion, serves to
mediate between fiction and memory. It provides a sense of immediacy that intensifies, rather than intrudes upon, history. In this
way, *The Courage of the People* has become a powerful model of
popular cinema. It is an expressive testimony of history that is designed to be, in the words of Domitila Barrios de Chungara, "useful
for the working class and not only for intellectual people or for
people who only make a business of this kind of thing."[74]

The notion of popular cinema as developed by Latin American
filmmakers (film as an agent of change, requiring political choices
and innovative aesthetic options to release popular creativity) reflects a tension between tradition and modernity. Not only has this
popular (and reflective) cinema reconstructed the subversive power
of popular traditions and historical memory, but deconstructed the

representations and discourses that have limited the self-representation of Latin American peoples. In their films Latin American filmmakers celebrated class struggle, recalling past and present victories and defeats, and looked toward the people themselves as the revolutionary vanguard.

In the films studied in this chapter, I have shown how, armed with a revolutionary and anti-imperialist notion of popular cinema, filmmakers sought to establish new forms of dialogue and contest master narratives of the status quo. In the 1960s filmmakers themselves recognized the need to engage politically in the cultural arena. They turned their cameras toward the dark side of underdevelopment and neocolonialism, denouncing their effects and causes through their films. They also questioned the illusion of progress and democracy, scrutinizing the realities of discourses that benefited few but disenfranchised the majority of Latin Americans.

Cultural Difference and Representation

As pointed out in previous chapters, the New Latin American Cinema has promoted a political and aesthetic rearrangement of the terms that have served to construct national identities. Through popular cinema, the movement has acknowledged and attempted to redress the erasure of marginal experiences from class-informed constructs of national identity. Although filmmakers have taken a position in regard to class inequalities, they have tended to overlook the racial underpinnings of social oppression. By the late 1970s and into the 1980s Brazilian and Cuban filmmakers, in particular, had begun to advocate a need to review historical and cultural elements belonging to racially distinct groups that have contributed to the shaping of collective identities.

Therefore, it is useful to investigate how cultural difference has been drawn into the politics of representation of the New Latin American Cinema—in other words, to understand how issues of ethnicity have been incorporated into the films of the movement and how filmmakers are struggling to articulate the paradox of an intellectual legacy that has overlooked the histories of racial inequality in Latin America. Given that the movement itself has not addressed ethnicity in a direct way, any critical approach to this issue requires a preliminary sketching out of conceptual and historical terms of references.

On the one hand, I propose that the notion of ethnicity opens a critical space for a better understanding of how cultural difference, identity, and otherness have been shaped in and by history. Insofar as ethnicity presumes an awareness of cultural difference, it has as much to do with sociocultural organization as with representation. Instead of seeing ethnicity only in terms of the systems through which identity has been represented, one could locate ethnicity in existing patterns of power relations and with regard to marginal and subaltern experiences of alterity.[1]

On the other hand and insomuch as ethnicity in Latin America has tended to be subsumed in the notion of *mestizaje,* this term requires further elucidation. The term *mestizaje,* as William Rowe and Vivian Schelling suggest, dates from the early colonial time and was used to refer to the miscegenation of Spanish and Indians. "The difficulty with the idea of *mestizaje* is that, without an analysis of power structures, it becomes an ideology of racial harmony which obscures the actual holding of power by a particular group."[2] I will return to this term later. For the moment, it seems appropriate to understand *mestizaje* as a race-relations narrative that has been historically mobilized to represent the multicultural foundations of Latin American societies.

Ethnicity and *Mestizaje*

On a continent where cultural production has been determined by conquest, colonization, and genocide, and where cultural diversity is the result of hybridicity, difference has been crucial to the imagining of national identities. But cultural difference, as Homi K. Bhabha suggests, is not the same as cultural diversity. The second term subsumes the articulation and exchange between old, new, and hybrid forms of culture, while the first "focuses on the problem of the ambivalence of cultural authority."[3] Therefore, and given that the cultural history of Latin America has operated within two distinctive forms of exchanges—*mestizaje* and syncretism—I would suggest that the ideology of *mestizaje* is precisely the site of cultural difference, while syncretism—the selective alliance of indigenous and nonindigenous elements—is the location of cultural diversity.

The syncretism of Afro-Cuban music, popular religious practices in Mexico, and the dialectical speech patterns of the Rio de la Plata are some instances through which the violent encounter between races, classes, and cultures can be traced. Shaped in the exchange and through the struggle between native, African, and European cultures, these practices are the result of processes of hybridization and deterritorialization—in other words, of formal rearticulations of existing practices and relocation of dislocated practices.[4]

Moreover, Latin American cultural practices have been molded by social relations whereby patterns of exclusion and inclusion have operated within competing versions of history and popular memory. Hence, the questions concerning who speaks and for whom have historically informed, legitimized, and empowered the constructions of national identity. These questions are the site where the struggles for Latin American identities have played themselves out, and where open or fixed relations between self and other, between subjective and collective locations, are articulated and images are produced.

Angel Rama, the Uruguayan essayist and critic, has pointed out that the cultural history of the continent has been characterized by a modernist impulse, a dialectical synthesis of otherness and universality, and regional resistances to unifying narratives of class and culture. The specificity of Latin American narrative can be found in a process that Rama calls "transculturation," whereby literary forms are transformed by invention and innovation.[5] Similarly, Claudio Solano suggests that "it is at the meeting of . . . (class and culture), at the crossing of a specific social/economic REALITY and cultural/ artistic/mythical FANTASY that we can find the most representative aesthetics of Latin American Cinema in the last three decades. This 'most representative' refers less to the quantitative and more to what I believe to be one of our strongest features: the cultural/mystical syncretism of our continent."[6]

Neither Rama nor Solano acknowledges ethnicity in the construction of Latin America's distinctive literary or cinematic practices. Therefore, it seems appropriate to try to disentangle some of the historical factors that have contributed to the collapsing of cultural identity and cultural difference into class rather than ethnicity. Moreover, and insofar as some Cuban and Brazilian filmmakers are attempting to reclaim the place of ethnicity in representation, it is equally pertinent to understand how their films break through class-bound ideas of race.

Pervasive miscegenation has camouflaged racial distinctions, contributing to the tendency to overlook ethnicity in favor of class distinctions. Racial inequality has been so profoundly embedded in social relations that class awareness has inhibited ethnic consciousness. Although colonial Latin American societies had been shaped by the dialectical intersection of race, class, and culture, the issue of race surfaced again after independence and converged obsessively with the nationalist ideologies of emerging nation-states. Between 1870 and 1940 racist thinking first delayed the abolition of slavery (Brazil and Cuba) and later affected immigration policy (Argentina, Brazil, Cuba, and Mexico). Social Darwinism played a role in the marginalization of mulatto and mestizo populations and justified massive land appropriations all over Latin America.

Richard Graham points out that intellectuals have been rather unsuccessful in negotiating the racially mixed reality of their countries and the racial determinism inhered from colonialism.[7] As Aline Helg writes, "They tried to build up an imaginary and stereotyped world that would function according to permanent and logical bio-psychological laws. It would be a world with acknowledged enemies and myths. A 'scientific,' 'rational' world, when a confusing and rapidly changing reality made it difficult to find one's identity."[8]

In Brazil, for instance, the preoccupation with the multiracial foundations of nationhood has generated since the 1940s a particularly strong myth of "racial democracy." This myth is so pervasive that, as Thomas E. Skidmore argues, even in the 1980s "Brazilian opinion makers are still living with the intellectual legacy of the compromise their parents and grandparents struck with racist theory. . . . They have inherited a richly complex multiracial society but have not yet found a new rationale to describe or justify its nature."[9]

In Cuba, and in spite of the antiracist positions of José Martí and the participation of blacks in the struggle for independence in the nineteenth century, the acceptance of an African heritage was limited to commercial and nonpolitical cultural practices (such as music and Carnival). But even with the 1959 abolishment of overt forms of racial discrimination, Cubans are still struggling with a historically based sociocultural hierarchy. As Lourdes Casal points out, "the egalitarian and redistributive measures enacted by the revolutionary government have benefitted blacks as the most oppressed sector of the society in the pre-revolutionary social system. This does not imply that all forms of prejudice have been banned or that the consciousness of all the people has been thoroughly transformed."[10]

As the New Latin American Cinema struggles to integrate ethnicity into the politics of representation, it might be counterproductive to see ethnicity as an alternative to stereotyped images. Because the notion of stereotype presupposes from the outset the possibility of positive—or even authentic—images of cultural interaction, the redressing of negative representations of ethnicity tends to entrench ethnic representability, or what black British filmmakers Isaac Julien and Kobena Mercer call a "restricted economy of ethnic enunciation."[11] Therefore, it might be more appropriate to explore how cinematographic representations of ethnicity contest *mestizaje*, how these images engage in the replotting of race relations, and how representation is mobilized to reimagine history. What is at stake, as suggested by Julien and Mercer, is "the culturally constructed nature of ethnic identities, and the implications this has for the analysis of representational practices."[12]

One of the characteristics of the New Latin American Cinema has been the capacity to speak from a socially pertinent position, to articulate social, political, and cultural aspirations within nationally specific forms of expression and affectivity. From this perspective, it is interesting that some black filmmakers have begun to reexamine the stifling interrelation of race and class. Sergio Giral, for instance, has said about a recent film: "The philosophical underpinnings of the film *María Antonia* [Cuba, 1990] are the philosophical underpinnings of the Yorubá culture. Of its ethics and even its aesthetics. This is particular to our cultural syncretism. I believe that from the time African slaves were first brought to Cuba, many of the Yorubá, up to the present, have bequeathed to us a strong ethic of resistance, which has survived every kind of adversity: slavery, bourgeois contempt, and dogmatic incomprehension."[13]

The films in this chapter present different ways of dealing with ethnicity and with distinct experiences of oppression. They are attempts to explore the dialectical relation between cultural experiences of ethnicity and social development by drawing attention to the conflict between historical and contemporary patterns of social relations. These films also move away from ahistorical presumptions of identity and from romantic celebrations of difference either by connecting ethnicity to emerging cultural and social movements or by providing alternatives to historical representation. The films analyzed in this chapter, in spite of their shortcomings, represent a struggle to come to terms with the mythologies of *mestizaje* and the possibility of rearticulating the master narratives of national identity.

The Dialectics of Race and Class: *One Way or Another*

One Way or Another (*De cierta manera*, 1974–1978) was made by Sara Gómez, who at the time was the only woman director working at the Cuban Film Institute. The film juxtaposes documentary and fictional modes in a manner characteristic of Cuban filmmaking to explore the dialectics of class, ethnicity, and gender. A black woman, Sara Gómez nevertheless avoided the idealization of race as a means of presenting the marginal status of Havana's predominantly black and mulatto subproletariat.

At a time when colour stock had become a prevalent feature in Cuban cinema, the film was shot in black and white and blown up from 16mm to 35mm. Its mode of production was akin to documentary. Sara Gómez, a musician by training, began working at the Cuban Film Institute in 1964. After having made a number of documentaries, she had the opportunity to direct her first feature film in 1974.[14] Her untimely death, from asthma, delayed the completion of the film. Julio García Espinosa, Tomás Gutierrez Alea, and Rigoberto López supervised the final mix and the postproduction. The negative of the film, damaged during processing, had to be repaired in Sweden. *One Way or Another* was finally released in 1978.

From the late 1960s and well into the mid-1970s, Cuban cinema placed a particular emphasis on Afro-Cuban culture, and filmmakers undertook to restore black heritage to its rightful historical place. While a great number of documentaries, for example, dealt with the syncretic origins of popular music and drew biographical portraits of black performers, feature films took a historical perspective. *The Other Francisco* (*El otro Francisco*, Sergio Giral, 1974) inaugurated a series of feature films dealing with slavery in Cuba that included *The Last Supper* (*La última cena*, Tomás Gutierrez Alea, 1976). These films were crucial to a project of historical rehabilitation. As Ambrosio Fornet explains, slaves had traditionally been seen as secondary figures in Cuban history until freed slaves joined the wars of independence (1868–1898). However, and rather than being affiliated with the rebellious *cimarrón* (runaway slaves), black resistance was emblematically linked to the rebel *mambí* army.[15]

From this perspective, *One Way or Another* appears to be an exception. It places Afro-Cuban culture in a contemporary context. The film analyzes the psychological, moral, and cultural behavior of communities that remain outside the mainstream. When Sara Gómez made this film, the Cuban government's attempts to integrate marginals into the social process (mainly through improvements in housing and education) were not necessarily followed by changes in attitudes of and toward marginals. The filmmaker chose to approach marginality through the historical conditions that generated it. She revealed how social relations in underdeveloped countries are distorted by inequality and discrimination.

Gómez linked deviant forms of behavior (such as male chauvinism and delinquency) to poverty and social alienation. These forms of behavior are shown to be, as Carlos Galiano writes, "the most difficult and protracted hangovers to eradicate once a new social order is established in which the economic conditions that gave rise to them no longer exist."[16] However, by interconnecting characters of different social extraction, the film also reveals forms of behavior which are not exclusive to lower-class or specific ethnic groups. It promotes reflection on prejudices that permeate the fabric of underdeveloped societies and that are rooted in patriarchal, religious, and racial ideologies.

One Way or Another follows the love story between Yolanda (Yolanda Cuéllar), a middle-class teacher assigned to a new school, and

Mario (Mario Balmaceda), a worker in a bus factory. Their relationship is affected by the tensions that each has to resolve in the workplace. Yolanda confronts the reality of the neighbors who live in Miraflores, a new community on the outskirts of Havana. At the opening of the film and speaking directly to the camera, she admits having discovered "a different world, one I thought no longer existed." Yolanda's attitude toward her pupils is challenged by her coworkers because—even if she wants to help the boy Lazáro and his mother La Mejicana—she is insensitive to their personal histories. Mario jeopardizes his friendship with Humberto (Mario Limonta) when he reveals the truth behind his friend's frequent absences from the factory. Mario feels torn between a social morality and a male code of honor. Rather than assuming responsibility for his action, Mario makes unreasonable demands on Yolanda. She breaks off the relationship, and the film ends when Mario seeks her out on the street.

Although the romance between Yolanda and Mario is crucial to narrative development, it also serves to explore the intricate issues of social marginality. Through each one of the characters, One Way or Another outlines the conflict between collective demands and subjective desires. The issue of loyalty, for instance, is framed by the antagonism between a revolutionary ethic and the old-fashioned codes of machismo, between a communal solidarity that does not admit duplicity and individualism. In this way, Sara Gómez has investigated the effect of historical elements of black and mulatto culture on contemporary forms of social and political engagement.

Before 1959 the history of blacks and mulattos in Cuba was affected by social, economic, and political exclusion. The revolutionary government implemented policies to eradicate class discrimination and racial prejudice. Sara Gómez draws attention to quantitative changes in health, education, and housing but also to unresolved issues, particularly those that involve social acceptance and consciousness. As Osvaldo Sánchez Crespo points out, "One Way or Another is the story of a transition, of a painful process by which people recognize their ability to break with outdated colonial ethics, with their resistance to change and with their individualism. Seeking a dialogue within their marginal world, Sara Gómez explored the reasons for their resistance, and its relation to the defense of Cuban popular traditions and popular culture."[17] Therefore, without neglecting the feminist concerns of this film, it is useful to consider how issues of gender intersect with those of ethnicity and class.[18]

The combination of documentary and fictional modes and the participation of nonprofessionals along with professional performers in

One Way or Another have a political and aesthetic function. On the one hand, this juxtaposition sets up a complex dialectic between the patterns that regulate social relations and representation. As Julia Lesage writes, the film "refuses to contribute to segmented knowledge and segmented existence."[19] The strictly documentary sequences are given different functions within the film. These sequences serve to inform or comment on the effect of historical formations on subjectivity. The integration of documentary sequences into the fiction contests the authority of the documentary modes of address, and the film expands—rather than controls—the range of meanings.

On the other hand, *One Way or Another* demonstrates the radical potential of a mixed mode of filmmaking.[20] This mixed mode contests the social immediacy of documentary through a semifictional design. The film deconstructs the didacticism of documentary and the arbitrary arrangement of the fictional anecdote. In addition, the filmmaker uses either mode to destabilize address and narrative continuity. These self-reflective options connect creative expression to social change and promote a dialectical relationship between the film and its audiences. In this way, the film presents unspoken and unseen realities to restore everyday experiences to the historical consciousness of the Cuban Revolution.

Sara Gómez rejected a closed model of filmmaking on behalf of an innovative critical realism. She refrained from subordinating one mode to the other, and used documentary and fiction to articulate different levels of social location, experience, and awareness. The filmmaker's concern with representation and self-representation takes into account syncretic forms of expression, *mestizaje,* and cultural interaction. The vernacular used by the protagonists, combined with the melodies of the *son* and the *guaguancó,* is given a sociocultural dimension that, while rooted in a colonial past, is integral to Afro-Cuban popular culture. Moreover, the highly expressive intonations of the dialogue and the music contribute to the rhythm and agility of the film. The performances of the characters communicate the humor and pathos of black and mulatto culture, thus empowering racial difference as an element of social change.

The film proposes, as suggested by its Spanish-language title, a certain way of looking at individual and collective reality. By using a documentary on underdevelopment and neocolonialism as a point of departure to explain who the people from Miraflores are, *One Way or Another* roots social change in the achievements of the Cuban Revolution. Candito (Mario's father), for instance, is introduced in a documentary sequence, and later he addresses the camera directly. He speaks for the shantytown dwellers who see in the revolution the possibility for improving their lives. As the stories of individual characters are revealed, the film attempts to reconsider other forms of social exclusion. Although Candito has become a community and labor leader, his self-respect is undermined by Mario's inability to reject incompatible views and prejudices.

Therefore, the recurrent shots of old buildings being demolished to make space for new housing play a symbolic role. These images initially introduce the setting of the film, but also serve to associate physical leveling with moral renewal. The images of demolition are inserted again between a documentary biography of Guillermo Díaz (a black boxer whose career ended as a result of crime) and shots of Mario, Yolanda, Candito, and others cleaning up the schoolyard. This contrast between shantytown delinquency and neighborhood solidarity alludes to the past of the members of the Miraflores community who once lived in the slum of Las Yaguas. Like previous shots of Havana's slums, the documentary on Guillermo gives a conventional vision of poverty, suffering, and violence. But rather than invalidating the past, these images suggest—as Guillermo advises Mario—that it takes more courage to reject your background than to condone it.

One Way or Another furthers an awareness of marginality that is both empowering and critical. Inasmuch as the film draws attention to the persistence of marginality within the revolution, it frames the marginals' resistance to change within a history of intolerance and double standards of morality. This is achieved simultaneously through the spectators' familiarity with the discourses that inform racial and social relations in Cuba and with the textual operations of the film. What is interesting is that Sara Gómez, rather than sanctioning documentary address as a primary critical device, authorizes self-representation and, to a certain degree, is critical of publicly sanctioned assumptions about marginality. The romance between Mario and Yolanda, the friendship between Mario and Humberto, and the relationship between Yolanda and Lázaro serve to elucidate the distance that separates personal and public forms of awareness.

In the first case, when Mario begins courting Yolanda, the fictional narrative is interrupted by a short documentary on the Abacuá society in which atavistic rituals, social exclusion, and *machismo* are associated. The documentary is prompted by Yolanda's surprised reaction to Mario's disclosure that once he contemplated becoming a *ñañigo* (a member of a secret society). However, Mario's engaging account of his life counters the didactic voice-over of the documentary, thus constructing Mario's emerging awareness.

Through the editing and the alternation of close-ups of both characters, Mario's own indulgence and lack of political consciousness
is given by an oblique comment about the revolution ("and then it
came"). When Yolanda compels him to explain, Mario's reply ("The
school was rough" and "The military service saved me") contains the
realization that, without coercion, he would still be in the slums.

In the second case, Mario decides that he is incapable of defending
Humberto's derelict behavior. The confrontation between the two
characters is given twice in the film. The pre-credit sequence starts
with a speech by Humberto and, after Mario's rebuttal, ends with
Humberto's mocking smile. The entire situation is repeated later in
the film and is framed by Mario's self-questioning. Mario is torn
between Humberto's remark ("The teacher has brainwashed you,
made you a Komsomol") and his own remorse ("I acted like a
woman, turning him in"). But a discussion between mostly black
workers, filmed according to the protocol of documentary, disputes
the characters' perceptions. In this sequence, as Michael Chanan
writes, the factory workers "are no longer simply actors in a story,
but representatives of the audience watching the film . . . at the
same time participant observers and observant participators in the
dramas of daily life."[21]

In the third case, Yolanda's inability to deal with one of her young
pupils is set against the background of her ignorance about the sociocultural origins of the people of Miraflores. In a series of semi-
documentary sequences, Yolanda comes in contact with Lazáro's
personal and public story. His single mother (La Mejicana) explains
why she is unable to take care of him, and the social worker tells
Yolanda about Lazáro's stay in a home for delinquent youths. By
intercutting direct-address shots of the mother and the welfare official with Yolanda's reaction, the film constructs a process of evaluation that moves from the fictional characters to the spectators of
the film.

By personalizing marginality, *One Way or Another* empowers
forms of social experience that are grounded in gender, ethnicity,
and class. The film permits different levels of reading because identification is directed toward several characters. As Michael Chanan
suggests, the film establishes a "symmetrical set of structural op-
positions" between characters.[22] The tensions between Humberto
and Candito and between Lazáro and La Mejicana, for example,
serve to underline values that were once acceptable but are now inappropriate. In addition, the affinities between Humberto and Lazáro draw attention to family instability. Class inequity and racial
discrimination, as Osvaldo Sánchez Crespo suggests, produced a pa-

triarchal notion of family among Afro-Cubans. This notion was imposed during slavery when African family traditions were displaced by Catholic and Hispanic values.[23]

In this way, the dramatic conflict hinges on the individual stories as well as on the class and ethnic position of the characters. The sequence in the restaurant, for instance, parallels Yolanda's relationship with Mario to that of another couple, Joe and Migdalia. Scenes between the two women (in the restaurant's washroom) and the two men (at the bar) foreground how class differences hinder even the most self-evident and socially sanctioned forms of gendered bonding. As the group later walks along the ocean boulevard, Migdalia is left behind. A long shot of Migdalia against the darkened background, followed by a freeze frame, hints at her double marginalization. Migdalia's position, as a dark-skinned woman, is made more intense by a preceding scene in which she criticizes Yolanda's relationship with Mario.

In this way, the film connects women's inferior social position to pervasive sexist attitudes that, when linked to racism, are not exclusive to urban subproletarian male culture. Rather than blaming blacks and mulattos for their *machismo, One Way or Another* disputes assumptions (like those given in the Abacuá documentary) that produce class- and ethnicity-based stereotypes. Although Yolanda never confronts Migdalia's behavior, later in the film Mario discusses with Joe his conduct during the workers' assembly. This conversation takes place in a park underneath an equestrian statue of General Maceo, the black *mambí* hero of Cuban independence known as the "Bronze Titan." As Michael Chanan points out, this location carries distinct ironic overtones.[24] But I would also add that Mario's comment ("After all, it's men who made the revolution") places his self-awareness within a racial and gendered identity.

Moreover, this conversation follows a sequence between Yolanda and Mario in a hotel room. Yolanda mimics Mario's self-confident stride when he strolls around with his friends, pointing out how differently he acts with her. As Mario admits, "I am scared shitless"; his anxiety at the prospect of disclosing Humberto's lies is framed by a moment of intimacy between the lovers. By giving expression to Mario's doubts in a private place, the film reveals the antagonism between gendered, racial, and political values and romantic love. By placing the values that inform Mario's identity and conduct in conflict with his love for Yolanda, the film also makes these values self-conscious and problematic. As Julia Lesage indicates, the "personal sphere is revealed as the place where individuals struggle to know what they want, and this struggle is always incomplete."[25]

As the romance between the two characters becomes more and more strained and each encounters the hostility of co-workers, the film explores the way in which both are challenged to change. The conflict between Yolanda and Mario remains dramatically unresolved but, as the film has been insinuating all along, transformation is possible. The last scene of the film is edited to the ballad previously performed by Guillermo Díaz. Shots of Mario approaching Yolanda on the street are intercut with images from the shantytowns while the lyrics urge

Leave your world
that does not care,
that has no flowers,
only bars show its power.
Leave it
and never let it find out
what you have been doing on your own.

Because this appeal comes from a black man who has left the life of the slums behind, it places consciousness simultaneously within race and class.

Sara Gómez participated, with the making of this film, in a project (to quote Sergio Giral) "to retain the concept of race as an historical, social category."[26] Rather than endorsing such notions as "There are no whites and no blacks, only Cubans," which often conceal racism, the filmmaker called for a critical understanding of racial formations in Cuba.[27] The social edifice that promoted racism has been demolished by the desegregation laws of the Cuban Revolution. Even so, Gómez recognized and explored the conditions that prevent the integration of blacks and mulattos into the revolutionary process. *One Way or Another* proposes a dialectically empowering perspective on gender, ethnicity and class as a means of eliminating prejudice and inequality.

Metaphor and Difference: *Iracema*

Iracema was directed by Jorge Bodanzky and co-produced by Orlando Senna (Brazil) and Wolf Gauer (Germany) in 1974. The film takes its name from the romance novel entitled *Iracema, lenda do Ceará*, written by José de Alencar in 1865. Although the novel has been adapted many times to the screen, Bodanzky's version differs from the other adaptations. The filmmaker retains the novel as a frame of reference but not the plot details. He uses a modernist approach to map out moral and social alienation, and relies on historical codifications of gender and ethnicity to explore national identity.

Iracema was produced during a period in which government incentives to settle the Amazon brought about vast population displacements. Shot in the Amazon region, the film shows the systematic destruction of the rain forests to denounce the breakdown of social formations in the region. Iracema, an anagram of America, is the name of a young girl who leaves her family behind and travels in the company of a truck driver. With its intricate narrative structure that combines documentary and fictional devices, the film uses metaphor to construct a critical intertext on Brazil's self-image as a nation struggling to enter modernity.

Iracema was shot in 16mm and picked up for distribution by German television. Due to technical difficulties, the film was finished in Germany and the National Film Institute (Instituto National de Cinema) refused to classify it as a national production. As Randal Johnson points out, the film "entered a sort of catch-22 situation; it could not be exhibited as a Brazilian film . . . nor could it be submitted to censors as a foreign film."[28] The film was suppressed in Brazil until 1980, although Embrafilme was actively distributing other films based on recognized literary works.[29] Political motives were probably as important to the banning of the film. Its release in Brazil coincided with the *appertura* that followed the revocation in 1979 of the antisubversive laws of 1968. Despite what amounted to a clear case of censorship, *Iracema* was exhibited internationally in Europe and in North America.

The romance novel written by José de Alencar (1829–1877) is a major work of the indigenist tendency of Brazilian literature. It is still recognized as a classic and has been reprinted many times.[30] *Iracema* is set during the colonization of Ceará in 1611 and is the love story between an Indian princess and a Portuguese soldier who at the end of the novel takes with him the mestizo child. Alencar offers an idealist view of indigenous people, and, as Pedro Henríquez Ureña pointed out, the writer chooses "the moment at which the Indian faced the European conquerors and when contrast weights in favor of description; it is also a most pathetic moment."[31] Moreover, as David T. Haberly explains, for Alencar "Indianism was simply a logical and effective strategy in the struggle to create a meaningful and complete national history, to establish a consciousness of national separateness and worth, and to defend that new identity against powerful cultural pressures from abroad."[32]

Alencar's views on race reflect the debates that followed the 1831 banning of the slave trade and its reinstatement in 1845.[33] As a politician, minister, state councilor, and slaveowner, Alencar advocated the continuation of slavery. But in his literary work, he promoted the miscegenation of Indians and Portuguese as the ethnic foundation of Brazil. Doris Sommer suggests that Alencar "may be writing about integrating Indians in order to avoid writing about Blacks."[34] In terms of genre, the writer adhered to the conventions of romance novels which, as Haberly explains, "should contain fantastic and exotic elements, raising the reader above the banalities of daily life. At the same time, the reader should be able to identify with the characters as real people, and the action should remain within the realm of the possible and the moral to maintain involvement and avoid corrupting the innocent."[35] Alencar's contribution to the romance genre also comes from his inventive use of language: he blends the archaic sonorities of Portuguese with regional variants of Tupí terms. Alencar's extensive notations are part of the fiction, although they are used to authenticate Indian language and history.[36]

With its blend of didactic and legendary elements, *Iracema* constructs ethnicity and gender as conciliatory elements of national identity. This mythical vision of national history corresponds, in Antônio Cândido's words, to "the profound Brazilian desire to perpetuate a [fictional] convention that gives a nation of half-breeds the alibi of a heroic racial past and which provides a young nation with the resonance of a legendary history."[37] It is therefore not surprising that the romance *Iracema* would be filmed many times, particularly at the beginning of this century when the new republic was again preoccupied with national identity.

In the early period of Brazilian cinema the novel was adapted by Vittorio Capellaro in 1919 with Iracema de Alencar in the main role. Luiz de Barros, who made a film based on the novel in 1917, adapted two other romances by José de Alencar: *A Viuvinha* (*The Little Widow*) in 1914 and *Ubirajara* in 1919 with Carmen Santos (later a renowned producer) in the leading role.[38] In the sound period, the novel was used three times. Jorge Kouchin directed *Iracema* in 1931, Gino Talamo and Vittorio Cardinali in 1949, and Carlos Coimbra in 1979. Joao Carlos Rodrigues points out that in none of these versions was an effort made to engage performers with Indian features. As in the early films, the choice of actresses (Ilka Soares in 1949 and Helena Ramos, a popular star of soft-core erotic comedies, in 1979) reflected prevailing ideas about beauty.[39]

In 1974 Jorge Bodanzky alludes to the novel and questions a contemporary political project that seeks to consolidate identity through territorial nationalism. He presents an alternative vision of a massive development project that began in 1964 and peaked in the much-vaunted economic miracle of the early 1970s. This enterprise focused on the Amazon and included major financial incentives to colonize Brazil's last frontier. The construction workers of the highway linking the Amazon to the industrial zones of Brazil, for instance, were conspicuously compared to the *bandeirantes* who in the 1700s discovered gold on the southern border of the Amazon. As Susan Hecht and Alexander Cockburn write, the *bandeirantes* "were the scouts and pioneers of national integration. [They] represented the coarse delirium of pioneering empire."[40]

The film denounces the effects of nationalism on the social, cultural, and ecological fabric of the Amazonian interior. Jorge Bodanzky obviously took a political risk by making direct references to issues that transformed the nature of social relations and marginalized vast sectors of the population. By taking Alencar's novel as a point of departure, the filmmaker seeks to question the mythic vision of the Amazon. As Ismail Xavier suggests, the "matter-of-fact, and matter-of-representation, the empirical world touched by film's mediation . . . dialectically reveal[s] the process of invasion and contamination that turns nature and people into representation."[41]

The narrative of *Iracema* is structured around the protocol of documentary and combines a few professional with mostly nonprofessional performers to tell a fictional story. From a fictional perspective, the film also relies on the conventions of road movies by having the characters move constantly from one place to another. Thus Iracema's journey inland from the estuary and the island of Marajó takes her along the trans-Amazon highway to a land that is nowhere. As the geographical allusions are gradually reduced, identification shifts from the character into the landscape. The drama is displaced toward the region and away from Iracema's fate.

The film's tendency to allegorize is the result of modernist strategies, in particular through self-reflective and participatory devices that draw attention to the antidemocratic discourses and the official representations characteristic of the period. This approach establishes, as Ismail Xavier remarks, that "social, economic and cultural domination are not only the theme of the discourse but also the organizing principle, the very process at the centre of the mise-en-scène."[42] However, as I would like to argue, Bodanzky's modernist options undermine any possibility of empowerment capable of reversing the asymmetry of social relations.

The plot is arranged into three distinct dramatic sections. The first presents Iracema's move into urban culture; the second follows her trip on Tiao's truck; and the third shows her downfall. The broader ramifications of Iracema's hopeless journey are anchored in the dialectical relationship between the documentary and fiction. In this way, address and point of view are destabilized and meaning is shifted away from the main character. As suggested above, the film imagines Iracema's world through the collusion of social and cultural forces she cannot control.

In the opening sequences random images on the river are combined with the voice of a radio announcer. The waterways and the broadcast are established as the lifelines that bond communities and families together. The documentary point of view stresses a social topography. The only personalized actions serve to introduce Iracema (Edna di Cassia) and her family, traveling on a barge to the port of Belém do Pará. This pattern continues in the sequences where Iracema is shown strolling in the Belém market. In keeping with the documentary exposition, the trucker Tiao (Paulo César Pereiro) is first shown on the docks, where he introduces himself to a boat owner as Sebastiao da Silva. This sequence combines the improvisational properties of on-camera interviews with the shot-counter-shot figure of fictional acting. The exchange between the two men is punctuated by overused phrases such as "Nature is the mother of all" or "Brazil is a rich land." Tiao responds to the boat owner with clichés such as "Nature is my truck" and "Where there is wood, there is money." When the conversation ends, the trucker says, "I am Tiao Brazil Grande."

These self-reflective (and ironic) qualities are absent from Iracema's performance. Her actions are reactive rather than interactive. She is shown in the market. Drifting in and out of the stalls, Iracema guides the viewer through the urban setting. Later she is shown—among the spectators of a procession—being pushed back by soldiers controlling the crowd. A short scene showing a woman bargaining her way out of a trucker's proposition at the town fair further stresses Iracema's marginality. Her character is subordinated to the observational protocol of documentary and is restored to the plot only in a scene in a flophouse where—in the company of Teresa—she puts on the makeup and the clothes of a prostitute.

To the extent that documentary codes are given a fictional function, the film avoids pathos. As Ismail Xavier points out, "Pereiro's theatrical intervention also undermines the audience's demand for identification, melodrama, compassion."[43] Power relations are determined by Tiao's performance and dialectical position within the narrative. He plays the role of an interviewer when he talks to truckers, loggers, or peasants who, for all purposes, are the social protagonists of the film. In contrast, he has a purely dramatic function in the sequences with Iracema.

Throughout the film Tiao shows contempt for Iracema. He calls her *burra* (stupid) and insists on addressing her as "Jurema."[44] Iracema's attempts to defend herself are ineffectual. She responds to Tiao's mocking remarks about her Indian origins by maintaining that she is Brazilian. The dialogue between the two characters establishes her dependence and his autonomy. Moreover, Iracema's role as an Indian woman, a migrant, and a prostitute confirms her marginality in relation to Tiao, who comes from the south and is able to claim the complementary advantages of being an outsider and a male.

In the second part of the film, Iracema's journey away from the life-giving river into the barren landscape of the trans-Amazon highway is intended to draw attention to exploitation and deceit. In the sequence where Tiao stops at a logging camp to negotiate a payload, for example, the harsh reality of landless settlers lured by the Amazon's riches is presented. While Iracema empathizes with the woman who speaks about the infertile soil and shady deeds, Tiao is oblivious to the distress of the man who hauls—in spite of a government ban—solid wood from the forest.

In this part of the film (as well as in the third part) the observation code of documentary links oppression with ecological breakdown. This second part begins with a long tracking shot that frames Iracema's shoulder in the foreground and the burning forest in the background. In this scene, as in the aerial shots of calcinated trees, the road's promise of richness and the fertility of nature are negated. The character of Iracema is left to symbolize social and environmental degradation; in this way, her subjectivity is confined within the gendered representation of the Amazonian myth of plenty. In spite of the rhetorical and stylistic shifts characteristic of modernist filmmaking, Iracema remains a victim and a disposable commodity, not unlike the anagram suggested by her name. When Tiao throws her out of the truck, Iracema is dressed in red and white shorts with a Coca-Cola logo and her figure is lit by the headlights of the truck.

Tiao's role as intermediary between documentary and fiction is supported by the identification of his character with the slogan *Brazil grande*. Not only does Tiao act as the mouthpiece for government slogans, but his truck is decked with stickers publicizing the same slogans. Tiao adds a new decoration (a decal of the Lady of Nazareth) on the windshield, explaining to Iracema that "every girl who stays in my hotel has to leave a sticker." Tiao rearranges the insignia on his vehicle, each new sticker recreating the encounter between the developed south and the agrarian north.

Moreover, this encounter is also reflected in forms of popular culture that celebrate progress and freedom and the mythical status of the Amazon. The songs that accompany the shots of the truck traveling along the highway, for instance, speak of pioneers who hope for a better future, while the walls of the bar where Tiao meets Iracema are decorated by drawings of Indian warriors imagining the forest as a place of bravery and romance.

In the third section, the film focuses exclusively on Iracema. The last leg of her journey includes scenes of abuse and disempowerment in which prostitution and slave labor are complementary forms of exploitation. When Iracema meets Teresa again, they are taken by airplane to a large ranch. They witness a deal between a foreman and a trafficker, and the women are forced to ride in a truck with a group of *sertanejos*. Iracema is left at the side of the road. She continues her journey because, as she replies to a woman willing to teach her a skill, "God doesn't want me to be a seamstress, but to travel around." This time around she is driven away and ends up in a shack with a group of older women.

Insofar as Iracema's subjectivity as a character is consistently allegorized, her alienation is expressed through uncritical and fatalistic comments. In the last sequence, Iracema and Tiao meet at a roadside shack. Her dress and face are dirty. Again he addresses her as Jurema and pretends not to know her. She is left alone at the edge of the highway while his truck drives toward the horizon. By avoiding affectivity and closing with a despairing view, the film denies Iracema any affirmative or redemptive function.

The film is problematic because, notwithstanding irony (or precisely because of it), it fails to go beyond the discourses and representations that have oppressed women and ethnic minorities. In fact, Iracema enters the plot through masquerade, and her despair is the result of futile attempts to survive as a prostitute. As an Indian and a female, Iracema is left outside of history: she is not allowed to speak as everyone else speaks for her. She is constantly being rewritten as an object. Although the film predictably rejects romantic notions of social harmony and racial accord, it opts for a metaphorical construction that disempowers subjectivity.

At the same time, the film is a critique of a modernity that excludes gender and ethnicity and erases difference. As the forest is being burned and bulldozed, its difference is being remapped and reconstructed to serve a nationalist economic agenda. Modernization and development dehumanize the landscape and objectify people. In a sense, by invoking José de Alencar's romance, *Iracema* contests the romantic underpinnings of a national metaphor. While placing myth at the service of a modernist rewriting of history, the film struggles to detach itself from the representational systems on which national unity has been founded. In the process, the official vision of modernization is imagined as ecological devastation and human downfall.

The Aesthetics of Carnival: *Quilombo*

Quilombo (Brazil, 1984), directed by Carlos Diegues, is a film that seeks to connect the history of blacks with contemporary Afro-Brazilian culture. The filmmaker draws on elements of popular culture (particularly music, carnival, and *candomblé*) to represent the resistance of maroons in the settlement of Palmares in the seventeenth century. Although Diegues had directed two other films dealing with slavery in colonial Brazil—*Ganga Zumba* (1963) and *Xica da Silva* (1976)—*Quilombo* is far more ambitious in its attempt to celebrate Afro-Brazilian collective memory.[45] It reconstructs the story of Palmares by putting the musical, performance, and religious expressions of black culture at its center. This film was one of the most expensive films produced in Brazil in the early 1980s with a budget of $1.2 million.[46]

From the mid-1970s on, filmmakers such as Nelson Pereira dos Santos (*Ogum's Amulet*, 1975; *Tent of Miracles*, 1976), Walter Lima, Jr. (*The Lyre of Delight*, 1978; *Chico Rei*, 1982) and Carlos Diegues showed an increased engagement in Afro-Brazilian culture. They acknowledged historical forms of racial exclusion often overlooked during the *cinema nôvo* period. In this way, Brazilian cinema began to align itself with the resurgent consciousness of and commitment to black historical experience as exemplified by a variety of artistic practices. David Brookshaw points out, for example, that the Quilombista poetry which emerged in the 1970s "corresponds to a search for black cultural roots and for a tradition of cultural resistance to the ideology of 'branqueamento' [whitening] buried deep in the recesses of Brazilian popular culture."[47]

In a period when Brazilian filmmaking was faced with an impending crisis, the production of *Quilombo* inaugurated a trend to rehabilitate cinema as a spectacle. As Robert Stam points out, "The film evokes comparison, not always to its benefit, with Hollywood epics, even if it was made for a fraction of a normal Hollywood budget."[48] Diegues and producer Augusto Arraes looked for a new way of financing their film by setting up a joint venture between CKD Productions, Gaumont (France), and Embrafilme. With Brazilian films doing well in foreign markets, these organizations were willing to arrange co-production based on distribution advances rather than production costs.[49] To reconstruct the legend of Palmares, a large crew of technicians had access to sophisticated equipment and thousands of extras. The lavish art direction was meticulously conceived to reflect the period, with artisans hired to manufacture the pottery, costumes, and sets.

By casting some of Brazil's best known black performers, musicians, and dancers, Diegues reversed the tendency within popular media to marginalize blacks. As Zelbert Moore points out, even the handful of entertainers and performers who have gained national or international exposure are systematically discriminated against or relegated to socially demeaning roles.[50] The score of *Quilombo* was composed by Gilberto Gil, one of the most prestigious Afro-Brazilian musicians and performers, and the lyrics by Waly Salomao. As promoters of what Salomao has called *blackitude,* these two musicians created a musical score in which Brazilian expressions are blended with rhythms associated with black consciousness such as Jamaican reggae, Nigerian juju, soul, and funk.[51]

This syncretic mixture of African, Afro-American, Caribbean, and Brazilian music establishes a celebratory mood akin to the predominantly black carnival festivities that emerged in the city of Bahia in the mid-1970s as an alternative to the commodified forms of the Rio de Janeiro carnival. Through the participation of dancers from the *afoxé* Filhos de Gandhi (The Sons of Gandhi)—with whom Gil has regularly marched since 1975—the Candomblé Ilé Axé Orio from Bahia, the Escola da Samba Imperio, and the Capoeirao Feitiço de Caixas, *Quilombo* adds a religious perspective to one of the most festive and popular manifestations of Afro-Brazilian culture.[52] By drawing on the pre-Lenten carnival, the film establishes a second level of reading that depends less on the historical anecdote than on the highly ritualized forms through which blacks have narrated their history.

Whereas traditional accounts of the largest maroon settlement that ever existed in the Americas (and which lasted for almost one century) emphasized Portuguese military tactics, *Quilombo* is based on new research and the work of Decio Freitas, who authored *Palmares, War of Slaves* (1974). Recent studies on Palmares have privileged a black perspective and its historical and cultural bearing on Afro-Brazilian culture. Although Diegues sought advice from prominent black scholars and historians, such as Lelia Gonzalez, Beatriz do Nascimiento, and Joel Rufino dos Santos, the film was not exempt from controversy. Dos Santos criticized the film because it underscored the heroism of Zumbí (the legendary chieftain who led the final battle against the Portuguese), who is the emblematic figure of resistance and pride for the Black Movement Unified against Racial Discrimination (Movimento Negro Unificado Contra a Discriminaçao Racial—MNU).[53]

Spanning almost a century, Palmares was founded in 1605 and destroyed in 1694. It withstood repeated attacks first by the Dutch and then by the Portuguese. Historians have recognized that this settlement constituted a prototypical African state that served as a model to other communities. To oppose the system of slavery based on the destruction of traditional forms of bondage, the blacks of Palmares created social, political, and religious structures to fit the multiethnic origins of the community.[54] Agriculturally self-sufficient, the Palmarinos traded with area settlers and welcomed poor whites and Indians. Neither the Dutch nor the Portuguese were willing to relinquish territory, and, as the power of Palmares grew, the captaincy of Pernambuco waged a war to exterminate the rebellious colony. The bravery of two chiefs—Ganga Zumba and Zumbí—spread across the Americas, and November 20—the anniversary of Zumbí's death—is celebrated in Brazil as the Day of Black Consciousness.

In its attempts to strike a balance between historical and mythic elements, the plot of *Quilombo* organizes the enduring legend of Palmares around a series of episodes that evoke in its form the *samba de enredo*—a specific form of samba composed for carnival processions in which a historical event is narrated. As Robert Stam points out, Diegues used a structure in *Quilombo* (and *Xica da Silva* previously) "analogous to the collection of songs, dances, costumes, and lyrics that form part of that popular narrative form called a samba school presentation."[55] While the mise-en-scène is characterized by a spacious use of landscapes and settings, the choreography serves to communicate the vital links between traditional and contemporary Afro-Brazilian cultural practices, and every element of the film is designed to celebrate resistance and freedom.

The film begins in a cane field with the escape of a group of slaves. While some want to find the way back to Africa by walking toward the sea, others decide to go to "the land of free men." When they arrive, the man (Toni Tornado) who has led them to the inland valley is recognized by the aging female leader Acotirene as the Ganga Zumba—king and spiritual guide. The peaceful life of the community is broken when Portuguese soldiers attack, killing the elder Babá (Grande Otelho) and kidnapping a male child born on the trip to Palmares. Fifteen years later, while the night sky is lit by a shooting star, a young slave Francisco (Antonio Pompeo) runs away to Palmares. Ganga Zumba identifies him as his missing godchild and names him Zumbí—a war chief. Dandara (Zezé Motta), who has successfully led an attack against a white village, mediates between Ganga Zumba, who wants to negotiate with the Portuguese of Pernambuco, and Zumbí, who wants to fight them. Following Ganga Zumba's failure to secure peace and his suicide in the valley of Cucaú, the young chief prepares the defense of Palmares. After the final attack, led by Domingo Jorge Velho (Mauricio do Valle), a *bandeirante* from São Paulo, Dandara jumps off a cliff, but Zumbí manages to escape into the jungle. His ambush and execution mark the close of the film.

In spite of its important budgetary resources, *Quilombo* uses a limited number of locations. As the film's narrative moves from bondage to deliverance, the landscape takes on an emblematic and symbolic value. The cane field evokes the hardship of plantation life. The perspective of the neatly planted rows of sugar cane is broken by a road that cuts through it like an open wound. On this road the slaves overrun a group of Portuguese and the *bandeirantes* are welcomed by local authorities. Standing on this road, Zumbí decides not to attack the city of Recife because, as he says, "We would have to take slaves and become like them." As a dividing line between freedom and oppression, this road plays an equivalent role to the boulderlike mountain that marks the territorial boundaries of Palmares. This mountain dominates the inland valley, and it signals emancipation. Those who climb it (like Zumbí) are rewarded with freedom, and those who fling themselves over its edge (like Dandara) are granted immortality. The fertile jungle protects and feeds Zumbí during his escape. In contrast, the sandy dunes of the Cucaú valley are the setting where Ganga Zumba's vulnerability is exposed.

In terms of the mise-en-scène, *Quilombo* sets up distinctive patterns for each location. The cane field and the dunes of Cucaú are mostly shown in long shot with the horizon as a compositional barrier that fragments actions and characters. The rock of Palmares is also shown in long shot, and its centrality within the frame signals its representational power. The medium and close-up shots of the jungle, in contrast, suggest physical and spiritual bonds with the natural world. The lush foliage of the jungle that shelters Zumbí's birth and his death—both set by a stream—establishes the renewing power of nature. In the settlement itself, the mise-en-scène favors the spaces where decisions are made and religious rituals are enacted. The Palmares sequences highlight performance aspects of collective interaction and downplay individual exchanges. The formal design places characters within sheltered places (even in the outdoor sequences) that symbolize freedom and resistance. Thus, at the beginning of the film, the Palmarinos are shown tending an orchard set among tall trees. While young people and women work, Babá teaches children about herbs and medicine. When the mercenary Rufino (Joao Nogueira) attacks, the children counterattack. During this collective defense, the movements of the children are choreographed to the *capoeira*—a ritual martial art practiced mainly in the city of Bahia.

In addition, the day and night sequences are enhanced by colored filters and smoke. Red, blue, and yellow filters are used to light Ganga Zumba, Zumbí, Acotirene, and Dandara, emphasizing the transfiguring power of legend. Acotirene's death in the jungle is signaled by a burst of smoke that literally transports her to the land of spirits. Francisco's flight is bathed by the blue glow of a shooting star, and his transformation into Zumbí the warrior is illuminated by a burning spear. Ganga Zumba's red-lit spirit appears during the final siege to announce that "Palmares is immortal." The black heroes and heroines inhabit distinct realities. Represented as strong warriors and wise leaders, their mythical and spiritual powers are revealed through the mise-en-scène. Using theatrical devices and lighting individual characters, *Quilombo* differentiates between historical reconstruction and mythology, realism, and metaphor.

As opposed to the monochromatism of the secondary colors (maroon, brown, and gold) that prevail in the sequences recounting historical episodes, primary colors dominate the sequences fusing historical and mythical representation. Hence outfits, headdresses, makeup, and hair styles are arranged by colors and textures into a dazzling pageant suggesting the multicolored *fantasia* of carnival. *Fantasia* is the Brazilian word for costume and refers simultaneously to the costumes of carnival and the illusory reality represented by the dress. And as Roberto de Matta points out, the meaning of costumes—like the carnival itself—invokes a polysemic universe that is grounded in the symbolic subuniverses of Brazilian society.[56] The choreographic patterns of these sequences are akin to the movements performed by the *afoxés*, the *escolas de samba*, and the *afro-blocos* groups that parade in Bahia.[57]

Quilombo draws on distinctive performance and musical forms of carnival and integrates them into the mise-en-scène. The meanings generated by the patterning of cinematographic and carnival representation (or what anthropologist Morton Marks calls "metaphorical switching") create a syncretic and ritual setting for history.[58] This aesthetic choice is appropriate insomuch as carnival has preserved and revitalized the practices forcibly transplanted to Brazil. During carnival, the streets of Bahia and Rio de Janeiro are "Africanized" through a highly ritualized, spectacular, and communal display of Afro-Brazilian culture. As Robert Stam suggests, meanings and symbols otherwise "marginalized and excluded . . . take over the centre in a liberating explosion" and "enjoy a symbolic victory over all that oppresses and restricts."[59]

However, Diegues has privileged the more introspective aspects of Brazilian carnival (as opposed to the sensually excessive festivities promoted by mass media), thus pointing to the interrelationship between *candomblé* and black resistance.[60] The filmmaker uses carnival forms to celebrate spirituality and struggle, but also to imagine how daily life was organized in Palmares. Unfortunately, the effect of these sequences is often reduced. The arrival of Francisco/Zumbí to Palmares, for instance, begins with a long shot of dancers moving around the village. Once the choreography is taken up again (inside the main hut), groups in different-colored attire perform an exchange of goods and food, suggesting the activities taking place in a market. The abrupt shift to Ganga Zumba with his young lover Namba (Namba Santos) at the edge of the cliff distracts from the spectacular choreography.

As Paulo-Antonio Paranagua has indicated, the film's original project was reduced during production. This might explain why virtually all the sequences involving large groups of dancers and performers are shortened, and why main characters are not allowed to develop.[61] Although the plot of *Quilombo* centers on black characters and the resistance of Palmares, it treats historical characters in a conventional way. The conflict between Ganga Zumba and Zumbí, for instance, is given through contrasting political and generational attitudes. Ganga Zumba's benevolent idealism is sustained by democratic consultation in contrast to Zumbí's radicalism, which is quite modern in its alignment with a revolutionary vanguard. And while Dandara (who, like Ana de Ferro, is adept at war and negotiation) plays a mediating role, only the actions of black male characters are given a political and military function, with the female characters occupying secondary roles.

This unidimensional portrayal also affects other characters that personalize various reactions toward Palmares. The Jewish immigrant Samuel (Samuel Bloch) and the white woman—identified by Carrilho as a prostitute—Ana de Ferro (Vera Fisher), for example, represent marginal groups. By choosing to join the blacks, instead of fighting against them, these characters establish how the mystique of Palmares overflowed to other racial groups. Predictably the Portuguese soldiers, such as Fernando Carrilho (Daniel Filho) and Domingo Jorge Velho, are portrayed as racist zealots. Even secondary black characters, such as Acajuba (Antonio Pitanga) and Katambo

(Marcos Konká), remain dramatically undeveloped and their actions subordinated to Ganga Zumba and Zumbí.[62]

The struggle between the blacks and the representatives of Portuguese colonial power is predictably resolved in the final battle. Shot in a conventional way and by alternating points of view, the battle sequences look like those of a mainstream epic, except for the sequences that evoke Zumbí's legendary status. The mise-en-scène stresses what he sees (a dream) or hears ("Palmares will never die")—in other words, a world of spirits that nourishes Zumbí's bravery and sets his spear in flames. The sweet song that drifts in the fog-shrouded night and leads Zumbí to Camunga (Eduardo Silva), unlike the epic soundtrack over the raids led by Dandara earlier in the film, is tinged with melancholia. When Zumbí is killed, the sound of gunshots is punctuated by images of blood staining stones and leaves, and the screen turns red when he tosses his spear skyward. Therefore, as the film closes, the tone shifts from history to mythology.

To the extent that the drama *Quilombo* is organized around warfare and resistance, the collective, performance, and utopian significance of Palmares appears confined to its most ornamental aspects. The choreography (and even the music) is given a secondary role and—in spite of its vitality—evokes a musical extravaganza. As Robert Stam and Ismail Xavier point out, "One senses in *Quilombo* a nostalgic utopianism combined with a disenchantment with occidental political models, including a Marxism often guilty of a certain ethnocentrism."[63] As the film exalts the roots of Afro-Brazilian historical and cultural consciousness, it remains problematic in its representation of ethnicity. It is ironic that Diegues directed a high-budget film to celebrate Afro-Brazilian popular culture but remained attached to an idealist representation by overlooking the historical relevance of the *quilombo* of Palmares to Afro-Brazilian history.

Immigration and Identity: *Gaijin: The Road to Liberty*

Gaijin: The Road to Liberty (*Gaijin: Camino da liberdade*, 1979) was directed by Tizuka Yamasaki, a Brazilian filmmaker of Japanese origin. In her first feature-length film, Yamasaki connects the reality of Japanese immigration to that of other national and ethnic groups who labored in the coffee plantations of southern Brazil during the early part of this century. This multilingual film is based on the life of Yamasaki's grandmother and mother. This autobiographical framework is enhanced through the integration of other stories that are part of the historical experience of Brazilians of Japanese origin.

Through a reflection on culture and identity, the film draws a moving portrait of a young woman who arrives in Brazil as an immigrant and laborer.

Tizuka Yamasaki belongs to a generation of women filmmakers who began working in the 1970s, such as Tereza Trautman, Ana Carolina, Suzana Amaral, Vera de Figuereido, and Maria do Rosario.[64] In her films—including *Parahyba Mulher Macho* (1983) and *Patriamada* (1985)—Yamasaki seeks to redefine conventional images of femininity. She places gender, but also ethnicity and class, in relation to historically distinctive patterns of inclusion or exclusion. By simultaneously redrawing the boundaries of representation and self-representation, public and private, as Julianne Burton suggests, the filmmaker stresses "variations within the 'self' rather than explorations of the 'other.'"[65]

High taxes, land shortages, and drought during the Meiji Restoration (1868–1912) forced rural workers to emigrate. They moved to other regions in Japan or overseas. Between 1908 and 1924, the coffee plantations in Brazil and the cotton farms in Peru became alternative places of immigration because discriminatory regulations barred Japanese from entering Hawaii and the United States.[66] The coffee planters had been importing laborers even before the abolition of slavery in 1888 and demanded changes in immigration policy to guarantee a steady supply of laborers. Given the rise of anarcho-syndicalism among Italian and Spanish immigrants, plantation owners (in spite of prevalent prejudices against Asians) preferred Japanese because they were regarded as reliable and docile. By 1926 more than 30,000 Japanese had arrived in Brazil through an agreement signed between the government of the state of São Paulo and Japanese immigration companies.[67]

The history of early Japanese immigrants tends to be explained either from a historical perspective (Brazilian immigration policies designed to replace blacks on the coffee plantations) or from a sociological perspective (agricultural patterns and communal organization developed by Japanese settlers from the 1930s on). *Gaijin: The Road to Liberty* presents an alternative view. The film stresses the difficulty faced by migrants to conserve the values of their culture in a new society. It individualizes ethnic and sexual difference without losing perspective on distinctive patterns of oppression. The film follows the departure for and arrival in Brazil of Titoé and her extended family. The group attempts to cope with the new environment. The contacts with other laborers allow the Japanese to realize their exploitation. After the death of her husband, Titoé leads a small group through the forest to escape from the harrowing living and working conditions. The film ends in São Paulo, where Titoé works in a textile factory. *Gaijin: The Road to Liberty* is a story of displacement, struggle, and transformation. Through a remarkable attention to detail in the mise-en-scène, the film reconstructs the harsh material conditions found by immigrants in Brazil. As Paulo Antonio Paranagua writes, the film places the integration of immigrants in conflict "with the enduring myth of Brazil's 'racial democracy.'"[68] The film approaches ethnicity through altering patterns of social and cultural exchange, and ethnic representation is divested of the oppressive homogeneity of the stereotype.

The imaging system of the film is not exclusively tied to a concern for historical accuracy. *Gaijin* re-creates the process through which immigrants forfeited *shumi*—the preference for an artistic nature characteristic of Japanese culture. As Tomoo Handa points out, the transient state of immigrants in the coffee plantations led them to adopt Brazilian customs of lodging, dress, and food only to lose the artistic sense through which daily life was organized.[69] On the one hand, the film places an emphasis on landscape, dress, and speech through a point of view that privileges the Japanese characters' reactions to the new environment.[70] On the other hand, the film illustrates that *shumi* is accessible only through memory. As a second generation *nissei*—a Japanese born in Brazil—Yamasaki also uses flashbacks to evoke the aesthetic affectivity lost by immigration.

Gaijin develops a sense of location that is tied to historical formations and presents the struggle between tradition and integration, between the actions of individuals and the values that regulate their behavior. Through each one of the characters, Tizuka Yamasaki presents individual—yet shared—experiences of thousands who, like her, and as the title of the film suggests, are branded foreigners. *Gaijin* is a pejorative term in Japanese used (like *candangos* and *paus de araras*) to belittle people who come from another country or region. As Yamasaki states, she also wanted to show that "we are all *gaijines*—that is foreigners said in a derogatory way—for the [Brazilian] Indians, because we took their land away as if it was ours."[71]

By staging three temporal and spatial realities, the film connects the multicultural and multiracial present of Brazil (contemporary São Paulo) with the personal past of a young girl (Titoé's story and her memories of Japan). The credits begin with images and sounds of São Paulo, Brazil's most populous and cosmopolitan city. The presence of Asians in Brazilian life is indicated either by people walking on the street (including a Brazilian man and a Brazilian Japanese woman) or signs on stores and restaurants.[72] The film cuts from these documentary images to a Japanese village where children and adults find out about the possibility of emigrating. Over shots on a country road, the voice of Titoé (Kyoko Tsukamoto) introduces the group that left for Brazil in 1908. Speaking of her own apprehension, she also says, "So many things have happened since. This past is now part of my memories." Although Titoé's voice-over in Japanese is a bracketing device (reappearing only at the end of the film), it establishes her dramatic centrality and sets up a point of view that is anchored in gender and nationality.

As the credit sequence ends with a shot of the immigrants disembarking, the film has already established a narrative pattern in which memory is related to personal and collective history. The sequence set in the São Paulo coffee stock exchange complements the village and boat scenes. The discussion in English between a stockbroker and a plantation owner reveals how the abolition of slavery in 1888, with its ensuing labor shortage and the collapse of coffee prices, justified the hiring of Japanese laborers. In this way, *Gaijin* establishes a socioeconomic and historical background to the dismal working conditions that will finally propel Titoé and others to escape from the plantation. As the filmmaker develops her main character from a frightened to a determined young woman, she stresses courage and solidarity. Hence the empowering perspective that the filmmaker brings to a film that would otherwise be simply a testimony of immigrant experience.

As she follows the arrival of Titoé at the Santa Rosa plantation, where she finds herself in an alien world, Yamasaki mobilizes every single element of the mise-en-scène to convey the trauma of displacement. The wretched working conditions and the inhospitable landscape are presented through a series of traumatic events: the death of a child on the train, the arrival at the plantation, and the first day of work. The initial trauma gives way to a gradual process whereby subjectivity is activated by the encounter of the immigrants with other laborers: Tonho (Antonio Fagundes) and the foreman Chico Santos (Alberto Freire), the Calabrian laborer Enrico (Gianfrancesco Guarnieri), and the migrant Ceará (José Dumont). Through these characters the film represents different degrees of abuse and solidarity. By avoiding a simplistic portrayal of the Japanese characters, *Gaijin* contests the image of the docile and passive Japanese immigrant. Ueno's dissenting and Nakado's fatalistic behavior, for instance, are contrasted with the initial desire of Ryuyi (Titoé's husband) to adjust.

While the actions of male characters establish their adversarial relationship to the Brazilian context, those of female characters are filled with gestures of awareness and self-discovery. In this way, the film pays homage to—rather than simply rescues—the historical role of immigrant women. The film validates their strength and their capacity to grow outside traditional roles. Characteristically, the children play a pivotal role in the film. The little girl, who has been taught by her mother to address her in Portuguese, corrects her brother's pronunciation of "Brazil." At the end of the film, Titoé's young daughter voices her decision to stay in Brazil even if her mother decides to leave.

Even the inability of women to accept the new country is framed by self-affirmation. Before killing herself, Nakado's wife (the only character who wears the traditional kimono) has a vision of Japan. The melancholic image of the sea signifies a reality accessible only by self-induced trance and madness. Titoé's inner world is also revealed through a series of flashbacks that suggest the power of self-representation. As Titoé imagines herself in Japan, her memories restage communal celebrations. The scenes of playing children and dancing girls are imbued with beauty and charm, contrasting with the ordinary drabness of the plantation. In this way, the film locates Titoé's attempts to make her home and to maintain some sense of well-being in the desire to rescue the artistic affectivity she has left behind.

The interaction between migrants and laborers reveals a solidarity that goes beyond language barriers. Angelica's seduction of Ueno in an abandoned house emphasizes a youthful passion that does not need words. When Ceará explains how to harvest the coffee or talks to Ryuyi about his native state of Paraiba, these images convey his profound desire to reach out. In addition, the roles of Enrico and Tonho provide an even more distinctive space for solidarity. The Calabrian helps others to understand that, as Ceará says, "the fruit of the earth belongs to the laborer" and to demand proper wages. Enrico defies Chico Santos, who with his whip resembles a slave handler, not a foreman, and is beaten up. Although Ryuyi refuses to walk off the job, Enrico makes a gesture of friendship by taking his cap off to Ryuyi when he and his family are evicted from Santa Rosa.

Therefore, Gaijin develops a different perspective on intercultural relations, placing potential conflicts between groups within imposed structures of exploitation. Rather than presenting condescending situations, the filmmaker shows how the shift from a slave to a free work force (and from manual to mechanized labor) was determined by pragmatic plantation owners who selected manageable laborers. In addition, she presents a transitional perspective through the character of Tonho. Sometimes positioned as an observer (when Enrico demands an appropriate bonus from the plantation owner), a participant (when Enrico teaches the workers), or an accomplice (when he burns the forest to shield Titoé's escape), Tonho's role is gradually altered. Tonho's attitude toward Titoé, for instance, reflects a traditional outlook on Asian women. He sees her as a precious object and tells her "you look like a bibelot." In fact, this comment connects Tonho to other males in the film. When the immigrants arrive at the train station and a man grabs Titoé, the elder patriarch of the plantation remarks: "Their women are delicate and docile. Superb!" Enrico also assures Tonho that nobody will "touch the Japanese, not even with a rose petal." At the end of the film, Tonho (now a labor leader) recognizes Titoé in the streets of São Paulo. He takes off his cap to greet her. This gesture, paralleling Enrico's farewell, conveys a respect that was absent in earlier sequences.

This gesture is repeated twice. It opens and closes a montage of images of Titoé and Tonho in Santa Rosa. Since these images are now elicited by Titoé, his gesture of acknowledgment is displaced in favor of her memories. This shift of point of view is crucial to the film's representation of sexuality. In *Gaijin* female desire is presented as struggling to break with the historical subjection of women as objects of the male gaze. If Tonho is incapable of seeing in Titoé more than an unreachable fantasy, Ryuyi's forceful possession of her is also set within the husband's right to claim her body. In that sequence, Titoé turns her face away from Ryuyi and toward the camera, indicating her resistance. Rather than giving in to the facile eroticism that characterizes Brazilian filmmaking, Yamasaki draws attention to the containment of female desire.

Titoé's journey into freedom, as the title of the film implies, involves a struggle to overcome gender inequality, racial prejudice, and class exploitation. By locating her character's struggle against a historical background and by avoiding a condescending view of intercultural relations, the filmmaker has sought to empower the female immigrant experience. She uses the voice-over and flashbacks, as bracketing device and counterimages of the present, to represent memory. By presenting the traumatic confrontation of cultures and landscapes, the filmmaker provides an alternative to the sociological perspectives of the Japanese immigrant experience.

Mostly in the 1960s films stressed class struggle as the only possible way out of social injustice. To restore the subject into history, filmmakers systematically addressed in their writings national identity through the pervading usage of an all-encompassing notion of national reality. Yet the films studied in this book problematize the erasure of regional and social differences implied by the term *national reality*. The films examined in this chapter go a step further. By considering racial and sexual differences, these films privilege subjective and collective identities as embattled sites of representation and discourse.

The Cuban and Brazilian filmmakers have envisioned the layering of regional specificities (those inflected by locality). They have also questioned ahistorical presumptions and romantic celebrations of cultural difference in order to free ethnicity from the problematic notion of *mestizaje*. Their films expose the evolving, rather than foundational, essence of the national narratives and, in particular, the exclusion of native American and African populations.

Exile and Displacement

The exile of Latin American filmmakers has had an effect on the development of the New Latin American Cinema since the early 1960s. Fernando Birri, for example, left Argentina in 1963 after the military coup that overthrew the Frondizi government and traveled to Brazil, Mexico, and Cuba before settling in Rome. Upon his return to Latin America in the late 1970s, Birri began reformulating the conceptual framework of his own work. Moving between national and cultural contexts, the filmmaker redefined his practice and his filiation to the movement.[1] As more filmmakers were forced to leave their countries and, as exiles, began to draw on the cultural and political history of the Latin American exile, the New Latin American Cinema expanded its conceptual and aesthetic boundaries.

By the late 1960s and the early 1970s exile had ceased being an isolated occurrence. Fernando Birri, Edgardo Cozarinsky, Fernando Solanas, Octavio Getino, Gerardo Vallejo (Argentina), Alfonso Gumucio Dagrón, Beatriz Palacios and Jorge Sanjinés (Bolivia), Glauber Rocha (Brazil), Jorge Durán, Patricio Guzmán, Miguel Littín, Marilú Mallet, Raúl Ruiz, Valeria Sarmiento—among others—(Chile), Carlos Alvarez (Colombia), Walter Achugar, Mario Handler, Walter Tournier, and Ugo Ulive (Uruguay)—were among those forced to leave their countries because of political repression.[2] Even if exile was only temporary, these filmmakers were confronted with new audiences. Forced to communicate with and engage in new cultural (and sometimes linguistic) contexts, these filmmakers broadened the thematic concerns of their work and extended their practices beyond the affiliation with national communities.

Jorge Sanjinés and the members of the Ukamau Group, for instance, realized the importance of cross-cultural reception. The filmmakers had the opportunity to show *The Blood of the Condor* and *The Courage of the People* to indigenous and working-class audiences in Ecuador. The new audiences who saw these films were able to connect their own experiences to those enacted by the films' Bolivian protagonists. Sanjinés writes, "In our discussions with them, audiences have either insisted on the identi[calness] of the problems faced in Bolivia and Ecuador, or have simply ignored the nationality of the films, and discussed them as something of their own."[3] Furthermore, the success of *The Principal Enemy* (1973) and *Get Out of Here!* (1976) convinced Sanjinés of the importance of sustained transnational and intercontinental mechanisms of distribution and circulation.[4]

Therefore, exile (as notion and experience) is critically useful. It helps explain how geographic and cultural displacement has contributed to a decentering of views on identity, nationality, and difference and how the practices have been transformed and rearticulated in the New Latin American Cinema.[5] By looking at individual films (and filmmakers), it is also possible to evaluate how these practices in exile perform within what Julianne Burton has called the "dynamic and flexible typology" of the movement—in other words, how oppositional strategies "rather than becoming more cohesive over the past two decades, . . . [have] become more 'diffuse,' demonstrating varying degrees of marginality and oppositionality."[6]

Exile: Discourse and Representation

Exile is not simply a politically motivated form of emigration. It has social and political ramifications that affect subjective consciousness and inform cultural production. It might be useful to clarify what I understand by *exile*. It is a subject position conditioned by political, social, and cultural factors tending to disengage human activity in the public sphere. In its most institutional forms, exile is the harshest punishment for political opposition; in its most liberal forms, a means of social and political control.[7] No longer belonging to the originating cultural, social, and political formation, the exile is relegated to the margins of the old formation and equally isolated from the new one. Moreover, cultural identity is no longer circumscribed by roots and place. It acquires a portability similar to the document that identifies an individual's nationality.

Exile has played an important role within continental constructions of subjectivity and communality. The intellectuals and politicians, artists and writers banished from their countries of origin or forced into exile have produced an extensive body of work through which they have envisioned new approaches to identity and nationhood.[8] Writing in Europe, the United States, or Latin America, they developed practices that were rearticulated through a political commitment to their country of origin but also to the continent as a whole. Or as Julio Cortázar wrote, "When a writer lives at the periphery of local circumstances, outside the inevitable dialectic of daily challenge and response provoked by the political, economic and social problems of a particular country, which demand an immediate commitment . . . , his sense of the human process . . . operates by synthesis, attempting to see things whole."[9]

Therefore, as I have written elsewhere, these textualized responses to exile represent a productive space in which to identify the impact of exile on discursive formations.[10] By responding to the conjunctural elements which forced them into exile, the practices of these Latin American expatriates have been stimulated by exchanges, encounters, and confrontations otherwise impossible under normal conditions. And as José Donoso writes, "Exile . . . is one of those knots of live-wires, a shared collective experience, from which I think the greater part of Latin American contemporary fiction derives its strength."[11]

Their cultural production foregrounds a consciousness inflected simultaneously by structures of feeling and affiliation. The ambivalent merging of memory and otherness is a site of struggle where identification is dialectically anchored in nostalgia and resistance. The construction of this new political agency is aptly described by Eduardo Galeano. It involves a disengagement from anguish, silence, and stasis and a resistance to guilt, fear, and forgetting. With this process of acceptance and questioning comes the reformulation of individual and collective subjectivity because, as Galeano points out, "exile lays bare and makes evident the contradictions between the importance that the intellectual assumes and the real measure of his or her incidence on reality."[12]

At the same time, cultural and national identity is solidified either by a sense of belonging or difference. Cultural practice is rearticulated in contact with new contexts. It is not a matter of privileging one formation over the other, one position over the other. Thus, cultural idiosyncrasies are smuggled in and, through a process of bricolage, orchestrated into hybrid—yet politically distinct—alliances. As Donoso states, Latin Americans "write about our own Ithacas using the detritus of our different vernaculars still floating in our memories; in order to keep our Ithacas at a safe distance we recycle them into metaphors."[13] It is this process, evocative of a postmodernism *avant la lettre*, that characterizes Latin American cultural practices. Insofar as community associations are relocated, the specificity of cultural practices is renegotiated and filiations are rebuilt. While irrelevant elements are discarded, others are preserved or absorbed into a new context through a process of selection in which the lines of demarcation between the old and the new become extremely mobile.

Furthermore, in the 1970s exiled Latin Americans (filmmakers, writers, journalists, and painters) felt increasingly forced to take a position within the public sphere and to be representatives of that position. As Antonio Skármeta explains, "The mention of origin inscribes the writer in the general problematic of the country. It pressures and forces the writer into a pronouncement and an analysis. It does not admit any longer a bored grimace or a shrug of shoulders."[14] Therefore, filiation between the exiled intellectual and the originating community goes beyond situation and location. The exile is expected to be representative, and this representability is crucial to cultural production and reception insofar as it defines associations and expectations.

Exile has also meant the reconsidering of complex interrelationships between the ideals of a personal (or collective) project and the material prospects for its realization. Latin American filmmakers have faced the pressure of balancing individual needs with the political context that forced them to leave their countries. It is arguable that distinctive circumstances of exile have motivated equally singular perceptions of how exile affects individual practices. Therefore, rather than furthering a static stance, filmmakers have tended to emphasize the dialectics of historical and personal circumstance. Since the 1980s in particular, views on exile have been filtered through biography, thus validating the self as a reflective site.

In this process, personal memory and self-awareness are authorized but always perform within regional and communal narratives. Fernando Birri, for instance, has talked about his own struggle to recuperate the private and introspective aspects (rather than the public details) of his own experiences of exile. While stating that exile "has been resistance, a necessity to survive physically in time to be able to come back—like in the song of Carlos Gardel—with a new project, and not with interrupted aspirations," his own practice "continues growing after being uprooted and, as the *clavel del aire* and other plants of the orchid family, takes nourishment from the air."[15] Through this botanical metaphor, the traumatic uprooting of exile is altered by a regenerative understanding of creativity that is no longer grounded in one's own homeland but thrives in contact with new milieus.

Marilú Mallet explains that "exile implies confrontation but also comparisons. Leaving my country has given me more freedom to express my own culture in the same way as exile has allowed me to analyze other cultures."[16] By breaking free from historically conditioned models of filmmaking and coming in contact with new audiences, exiled filmmakers have been able to venture into new expressive territories. To present in a new setting narratives originating in another place implies intercultural and interrepresentational forms of dialogue. As ʀᴀ´ᶦ Ruiz explains, "I felt the need to explain Latin America to my European friends and Europe to my Latin American friends. [Some of my films] are bridges between the cinema I would like to do in Latin America and the cinema I make in Europe. This idea of a bridge came naturally when I got to know Portugal, which for me is a deformed mirror in regard to Spain and also to Latin America and Chile."[17]

It is from this perspective that filmmakers have enlarged the ideological and aesthetic outlines of their practices. But, as suggested above, these practices are also developed by concurrent historical and cultural attachments. "I am a Chilean and a Latin American filmmaker who is also a contemporary man," Miguel Littín says, and "Latin America is discovering imaginative solutions and answers vis-à-vis a sceptical humanity; it is a continent at the vanguard of a cultural and philosophical revolution that emerges after centuries of buried memories. I feel a participant of this movement, which is like an erupting volcano nobody can extinguish. In exile, our homeland extended and multiplied, but we never stopped being Chileans."[18] Because this process emphasizes reconnection rather than detachment, the practices of exile are projected into the center of the New Latin American Cinema.

As suggested above, the relationship between exiled filmmakers (and their films) and their new countries of residence is marked by a double marginality. No longer identified with a national cinema (other than through the previous experiences and status of its filmmakers), each one of the films analyzed in this chapter reflects the political impact and institutional priorities of the practices of individual filmmakers. Each serves to make sense of how exile has contributed to new alliances between nationality and identity. Therefore, each provides an opportunity to understand how territorial relocation has, in turn, underwritten diversity and difference within the New Latin American Cinema.

The Politics of the Personal: *Unfinished Diary*

Unfinished Diary (*Journal inachevé*, 1982) was made in Canada by Marilú Mallet. By fusing documentary and fictional devices, the film attempts to make sense of the manner by which the experiences of exile are reengaged in the personal. It is also a multilingual film in which characters speak Spanish, English, and French. Foregrounding the constant process of dislocation and reassessment characteristic of a cinema of exile. Mallet has made use of the personal diary in narrative form to present her struggle—as a woman, an exile, and a filmmaker—to come to terms with the past. In her attempt to politicize the personal, she has put a feminist agenda at the service of a culturally specific experience of exile.

Although exile dislocates individual experiences through the political representability that exiles have to assume, the autobiographical mode of *Unfinished Diary* expands the place of the subject in political representation. Bill Nichols suggests that in *Unfinished Diary* "the experience of place and subjectivity is tactile, everyday, corporeal. [The film] is not an exercise in imagination, an expansion of self by constructing an Other . . . . "[19] What the film does instead is to explore how individuals negotiate their place within communal forms of political engagement. Like Angelina Vázquez, another Chilean filmmaker who has lived and worked in Finland, Mallet has rescued some of the most ambivalent and fragmenting elements of exile and privileged modes of consciousness usually censored from collectively oriented presentations of personal politics.[20]

Shortly after her arrival in Canada, Marilú Mallet participated in a film about the situation of Chilean exiles in Canada produced by the National Film Board/Office National du Film (NFB/ONF). She directed *Lentement*, one of the segments of a long feature film entitled *There Is No Forgetting* (*Il n'y a pas d'oubli*, 1975).[21] Later she was contracted by the French production unit of the NFB/ONF to direct a documentary on Portuguese immigrants (*The Borges*, 1978). Although the filmmaker has admitted the apprenticeship value of her working experience at Canada's foremost filmmaking agency, she has also recognized that her position as a freelance director was far from ideal because, as she once explained, "What I was permitted to do was a film about immigrants since I was myself an immigrant."[22]

The project that became *Unfinished Diary* was initially conceived as a collaboration between Marilú Mallet and Valeria Sarmiento (the Chilean filmmaker living in France) and entitled *Letters from Exile* (*Cartas del exilio*). As Mallet explains, "It was a means of exploring a mode of communication that was then proper to our identity. Because exiles write to each other and exchange audiocassettes or Super 8 films, this project was an opportunity of developing new literary and visual forms."[23] However, financing for this film did not materialize, and Mallet decided to change the project and make her own film through Les Films de l'Atalante, Inc., a company she established with Dominique Pinel. Additional funding from federal government agencies, including the Canada Council, enabled her to complete *Unfinished Diary* in 1982.[24] In contrast to the problems encountered at the production stage, the film was extremely well received. It was awarded the Quebec Film Critics' Prize in 1983 and was shown as part of the Canadian Cinema celebration during the 1984 Festival of Festivals in Toronto.

The film begins with a series of still photographs of Montreal in winter and of the exterior of an apartment house situated in a pleasant residential neighborhood. Accompanied by classical guitar music in the background, a female voice-over says: "At the beginning, I would have wanted somebody to explain to me this place, which is so orderly and so organized." Over a series of tracking shots, the camera explores the sparsely decorated apartment. Introducing the brother (Octavio Lafourcade) as the guitar player who arrived with his guitar and his music, and the mother (María Luisa Segnoret) as the artist who has scattered her paintings everywhere, the voice comments on how "before we bought this house, I was surprised by the silence on Sunday afternoons." With these images, *Unfinished Diary* establishes that finding a place to live is the first experience of exile, even though "at the beginning all seemed so temporary."

In spite of the autobiographical mode of the film, it is important to distinguish between the authorial self (Mallet as producer and director) and the performing self (Marilú as main protagonist) of the film.[25] As Mallet writes, "The biographical aspect of *Unfinished Diary* was another challenge to overcome, because to 'show oneself' and to assume one's own reality demands courage: how to confront oneself as an exile, without roots, a woman or second-class citizen, mother of a child, wife of a filmmaker, and on top of that speaking in three languages."[26] Therefore, I will refer to the director of the film as Mallet and to the performer as either the filmmaker or Marilú. This same distinction will be made for the other protagonists of the film as the film's credits separate their fictional and social personae.

Although the rhetoric of the personal diary guides the film's address, it fixes an introspective point of view that partakes of the reimagined characteristics of fictional filmmaking. The real characters are changed into actors and their performances for the camera are reshaped by the evocative options of film editing. Brenda Longfellow proposes that "what is real, finally, is the process of the film itself, its consciousness of itself as a process through time and space."[27] This self-reflective quality of cinema, once put at the service of personal history, replicates the struggle to communicate the trauma of exile. Therefore, the film's development is not necessarily conditioned by a dramatic chain of events but by meanings produced in the layering of words, gestures, and images.

As the film moves through a variety of domestic and public situations that involve a filmmaker (Marilú Mallet) and other members of her family, images of the past are introduced to displace—even briefly—the matter-of fact exposition. For example, while the mother is seen painting in front of an easel, her calm gestures are disrupted by the sounds of marching boots and gunshots. A black and white back shot of two men and a woman (the filmmaker) with their hands against the wall follows. This figurative shift establishes a narrative and visual pattern whereby memory serves as a representational bridge between the here and there, between private and public forms of subjectivity.

As I have written elsewhere, the early films of Chilean exile displayed an overwhelming concern to explain the Popular Unity period and the military coup. Certain images (such as Salvador Allende addressing massive rallies, the bombing of La Moneda, the junta's soldiers burning books, the prisoners in the National Stadium, and the funeral of Pablo Neruda) and sounds (such as the political songs of the period and excerpts of radio broadcasts) provided an emblematic set of affective and political codes through which the past could be safeguarded and preserved.[28] In *Unfinished Diary*, these indexical signs of the Popular Unity period are rearticulated, and their historical function is shifted toward the personal. In a sense, the black and white shots that signal the past are used to disclose alternative histories.

The visit of Isabel Allende, for instance, establishes the impact of historical events on family bonds. The friendship between Marilú's father and Isabel's father is given through family photographs. But as Isabel recounts the last conversation with her father, Salvador Allende, the images of the burning Moneda palace are inserted. By shifting recall from collective to personal history, the archival footage is restored into Isabel's own history, acquiring the affective value of a snapshot in a family album. Later in the film, photographs of soldiers and dead people are edited in the manner of a slide presentation. The formal affinity of this sequence with the opening of the film suggests another level of reappropriation. The archival images are more than a reminder of the brutality that marked the end of a political process: they are elements in a personal scrapbook.

The black and white sequences are like obstacles thrown in the path of subjectivity and, like shreds of a fragmented past, they establish a point of view through which history can be reimagined. Therefore, the solitary organ grinder (Hugo Ducros) who appears several times in the film belongs to two distinct affective registers. When the filmmaker is prompted by her husband to talk about herself, a shot of the organ grinder postpones her account. His music spills over shots of the mother operating a printing machine in her studio and of the child (Nicholas Rubbo) riding on a shopping-center merry-go-round. This appearance of the organ grinder evokes childhood memories, and the music he plays signifies loss. Later he is positioned as a mute bystander to political violence: first through a color close-up shot of his hand covering the organ and the off-screen sound of a departing car and afterward through his look fixed in the shot of three people being detained by soldiers.

At the same time as Mallet uses the images of the organ grinder to symbolize the fear that gripped Chile, María Luisa Segnoret (the painter) reconstructs for the film her own vision of the military coup by meticulously working on a print. Representing the decayed brains of the Chilean military, the print (entitled "The Four Brains") is an insight into contemporary history. Hence, the different art objects in the mise-en-scène become additional elements of meaning. For instance, the marriage painting, inserted when Marilú talks about her loss of identity, represents a bride without a face. Although she says to Michael, "I hope [my mother] will one day paint my face," the skulllike emptiness of the face mirrors her incompleteness. In contrast to the sense of wholeness in the family snapshots that fill the wall of her study, this painting is a reflective surface where censored emotions are enacted.

As the filmmaker struggles with her husband's ideas about rationality ("Without it, everything would be confusion and disorder"), the camera pans slowly over an *arpillera*—a tapestry made with scraps of fabric—representing a fishing village. These tapestries have come to represent the resistance of Chilean women toward forgetting their disappeared relatives. Mallet enlists this distinctly Chilean mode of feminine expression to validate the film's introspective design. As Longfellow suggests, the aesthetics of "a life bound and constricted by the reality of oppression" is the site from which "the voice of a lived subjectivity [emerges], tethered to a particular body, that of the director herself."[29]

Although *Unfinished Diary* asserts the radical possibilities of personal expression, the film also stresses communal forms of communication. During a social gathering, a group of exiles improvises a *paya*—a dialogue in verse accompanied by a guitar—typical of Chile, Uruguay, and Argentina. Marilú participates as an object and subject of the *paya*. Reacting timidly when she is mentioned in a verse, Marilú responds with her own verse. While she takes part in the communal improvisation, Michael and Nicholas are mere spectators. In this episode of the film the gulf between cultures and languages, between the experiences of location and displacement, serves to heighten Marilú's isolation in the marriage. Inasmuch as Michael remains an outsider ("It is not my culture," he says when Marilú reproves his refusal to learn French, or Spanish, for that matter), he is unable to provide comfort and empathize with her uprootedness.

The tension between the Australian husband's self-assured, yet ironic, identification with Canada ("I didn't come to Canada, I came to the National Film Board") and Marilú's desire to put down roots is visually played out against a wall filled with masks. As Seth Feldman suggests, "The mask is an icon of the severing of ties between [Marilú and Michael]. . . . To Mallet, the mask is . . . the blank page on which the relationship between filmmaker and subject will be negotiated."[30] Rubbo's performance in this film (both as a documentary filmmaker who has consistently placed himself in his own work and as husband) foregrounds Mallet's own concept of filmmaking.

By restaging the process by which distinct social, cultural, and political experiences enter into conflict, Mallet has used cinema to stress difference. The eventual dissolution of the couple is secondary (in my mind) to the manner in which the director records this moment. In the much-discussed kitchen scene of *Unfinished Diary*, Marilú (Mallet) is forced to explain her idea about the film. Although Michael does not answer her question ("Why is it necessary to define the truth?"), her unexpected emotional breakdown reveals an unsettling truth. As Longfellow points out, "Uncanny in its spontaneity, it is a moment of heightened schizophrenia in which the director appears to lose control over her object, the representation of her image."[31]

This sequence is a turning point in the film. On the one hand, the contained emotions of the film are released, and the pervading melancholia is replaced by an energetic self-affirmation. On the other hand, the authority of the director is momentarily thrown into disarray by dramatic pathos. Therefore, through the spontaneous intrusion of documentary protocol in the kitchen sequence, the paralysing emotions of exile are liberated. The impossibility of exchange, both between two individuals and between different ideas about reality in film, turns out to be the film's most emancipatory operation.

Moreover, this sequence suggests that exile nourishes itself in the limits and extremes of cinematic representation.

Unfinished Diary makes use of the private environments and urban landscapes of exile to stage how emotions are stifled and creativity is inhibited by cultural difference. In addition, by integrating a variety of narrative forms, the film envisions the expressivity of exile as a dynamic and active exchange of modes of representation. Marilú Mallet has hijacked the literary mode of diary writing and reshaped it through a cinematographic juxtaposition of fictional and documentary devices. She has imagined exile as a scrapbook on which memory is constantly being recomposed. In this way, the authority of the film as a document on Chilean exile is displaced toward the critical reconstruction of conflict and crisis.

Spectacle and the Displaced Body: *Tangos: The Exile of Gardel*

Tangos: The Exile of Gardel (Fernando Ezequiel Solanas, 1985) presents the experiences of exile using the musical and danced forms of the Argentine tango. With its playful emphasis on spectacle and reliance on historically informed narratives of identity, the film operates through a dialectically provocative emphasis on spectatorship and pleasure. Its use of music as structuring element, extensive deployment of visual devices (blocking, wipes, irises, and intertitles), and emphasis on performance is characteristic of the expressively innovative—rather than the critically realistic—practices of the New Latin American Cinema.[32]

Fernando Ezequiel Solanas arrived in Europe following a significant directorial career in his country of origin. His status as a militant Peronist and political filmmaker did not facilitate what would eventually be a long and painful process of adjustment.[33] Forced to leave Argentina in 1976, he traveled first to Spain, where he wanted to shoot *The Winds of the People* (*Los vientos del pueblo*), a dramatic feature on the Spanish poet Miguel Hernández, who died in the prison of Alicante in 1942. After abandoning this project, Solanas went to Italy and then to France. When he arrived in Paris in 1978, Solanas began editing *The Sons of Fierro* and one year later directed *The Look of Others* (*Le regard des autres*, 1979), a documentary on the handicapped produced by the Conservatory of Arts and Crafts.[34]

The complexity of the Argentine situation and the political chaos that preceded the 1976 coup d'état did not encourage wide-ranging support for the initial wave of exiles who, like Solanas, settled in

France and became active promoting solidarity with the recent history of their country. The progressive disclosure of the viciousness of the Argentine military—including the systematic disappearance of women and children—contributed to dispel in part the mistrust of the European left toward Peronist militants. In fact, given the funding difficulties and the scheduling delays that plagued the making of his film, Solanas managed to concretize the production of *Tangos: The Exile of Gardel* precisely at the moment when civilian parties in Argentina launched a concerted effort to disentangle the country from the devastating consequences of military rule.

Solanas sought support from the National Centre of Cinematography (Centre National de la Cinématographie—CNC) and received an *avance sur recettes* in October 1980 underwritten by L.P.A. (Bernard Roland), Gaumont, and Tercine. He began shooting in November 1981 during a rally organized in Paris by the International Association for the Defense of Artists (AIDA) to honor one hundred missing Argentine artists. Although the rest of the shooting was planned for early 1982, Solanas lost the right to CNC funding and was forced to rewrite the screenplay. The project entitled *The Tangos of Homer* was renamed *Tangos: The Exile of Gardel*.[35]

After the collapse of the military regime in Argentina following the Malvinas fiasco and when Gaumont defaulted on its written promise, Solanas set up a co-production. By then, he had visited Argentina in August 1982 and was able to confirm the participation of Envar "Cacho" El Kadri as executive producer for Cinesur. Using the new Argentina-France co-production agreement, Jack Lang (through the Ministry of Culture) was able to complement the already available funds with a direct subsidy to Tercine. This company was set up by Solanas in Paris to distribute *The Sons of Fierro*, and in 1982—with Patrick Lemarie as manager and Yamila Olivessi (an Algerian writer and filmmaker) as co-production coordinator—it became the main producer of the film.[36]

When the Spanish actress Charo López decided not to play the leading role and until Marie Lafôret could be confirmed to replace her, Solanas was forced to postpone shooting until January 1985.[37] During the shooting stage, Solanas had to negotiate between the highly professional outlook of French technicians and the more flexible habits of the Argentine crew. As the filmmaker points out, his own team (director of photography Felix Monti and camera operator Aldo Lobotrico) was constantly scrutinized.[38] When he began editing, Solanas, as producer, was able to control the whole process of postproduction himself.

What needs to be emphasized is that, in spite of the renewed popularity of the tango, the reception of this film in Argentina and France was marked by ambivalent reactions toward its political intent and aesthetic options. Although most critics recognized the formal vitality of the film, others appeared unable to locate the film within distinctive filmic or thematic frames of reference.[39] If the film signaled the successful return of Solanas (and symbolically the homecoming of exiled *tanguistas*) to Buenos Aires, the exhibition of *Tangos: The Exile of Gardel* in Buenos Aires confirmed the filmmaker's peculiar status within Argentine cinema. This ambivalence can be explained by the complex relationship between Argentine cultural politics and the redemocratization process.

On the one hand, *Tangos: The Exile of Gardel* appears to conform to the overall intent of policies designed by the revived Institute of National Cinematography to foster, according to its director Manuel Antín, "a cinema based on the wishes of the filmmakers" and "an Argentine cinema that is broad and all embracing."[40] This insistence on personal options and on diverse modes of filmmaking was crucial to redemocratization because of the awareness, as Solanas points out, that the dictatorship "left us with the profound awareness of the need to preserve and defend a democratic and pluralist national space."[41]

On the other hand, film production assumed in 1983 the challenge to reclaim the painful past, in Nissa Torrents' words, "to articulate the lost voices of the nation."[42] Most of the twenty-two features made in 1985, particularly following the success of *The Official Story* (Luis Puenzo, 1984), dealt with events that had been silenced during the dictatorship. *Tangos: The Exile of Gardel*, however, turns away from specific contemporary situations—as a master narrative of redemocratization—and privileges a much broader historical metaphor. What might have appeared as a welcome change turned out to be a major handicap. Because Solanas's film remained an isolated instance, it was criticized for its apparently frivolous treatment of the country's recent trauma.[43]

A close look at *Tangos: The Exile of Gardel* could perhaps elucidate its problematic relationship to contemporary Argentine production. At the time when the process of redemocratization was in full swing, the film represents history—in Solanas's words—"as conflict whose meaning we are still deciphering in this nation and culture 'in trance,' as Glauber Rocha would say, still searching to realize its identity."[44] Rather than stressing consensus, the film looks at the process by which identity liberates itself from confining traditions and attempts to make sense of the multifaceted and shifting process by which national cultures and identities are constructed. The mixed opinions on Solanas's film (not unlike the re-actions to previous ones) are also linked to the filmmaker's un-compromising and revolutionary ideas: that "art [is] the risk of permanent invention" and that "the invention of a film is not the invention of a story but the invention of images."[45]

The story of *Tangos: The Exile of Gardel* is narrated by Maria (Gabriela Toscano), a young woman who has lived eight years in Paris as an exile, and revolves around two distinctive narrative axes. The individual trials and tribulations of a group of Argentine exiles intersect with the production of a *tanguedia*, a musical that incor-porates tangos and *milongas* (a faster, more satiric form of tango popular in Uruguay and Argentina) with tragedy and comedy. Switching back and forth between Paris—where Juan Dos (Miguel Angel Sola) lives—and Buenos Aires—where his alter-ego Juan Uno composes the *tanguedia* on scraps of paper—the film juxtaposes the struggles to produce a musical spectacle and to come to terms with exile. The yearning for Argentina and the desire to accept a new environment are acted out by characters of different ages: the actress Mariana (Marie Laforêt) and her daughter Maria (Gabriela Toscano) and by the aging writer Gerardo (Lautaro Murua) and Alcira (Mirta Camedeiros) and the musician Juan Dos respectively.

The film is divided into four chapters (or movements) structured around the performance and expressive modes of music, theater, cinema, and dance.[46] This structure serves to chronicle the stories of exile and allows for a highly self-conscious narrative form whereby artistic creation is integrated into a dramatic form. "Exile is multiplied in its meaning," as Solanas indicates, "I speak of the exile of those within their countries and outside their countries. . . . The children of exile are also exiled as adolescents, which is every-one's first experience of exile. Old age is our last. The other exile I discuss is that of creation. The authentic creation is an act of exiling oneself, moving out of the 'boarding school' where your parents put you, so to speak. If you get out of that culturally, you begin to live in exile."[47]

Each chapter (or movement) revolves around Maria—as narrator and protagonist—and Juan Dos—as producer of the musical show—and connects the anecdotal and the musical aspects of the film. In this way, *Tangos: The Exile of Gardel* establishes two distinctive performance registers. A series of humorous and poignant situa-tions, mostly presented in the form of short vignettes, establishes the effect of displacement on the lives of exiles, while the disheart-ening and empowering expressivity of exile is represented through the show's rehearsals. Nonetheless, the possibility of bridging what appear to be conflicting modes of representation is characterized by the *tanguedia.*

As Solanas explains, "The premise of the *tanguedia* was to constantly transgress and mix genres and languages. This intent to break patterns, blend messages, codes and images already occurred in *The Hour [of the Furnaces]* and *The Sons [of Fierro]*, but now the musical element became undistinguishable from the structure."[48] The musical spectacle being produced by Juan Dos and his friends includes traditional tangos of the 1930s and 1940s (made famous by Carlos Gardel and Discépolo) and avant-garde idioms (the compositions of Astor Piazzola and José Luis Castañeira de Dios). With its misty melodies, sentimental lyrics, and sensual choreography, the *tanguedia* narrates exile and rearticulates the meaning of past wanderings into a contemporary context.

Moreover, *Tangos: The Exile of Gardel* is characterized by shifts in tone that defer the apparent melancholia of both narratives. In the sequences that present the lives of the exiles, sadness follows euphoria and individual feelings are relocated into a collective. The efforts of Miseria (Jorge Six) to rig public telephones, for instance, are organized around conventions of slapstick comedy. But his amusing actions are subtly undermined by pathos. As the exiles wait to talk to their loved ones in Argentina, they enact their pains and hopes. The colored smoke that enhances the mise-en-scène in the train station places trickery at the service of dreams. It also announces the fire that later exposes Miseria's cunning to the police. The visual and aural gags convey the tragic-comic sense of exile, as in the sequence in which the money that Juan Dos's mother (Anita Beltrán) has brought from Buenos Aires is inadvertently flushed down the toilet.

During the solidarity meeting in which Alcira decides to travel to Buenos Aires to find her missing daughter and grandchild, for example, the anguish of her husband Gerardo is shifted toward the assembled group. The camera slowly pans over the faces of the Argentine exiles and their French friends. The feelings of grief that permeate this sequence are broken in the festive preparations for a rally that follows and in the communal show of support for the disappeared in Argentina. In these sequences, the mise-en-scène is dominated by a visually compelling choreography of banners floating above the crowds and a military truck full of cloth-covered mannequins winding along the streets.[49]

In contrast to these shows of individual or collective solidarity, the mise-en-scène of the *tangedia* seems to reinforce containment and fragmentation. However, the sense of loss produced by exile is constantly deferred by the expressive power of the tango and the affective performances of the dancers. The rehearsals are dominated by the vitality of musicians and dancers in contrast to the lifeless mannequins that are used to decorate the set. Shredded papers periodically float down from the balcony of the baroque set, and theatrical spots highlight the dancers and musicians.[50] The intricate steps of the dancers express a swirling sensuality, which, like the weightless papers, places choreography at the service of nostalgia and memory. However, visual gags are also integrated in order to deflect the reflective mood of the tango dance. Angel (Fernando Solanas) falls apart like a dummy and abandons the rehearsal, Juan Dos deflates like a balloon when he finds out that the French backers are pulling out, and Pierre (Philippe Léotard) snaps like a mechanical doll under the strain of the show.

The studio sets have an additional function in the film. They serve to reinscribe the spectacle and the tango into the drama of the characters. The ghost of Carlos Gardel (Gregorio Manzur) appears to Juan Dos and Mariana in the smoke-filled courtyard of the Palais Royal. The great singer's legend comes to life in this dreamlike setting as Gardel is called on as a character. Alongside Discépolo (Claude Melki), he coaxes the frustrated Juan Dos to finish the show because "the *tanguedia* will be our revenge." In a similar way, General José de San Martín (Michel Etcheverry)—the hero of the Argentine war of independence—appears to the ailing Gerardo, who is lying on a camp bed underneath the imposing dome of the library. The two old men converse about exile until Gardel reappears. The general beckons the *tanguista* to sing, and Gardel's voice (now relayed by a gramophone) interprets "Volver" ("Coming Back")—the quintessential Argentine tango on exile. Gerardo's own longing to return home is reinscribed into the film through this imaginative bridging of history, memory, and fantasy.

By blending performance and narrative sequences, *Tangos: The Exile of Gardel* replicates the lives of the protagonists. At the end of the film, for example, the dancers perform a memorable choreography of capture and entrapment on the balcony of the *tanguedia* set. The camera movement and the camera angles mediate the terrifying horror of political violence that evokes the disappearance of Maria's father and Mariana's husband (the only flashback sequence of the film). By articulating this haunting performance into history, the expressive and dramatic elements of the choreography (as in the rally sequence) connect again the distinctive representational registers of the film.

Hence, exile is presented as a means to bridge history and geography. In the sequence in which Gerardo takes Mariana and Maria to the house where San Martín died in 1850, the fog-shrouded cliff and the solitary oak in Boulogne-sur-Mer have an uncanny effect on the aging exile and his companions. Similarly, when Juan Uno writes the *tanguedia*, the rain-slicked streets of Buenos Aires (shot in black and white and connected by a series of dissolves) evoke a strange place. Because Juan Uno is the alter-ego of Juan Dos (like San Martín is the alter-ego of Gerardo), the highly stylized mise-en-scène of these sequences, as Solanas points out, places Juan Dos in a state "of reflection and consciousness always attached to a place" and to a dual sense of belonging.[51] This paradox of being simultaneously here and there—of presence and absence—is expressed in the sequence in which Juan Dos phones Buenos Aires and finds out that his mother has died. As he turns around, she appears in the snowy landscape beckoning him to approach.

This plotting of memory as invention suggests another aspect of the paradox of exile, its distinctive power to resist nostalgia. The argument between Pierre, who no longer wants to work on the *tanguedia*, and Juan Dos is set in an apartment decorated by a painting of Carlos Gardel on the ceiling. The singer is portrayed as a guardian angel with a devilish grin, and he visually defies Pierre's misgivings about Juan Dos's obsessive desire to change the rules. In contrast, Maria's painful confrontation with her mother is framed in a dazzling composition of doors and mirrors that mimics the daughter's resistance and Mariana's entrapment. The grayish hues of the apartment walls suggest, alongside its stark furnishings, Mariana's disabling and lethargic emotions.

The four chapters (or movements) of *Tangos: The Exile of Gardel* are activated by Maria and her group of young friends who sing and dance on the Seine embankments and parks, the terrace overlooking the former Halles, and the pedestrian mall of rue St. Denis. This partaking of musical film conventions and Brechtian antirealist traditions introduces critical and dissenting voices. Maria's narration and the lyrics of "Tango, Tango" and "The Children of Exile" (both written by Solanas) speak of an unwillingness to be coerced by nostalgia. Moreover, the traditional tango music is given an imaginatively modern feeling by a choreography that stresses a sense of belonging to a new place. While Maria and her friends dance in broad daylight, their bodies and gestures framed in and fixed by their surroundings, the couple in the credit sequence is encased in the blueish light of dawn. Their bodies seem to float phantomlike above the river, and their gestures are offered in a spectacular display of sensuality and passion. In this contrast between an everyday and a romantic Paris, Maria's (and the film's) narratives of exile contest a subjectivity that, as Jean A. Gili indicates, "grieves, splits, loses its points of reference, wavers between schizophrenia or inward withdrawal."[52]

Hence the importance of the body in *Tangos: The Exile of Gardel.* The body is suggestively dressed or exposed. Fixed in the choreography and bursting with energy, the body mediates the erotic and political meanings of the tango. Before the tango was accepted by the middle and upper classes in the 1920s, it was danced in the suburbs of Buenos Aires by immigrants mostly from the interior of Argentina. The couples, either two men or a man and a woman, enacted rituals of "male sexual domination, both contained and provocative, associated with the *machista* code of the *compadrito* and with an ambience of prostitution and knife-fighting."[53] But as Julie M. Taylor suggests, the choreographic style of the tango evokes—with its gendered affectations—a peculiar Argentine way of being in the world that is simultaneously introspective and life-affirming.[54]

The film harnesses this affectivity of the tango—mainly its melancholy and passion—but attempts to liberate the body from its fatalistic desperation. The bodies of the *tanguedia* dancers execute the traditional steps but not necessarily according to the characteristic protocol. The stiff upper body of the male and slightly tilted body of the female dancers are constantly rearranged, and the single figure of the dancing couple is broken. As the agile legs of the female dancers take an expressive life of their own, their bodies are freed from the classical gendered postures. Escaping from the man's embrace, the woman becomes an active partner, and, in keeping with the lexicon of modernist choreography, her body is feminized and sexualized. By interacting dynamically with their partners, the female dancers of the *tanguedia* rearticulate the gendered eroticism of the Argentine tango.

With its nostalgic orchestrations and a spectacular choreography, the film also expands the mythology of the tango. Exile serves to highlight how the commanding paradigm of Buenos Aires culture (*cultura porteña*) has historically blended national and foreign idioms.[55] Because it is used to evoke the contemporary reality of exile, the *tanguedia* counteracts meanings fixed by intercontinental appropriations of the tango. On the one hand, the political meaning and the eccentric style of the *tanguedia* upsets the Argentine friends of Ana (Ana Maria Picchio), who has come to visit Mariana in Paris, and puzzles the French director Jean Marie (George Wilson) and the actress Florence (Marina Vlady), who have offered to help. On the other hand, the *tanguedia* represents for Pierre and Maria the promise of amalgamating historically diverse forms of the tango and bringing its past and present together. The *tanguedia* places the contestational possibilities of the tango in solidarity, exchange, and synthesis.

Symbolized by the phantoms of Gardel and Discépolo, performed by the dancers of the ballet Núcleo Danza of Buenos Aires, and composed by Astor Piazzola and José Luis Castiñeira de Dios, the tango is a legendary, yet changing, signifier. The erotic charge of the tango, born in the red-light district of an immigrant port city, intersects with the reality of exile. The mise-en-scène of the tango in familiar (Paris) or spectacular (Buenos Aires) locations expresses hope and rejects despair because—as the title song says—"no tragedy ever lasts very long." Obsessed by stories of origins, *Tangos: the Exile of Gardel*—as the tango "Volver" is played on a gramophone by the ghost of Gardel—also celebrates the original investment of exile in the history of the Argentine tango.

At the same time, the title song of the film questions Gardel's idealist utopia of the return from exile. The lyrics of "Tango, Tango" are framed by a rhetorical question: "What country, where is the country?" which refers to a place where young people like Maria and her friends hope to be themselves. Hence, the song expresses the longing for a country that is yet to demonstrate whether dignity and respect are possible ("where you can work without begging" and "where your opinions are taken into account, even if you are a mouse"). Moreover, "The Children of Exile" (also written by Solanas and sung by Susana Lagos) pays homage to those crushed by old-fashioned values or persecuted by physical violence. In this way, the film addresses the young people yearning for a country they hope can fulfil their expectations.

With its culturally specific inscriptions and its formal rearrangement of the musical film, *Tangos: The Exile of Gardel* seeks to expand the meaning of national idioms and contemporary political events. Through musical, choreographic, and visual metaphors, the primal scenes of Argentine exile (San Martín) and Argentine tango (Gardel) are mirrorlike constructions reflecting history in an oblique, de-centered way. As Alicia Dujovne Ortiz writes, the tango is like Buenos Aires, which "exists only to the extent that Europe looks at it. The city was born in this play of mirrors, in this complicity of reflection."⁵⁶ While the axis Buenos Aires–Paris operates as its territorial boundary, *Tangos: The Exile of Gardel* journeys from a sense of loss into a critical awareness of its own eccentricity.

Phantasmagoria and Displacement:
The Three Crowns of the Sailor

The palimpsest effect of *The Three Crowns of the Sailor* (Raúl Ruiz, 1982) is grounded in a mise-en-scène that acknowledges its diverse cultural, aesthetic, and cinematographic sources. By playfully blending genres and modes of representation, this film makes use of pastiche not only as an ironic device but as a means to stage the psychological and physical wanderings of exile. The extreme fabulation of this film is the result of a process of decantation. The film is populated by romantic European sailor stories that intersect with mariner legends of the southern Chilean coast. In this way, images are transformed through contacts between elements of an original and a new formation. The characteristics of this film have contributed to solidify Ruiz's reputation as an experimental and modernist filmmaker whose practice is guided by a critical inquiry into representation and discourse.

The political solidarity in France with Chile was crucial to the making of Ruiz's first films in exile. After completing the editing of *The Expropriation* (1973) in Germany, he moved to Paris with his wife Valeria Sarmiento, a filmmaker in her own right. There he directed *Dialogue of Exiles* (1974). This humorous, flippant, and surreal treatment of the adventures of a group of exiles, compounded with a sketchlike narrative, was not well received in the highly charged political atmosphere that followed the 1973 military coup and that had forced many Chileans to leave their country. The film was harshly judged by political groups under the pretext of political opportunism and poor taste. This opinion trickled down into the community of Chilean exiles, many of whom had not seen the only existing copy of the film.⁵⁷

After *Dialogue of Exiles*, following a short period of relative inactivity, Ruiz produced an impressive number of films that were mostly broadcast on television or shown at film festivals. By the early 1980s, he managed to secure consistent funding from the National Institute for Audio-Visual Communication (Institut National de la Communication Audiovisuelle—INA) and the Centre Beaubourg. Ruiz himself has often insisted that his preference for small crews, condensed shooting schedules, and performers' improvisation was not precisely suited to the policies of the National Centre of Cinematography (Centre National de la Cinématographie—CNC). Therefore, he opted for accessing alternative sources of funding rather than the *avance sur recettes* method favored by most filmmakers in France.

Although Ruiz was forced in France to adopt a certain degree of professionalism, such as sketching a written scenario, he has explained that working in Europe has given him "an experience of production and a sense of craft that does not exist in Latin America, the idea of professional development and advancement, and the possibility of various technical skills converging into one."[58] Ruiz has not renounced the informal shooting methods of his earlier work, and as Waldo Rojas—a friend who has participated in various films—has written, the filming situation furnishes "a point of departure to break available standards and codes, to de-construct and re-construct them."[59]

The Three Crowns of the Sailor was produced by INA in partnership with French television (Antenne 2) and was based on a project written before the making of *The Suspended Vocation* (1977). Ruiz says that he presented the project to INA, which accepted it for script development. When the other film of the two underwritten by Antenne 2 was delayed and because shooting dates were already scheduled, he was asked to go ahead with his own film. The film was shot in nine weeks (two of which were used for special effects) and Antenne 2 agreed to co-produce in order to absorb costs generated by the shorter deadlines. "Of ten of my films at least nine have been made in this way, in other words I was not prepared and had to begin right away," he has commented.[60] It is arguable that the formal singularity of his French films has as much to do with available financial means as with the filmmaker's penchant for artisanal working methods, skillfully transplanted from Chile.

Given the scarcity of resources in Chile, he became used to working within modest means. Although during the Popular Unity period Ruiz received material support from existing organizations, like Chile Films (the national film institute), he could also count on the collaboration of friends who shared what Waldo Rojas calls his "involuntary marginality" and engaged with his "*realismo púdico*," a decorous and modest style of political filmmaking.[61] In contrast to the minimalist mise-en-scène of his Chilean films—*Three Sad Tigers* (1969), *Nobody Said Anything* (1972), *The Penal Colony* (1971), and *Socialist Realism* (1972)—the work of Ruiz in France reflects a cinematic virtuosity that belies his modest budgets and brief shooting schedules. With the collaboration of veteran cinematographers Sacha Vierny and Henri Alekan, the filmmaker has espoused a

highly aestheticized mode of filmmaking characterized by an astonishing variety of shots and complex setups that enhance wordy
soundtracks and theatrical performances. As Gilbert Adair points
out, "Ruiz *pays* his technicians by offering even the most minor
among them an opportunity to participate directly in a number of
complicated visual exploits."[62]

The prolific output and frenzied activity of Ruiz, beginning with
The Suspended Vocation (1977), drew the attention of France's fore-
most film magazines. In 1983 *Cahiers du Cinéma* dedicated its
March issue (no. 345) entirely to Ruiz to accompany a retrospective
of his films and the première of *The Three Crowns of the Sailor*.[63]
At the same time, his French work was available to only a handful
of Chilean and Latin American critics, mainly living in Europe, who
continued writing on his career.[64] Since the 1983 retrospective in
Paris, however, Chilean publications have regularly commented on
Ruiz's films. After 1984, when the French-Chilean Institute of Culture began showing his films in Santiago and the filmmaker began
to travel regularly to his country of origin, Chilean film critics (including those who knew his previous work) who might have been
suspicious of his Parisian *succès d'estime* began to appreciate his
work in exile.[65]

The reception of the films that Ruiz produced in France has been
characterized by an extreme ambivalence. On the one hand, this ambivalence is the result of an idiosyncratic and uncategorizable style
of filmmaking that has to do with the filmmaker's highly experimental attitude toward cinema. On the other hand, this ambivalence also comes from expectations about the filmmaker's work and
his status as a Chilean exile.[66] In 1978, when Ruiz's films moved
away from direct references to national origins, Chilean and Latin
American critics were puzzled by what appeared to be a thematic
break. This difficulty in identifying a cultural specificity was cer-
tainly compounded by the filmmaker's adoption of French as the
language of his films. It was precisely this eccentric otherness (and
avant-garde approach) that distanced Ruiz from his compatriots and
endeared him to European and North American critics. The responses of the latter have tended to look at the Chilean production
in a minor way, thus failing to make connections between the filmmaker's origins and his exile.[67]

By moving between a fascination with the European sources of his
own culture and his experience of exile, Ruiz has drawn on the capacity to select and integrate elements from distinct cultural formations.[68] As he points out, "Using narrative mechanisms and stylistic tics to establish a double translation, I have made films that

could be seen by two cultures. As the emotional element always tends to fail, I decided to tell—through metaphors and the multiplication of cinematographic rhetorics—stories of dispersed families in which the Latin American condition . . . is paramount."[69] The temptation to categorize his films as the quintessential cinema of exile is valid only insofar as the films tend toward cultural hybridicity. Nonetheless, it is inappropriate to pose Ruiz's exile in Paris as a definite break with his national origins. Through a study of *The Three Crowns of the Sailor,* it is possible to understand how the filmmaker has explored new expressive territories and renegotiated connections and differences between his country of origin and his country of adoption.

The story of *The Three Crowns of the Sailor* begins with a narrator's account of a young man's killing of a teacher in a Warsaw theology school. In a dancing hall the theology student (Philippe Deplanche) meets a sailor (Jean Bernard Guillard) who tells his story in exchange for three Danish crowns. The narration shifts from the third to the first person and another story begins, this time in Valparaiso. From there on, contained by a claustrophobic mise-en-scène, the film constructs a world of narrative labyrinths, a "nowhereness" of oppressive mazelike fictions. As David Kehr has pointed out, in *The Three Crowns of the Sailor* "patterns emerge within the stories (told by the sailor to the theology student), and patterns emerge around them."[70] Thus, the film escapes into an infinity of fictions that draw on multiple representational and literary sources.

It is precisely through these fictions that old and new stories (some Latin American, others European) come together and are reconstituted into heteroglossia, whereby "language becomes the space of confrontation of differently oriented social accents, as diverse 'sociolinguistic consciousness' fight it out on the terrain of language."[71] As a result, the narrative structure of *The Three Crowns of the Sailor* serves as a blueprint for a reterritorialization of origins. At the same time, by an intricate interweaving of classical cinematic codes with unstable signifiers of intercultural imaging, Ruiz imagines a space where an uprooted subject can belong.

The film is populated by marginal characters who inhabit strangely subterranean worlds, where social rituals are perversely enacted, and where everyday situations turn violent. *The Three Crowns of the Sailor* shares with *Three Sad Tigers* a gloomy, almost nihilistic feeling that reaches its climax in a gratuitous and violent murder. Characters are wanderers, social and cultural outcasts, who roam through taverns and seaports exchanging stories for money and for lodging.[72] Nonetheless, the characters of *The Three Crowns of the Sailor* are like phantoms who drift in and out of the stories told by the sailor who boarded the *Funchalense* in Valparaiso. As the film eventually reveals, the sailor must find somebody before dawn to take his place on the mysterious ship docked in the harbor.

This ship is manned by dead sailors, each having had to convince someone to take his place as the only living crewmember. The *Funchalense* is a phantom ship and suggests another phantom ship— the *Caleuche,* which appears in southern Chile seas. By invoking this mythical ship, the fictional world of *The Three Crowns of the Sailor* is merged with the regional imagination of the archipelago of Chiloé. The *Caleuche* belongs to the oral tradition of the fishing communities of Chiloé, and its story is told by those who have survived its sightings. As the legend goes, the *Caleuche* emerges—like a giant sea monster—during stormy nights and illuminates the dark sea. The music and happy voices coming from its hold promise protection to those who fear being shipwrecked. But those who know that the crew is made up of dead men warn that, before the *Caleuche* disappears, "our bones, like those of all who have seen it, will end up at the bottom of the sea."[73]

Like other oral narratives circulating among the people who navigate the southern regions of the Chilean Pacific, the stories of the *Caleuche* are exemplary stories about threatening phantoms or auspicious spirits. While fish provide material sustenance, the exotic creatures living at the bottom of the ocean embody the communities' affective attachment to the sea. This belief in supernatural monsters such as La Pincoya (a beautiful woman covered in algae who dances on the beach and leaves a plentiful harvest of crustaceans before returning to the sea) and the *Caleuche* are a source of inspiration and knowledge. As Gabriela Mistral wrote, "A real *chilote,* guardian of his archipelago, *chilote* weather-beaten by brine, always manages to succeed and will carry throughout life the lights of the ship in [his] dazzled eyes. This happy *chilote* will understand the romance or the *corrido* of the *Caleuche.*"[74]

This is the primal scene of *The Three Crowns of the Sailor.* The *Funchalense* serves as an intertextual container of national fictions, where a northern European sailor story intersects with a magic legend from Chiloé and where European romanticism and Chilean folklore are bound through biography.[75] By placing the logic of folklore at the service of cinematic narration, the phantasmagoric ship holds together the fleeting fictional fragments of the film. This playful fabulation is not just "a kind of surrealist shaggy-dog story" or "a pastiche of nearly every seafaring adventure saga."[76] It serves to replot a fiction of origins through a series of narrative digressions and cultural mediations.

When the mariner begins telling his story to the theology student, color replaces the black and white images of the dancing hall. Starting in Valparaiso, he recounts how he was recruited by a blind man (Frank Auger) and how he bid farewell to his mother and sister. The man warns him never to take money from someone without getting something in exchange, and the women beg him to remember. As the film shifts back to the dancing hall, the student impatiently comments, "All you have said is interesting, but it has all been said before." From there on, the sailor's stories become more surreal, and the settings and characters more fabulous.

The subsequent stories are driven by the sailor's attempts to acquire a surrogate family to replace the one left behind in Valparaiso. This time his stories take place in the tropical seaports of the Southern Hemisphere. As the *Funchalense* anchors in Tampico, Dakar, Singapore, and Tangiers, the fictional territory of the film is located between the American south and the European north. Thus the imaginary landscape of the film privileges the tropics, that visual and aural Other that constitutes the representational map of the Third World.[77] Thus, the characters of the film acquire the density of allegory. Their stories locate the characters in a world of poverty, debt, and exploitation, but these themes are mediated by fantastic metaphors. The child prostitute (Nadège Clair), for instance, has to pay a debt acquired by her family. The young boy (Tank N' Guyen)—as the honorary consul (François Ede) in Singapore explains—suffers from an illness that makes him grow younger when he is hungry.

In addition to these forlorn stories of children, the sailor tells about life on the *Funchalense*. The theology student becomes intrigued by the cryptic images evoked by the sailor, such as the tattoos on the sailors' bodies or the cabalistic letters on the walls. As the narrative axis of *The Three Crowns of the Sailor* shifts toward the enigmatic crew, the mise-en-scène changes to construct a gruesome visual universe. Representation is transmuted by trompe l'oeil images of the supernatural through depth-of-field photography. Rather than using any sort of special effects (like the dolls with glowing eyes that fill the foreground of Maria's room), Ruiz uses objects in the ship sequences that acquire monstrous qualities. An example is the mouth that fills the screen when the sailor tells how one morning he woke up in the body of another man. Ruiz explains the function of the foregrounding of background objects in this way: "Constant tension, which makes abstraction impossible in the cinema, is like a subterranean current accompanying any series of images which, when it is applied to identical or similar objects . . . , follows a story which is half contained in the objects shown and half provided by us."[78]

The ship narratives are impregnated by necromancy (the drunk first officer [Jean Badin] makes the sailor's dead mother available for hire to the others), fantasy (the sailors drink their tears when the ship's supply of salt runs out), or inversions (the boat emerges after rather than during the storm). But the most unnerving situations take place upon the sailor's return to Valparaiso. He finds that his house is boarded up because his mother is dead and his sister has committed suicide. A man dressed in white guides him through a mazelike tunnel, and at mid-point they must walk backward, as in the story of the *Caleuche* where, as Mistral wrote, the men disembark "topsy-turvy like those on board, but also without memory."[79] Moreover, two different versions of his sister's death are told. One is told by the salesman to the sailor and the other by the sailor to the crew of the *Funchalense.*

In spite of assurances that "nothing has changed," the Valparaiso of the sailor's return is another city. In a ballroom, he sees the show of Matilde (Lisa Lyon), the queen of the mambo. When they meet the next day and she takes off her clothes, she also removes her nipples and pubic hair. When the sailor returns to the ballroom, the body of Matilde appears in the glass from which he drinks his sorrows away, suggesting an imaginary but impossible rendezvous. This bizarre story upsets the theology student, who is repulsed by the idea of Matilda's single body opening—like the sailors' inability to defecate or their habit of eating the white maggots that come out of their bodies.

In this way, the sailor's narratives are overcome by horrific visions akin to those of a nightmare. Perverse images of female sexuality and bodily decay suggest a logic of desire that falls apart under the phantasmagoric excess of the cinema. If thus far *The Three Crowns of the Sailor* seems to suggest the reconstructive power of memory, at this point the film begins to slide obsessively toward a deadly climax. The film becomes a sophisticated parable of the imagination in which vision is interchangeable with death. Christine Buci-Glucksman points out that the highest reward of fiction is "its own freedom, its life. Tell me a story and I will kill you is the maxim of the [film's] romanesque ethics."[80] Now that the sailor has collected the three Danish crowns, he surrenders to the outrage of the theology student. In a violent scene on the docks, the sailor is beaten to death. Almost dead, he staggers about, singing "Mambo, que rico el mambo," and expires saying "This is pure poetry!"

While the fascinating exoticism of *The Three Crowns of the Sailor* suggests a regressive nostalgia, the *Funchalense* (like the *Caleuche*) is the repository of a memory unable to forget. And like the Chilean legend, the visionary power of the film empowers the dreamlike quality of recollection. The stylistic tics of the film—its historically dated techniques (such as gels, depth of field, voice-over) and its generic imprints—place loss in a variety of locations. The photographic effects characteristic of the French cinematic poetic realism of the 1930s are transformed into a distinctly Latin American imagining of the fantastic with its blend of fairy tale and horror. As Ruiz comments, "I am interested in the idea of images generated by other images and the logic that's involved. I'm not a surrealist. . . . But I am interested in surrealism on the level at which its technique can be used to examine different levels of consciousness."[81]

The disembodied and phantasmagoric subjectivity of exile is re-plotted through the imaginary of popular culture. The imagination of exile (like that of popular memory) is accessible only through the manipulations and the complicities of narrative effects. At the end of the film, the narrator of *The Three Crowns of the Sailor*—commenting on the murder of the sailor—says, "I understood that it was my duty to accomplish this abominable task." The intertextuality of *The Three Crowns of the Sailor* constitutes a maze of reflecting mirrors that, while concealing its cultural identity behind a hybrid practice, exemplifies what Paul Willemen calls "a way of inhabiting one's culture which is neither myopically nationalist nor evasively cosmopolitan."[82]

Therefore, in spite of its nihilistic stance, this film expresses a distinct sense of being in the world. The stylistic virtuosity of the film represents a self-reflective strategy of imaging whereby regional signifiers are reterritorialized and cultural identity ceases being solely attached to geographical codes. The aesthetic excess of The *Three Crowns of the Sailor* is located in an almost perverse fascination with tropical settings. Hence, the "mise-en-spectacle" of exile is located in a metafictional territory where subjectivity nourishes itself in the crisscrossing of parody and utopia. Maybe, as Ian Christie points out, the cinema of Raúl Ruiz is "a play between rhetorics."[83] But far from being impersonal, these rhetorics of representation originate in a desire to de-center address and reimagine identification through historically mediated codes of cinema and historically centered concepts of identity.

Hence, the deconstructive strategies of this film are anchored in the marginality of original imprints and competing narratives, or what has become a "Ruizian conundrum" par excellence. In an interview published in *Cahiers du Cinéma* Ruiz described three characteristic Chilean attitudes: "That of Lautaro, an Indian who was befriended by the Spaniards and who meticulously studied their methods for no other reason than to turn them against his masters. That of Jimmy Button, an illiterate Indian adopted by the captain of the 'Beagle' on Darwin's first voyage: although he learned English in three weeks, went to Oxford and was even called to the Bar, he forgot everything on his return to South America. And that of Valderamat [*sic*], the Chilean Oscar Wilde, who was the darling of the salons before drowning himself in a sewer. Asked which of them he identified with, Raúl replied 'I've the feeling I float from one to the other. . . .'"[84]

This contentious placement of Chilean and European is perhaps a crucial element of Ruiz's narratives of identity and culture. Inasmuch as exile de-centers language and representation, identity returns to its formative stages where difference struggles against containment, where the imaginary negotiates its placement in the symbolic. The word *destierro*, a Spanish-language word for banishment, denotes deterritorialization as much as geographical displacement. *The Three Crowns of the Sailor*, in spite of its bleak nihilism, is a site of resistance against this loss of place.

In this chapter, I have examined films directed by Chilean and Argentine filmmakers in the 1980s. Each film locates exile in the initial trauma of dislocation and in its subsequent rearticulations. Each deals in distinctive ways with displacement, marginality, and estrangement and operates dialectically to foster multilayered readings of identity.

Moreover, by redefining the constituting elements of identity, each reinvents and reimagines representational territories. However, the significance of each film does not stop at its innovational aesthetics. Each was affected by different modes of production, reception, and critical evaluation. As a result, each film has involved distinctive exchanges and each has operated within singular expectations about cultural representativity and political resistance. Furthermore, these films are neither assimilable nor assimilated to the new contexts; they are indicative of a dialogical integration rather than of assimilation into existing structures. As Edgardo Cozarinsky has observed, the films made by Latin Americans in France keep— despite their French fluency—recognizable foreign inflections.[85]

In these circumstances, it is not surprising that in exile Ruiz and

Solanas—and, to a lesser degree, Mallet—have wholeheartedly embraced marginality; it has granted them a space where identity can drift in and out, floating among cinematic and national signifiers. Filming in Portugal, Paris, and Montreal, the filmmakers have used locations as if they were a map. Upon this map they imagine subjectivity itself in a process of negotiation between original and new formations.

Conclusion. The New Latin American Cinema: A Modernist Critique of Modernity

The ideological agenda of the New Latin American Cinema cannot be detached from historical discourses on regional identity through which the specificity of Latin American cultural practices has been defined. Its distinctive profile as a cinematographic movement is grounded in the idea of unity within diversity. The movement developed historically within the recognition of dialectic interactions between regional expressions, national projects, and continental ideals, thus linking its project to the idea of Latin America as a historical entity.

This idea of Latin America, in the words of José Luis Avellán, "expresses the consciousness of a cultural unity capable of extending itself to the rest of the continent."[1] Furthermore, as Angel Rama pointed out, this idea "is founded on persuasive arguments and supported by concrete and powerful unifying forces. Most reside in the past and have profoundly shaped the life of nations ranging from a common history to a common language and similar models of behavior. Others are contemporary, their minority status is compensated by significant promise: they react to universal economic and political impulses brought about by the expansion of the dominant civilizations of the planet."[2]

The idea of a continental identity emerged as a means of questioning the positivist utopias of progress that displaced the colonial legacy after Latin American countries consolidated themselves as modern nation-states. This ontological search for distinctiveness was based on a sense of a shared destiny and a common identity. But, as Rama stated, "underneath unity, concrete as a project and real as the bases that sustain it, unfolds an internal diversity that defines the continent more precisely."[3] This diversity is made up of regional cultures that form, to quote Rama again, "a second Latin American map more accurate and concrete than the official."[4]

Latin Americans have assumed the history and envisioned the future of the continent in the layering of regional specificities (those inflected by locality) and through narrative negotiations of nation, class, race (of which the exclusion of native American and African populations cannot be overlooked), and gender. In this way Latin Americans have endowed themselves with a continental identity, "a grand historical narrative" that, as Gerald Martin writes, "is the continent's own dominant self-interpretation."[5] This continental identity has permitted Latin Americans "to move beyond the futile limitations of national identity in the direction of some humanistic continental culture as part of the global community of tomorrow."[6] By ascertaining the symbolic power of continental nationalism, this identity produces a sense of shared community that recognizes itself within interregional (and intraregional) variations, countering state-defined allegiances and differences.

Hence, this idea of Latin America is more than simply a myth or a utopia. It is a discursive formation whereby the history and imagination of the continent can be reclaimed. As a discourse, this idea operates both within the fleeting memories of the past and the material concreteness of the present. On the one hand, this idea has served to articulate regional autonomy and self-determination, countervailing the historical failure of countries to set up durable pan–Latin American political and economic organizations. On the other hand, the idea of Latin America is grounded in the desire of self-definition as well as the struggle for the control and autonomy of culture and identity.

This determination has as much to do with ideology as with the characteristic resilience of concepts of Latin American culture and identity. As Edward Said suggests, "Culture is used to designate not merely something to which one belongs but something that one possesses and, along with that proprietary process, culture also designates a boundary by which the concepts of what is extrinsic or intrinsic to the culture come into forceful play."[7] From this perspective, cultural historians in Latin America have consistently sought to discuss identity neither as an apparently obvious nor a transparent position of self-recognition.

If the idea of Latin America is a construct, an imaginative and evolving projection (not less imagined than the communities that are represented by it and represent themselves in it), it is "one possessing all the institutional force and affect of the real."[8] The search for means of representing national and continental realities, collective and individual identity, is the keyword that best characterizes the creative and political projects of Latin America. Nowhere is this search more explicit than in artistic practices, in visual arts, music, cinema, and literature.

Maybe a few examples are in order. The Uruguayan painter José Gamarra, as Oriana Baddeley and Valerie Fraser point out, "combines an ideal image of the tropical Latin American landscape with an acute awareness of the irony of the parallel history of conquest, colonization and exploitation."[9] Set within the luxurious jungle vegetation are tiny figures of people and objects, sometimes narrating an incident, like the beheading of a nun in *From the Series of Masked Aggressions* (1983), which refers to the rape and murder of American nuns by the Salvadorean army in 1980. In this painting, the tropical forest is invoked simultaneously as a mythical and an actual place, the site upon which Europe imagined the Americas and the place where Latin America's violent history is still being played out.

Another example of the powerful effect of the idea of Latin America can be found in *Barroco* (1989), a film by Paul Leduc that attempts a synthesis of what Gabriel García Márquez called the "outsized reality" of Latin America.[10] Based on *Concierto barroco* (1974), a novella by Alejo Carpentier in which the Cuban writer pays tribute to his lifelong passion for music, this formally ambitious and complex film celebrates the syncretism, the cultural cross-fertilization of the Old World and the New World. Juxtaposing high culture and popular art, indigenous, Afro-Caribbean, and European music, dance, and performance, the film explores the intertextual expressiveness of the Latin American imagination.

Moreover, the idiosyncratic distinctiveness of this construct (the idea of Latin America), in regard to more discrete formations like nations, is its composite character. The national becomes international, superseding—without overriding—individuation. To the extent that Latin America is imagined as a "Patria Grande," the mutual and interlocking awareness of diversity within a relative cultural homogeneity has (more often than not) been concurrently inflected by nationalism and internationalism. Promoted as a polemical objection to traditional nationalist or universalist ideologies, the idea has historically been a battlefield where national, regional, and continental identities are contested and renamed. It has been continuously questioned and redefined.

Debates about national (or, for that matter, continental) identity have often revolved around the values defined either as authentic or derivative. This dichotomy has tended to obscure the conscious acceptance of the ambivalent origins of identity, what Robert Stam calls the "ironic echo" of Latin American practices, and is suggestive of the fusion of European and Latin American modernism.[11] In other words, identity is both already available—in the form of historical traditions—and still to be achieved—in the form of a modernist break with the past. This de-centered, yet historical, notion of identity is reflective and self-reflective. It implies an awareness of a history determined by conquest and revolution, by dependence and autonomy.

The cultural consciousness of nations and regions, communities and classes, languages and representations has been forged against state-imposed hegemony and in resistance. As Carlos Fuentes suggests, "The complexity of the cultural struggles underlying our political and economic struggles has to do with unresolved tensions, sometimes as old as the conflict between pantheism and monotheism, or as recent as the conflict between tradition and modernity."[12] The idea of Latin America is obsessed concurrently with the past and the present, with narratives of injustice and protest. These narratives are essentially modern. They promote discourses aimed at locating, identifying, and engaging with concepts of progress and projects of modernization, either to commend or censure them.

To attach the idea of Latin America to modernity requires a clarification of what is meant by modernity. To this purpose, I favor seeing modernity in the terms suggested by the Mexican cultural critic Carlos Monsiváis. In his address to the prestigious Coloquio de Invierno held in Mexico City in 1992, Monsiváis remarked on the modernity (and liberating agency) of social and cultural projects motivated by criticism, free expression, and tolerance. Because, as he says, "in the debate of modernity, democracy is central to the renewal of the forms and contents of political and cultural life, and it may be, or not, a barrier against authoritarianism. . . ."[13] In other words, modernity is "an inevitable paradigm" that calls forth and contests visions of tradition and progress, and a site that "engenders a sense of the future, so irrefutable because it is so unstoppable."[14]

From this perspective, the distinctive effort of self-definition that characterizes the New Latin American Cinema can be seen as a conscious attempt to assume the idea of Latin America as its ideological foundation. Moreover, the movement has articulated its continental project within a modernist contestation of tradition. At its inception in the late 1960s, the movement broke with the national cinemas, such as those of Argentina and Mexico, that once dominated Spanish-language production. The manifestos and critical essays written by the filmmakers are polemical—even dogmatic—in their dismissal of what the filmmakers called the *old* cinemas of Latin America.

Through this conscious rupture with traditional cinemas, the New Latin American Cinema launched a project of cinematographic renewal that was defined from the outset as revolutionary and anti-imperialist. Through this agenda the movement asserted the creation of new expressive spaces and the rejection of traditional genres. The movement challenged the hegemony of North American and European models of cinematographic production and consumption. In this way, filmmakers advocated an oppositional and innovative cinema. As militants and artists, they saw themselves capable of transforming the existing structures of filmmaking. In the 1960s the movement's cultural politics converged (at least through its most militant practices) with left-wing insurrectional tactics that spread throughout Latin America after the Cuban Revolution. As I have written elsewhere, the films of the movement called for "direct political action: denouncing injustice, misery and exploitation, analyzing [their] causes and consequences, replacing humanism by violence."[15]

Concurrently, the movement addressed from the onset contextually specific and distinctive issues. Through discussions generated by filmmakers in different countries, the movement debated, as John King remarks, "the question of the appropriate filmic language for particular situations; the whole vexed question of what was a 'national reality'; the uneasy relationship between filmmakers (largely middle-class intellectuals) and the 'people' they hoped to represent; and the nature of popular culture."[16] In this manner, the movement furthered critical and reflective approaches to cultural production and representation. It sanctioned an aesthetic capable of rearticulating itself into the collective by breaking hierarchical modes of address. The films sought to assert new forms of dialogue and contest the master narratives of the status quo.

By bringing together filmmakers, the movement encouraged generational and regional solidarity. It also stimulated projects committed to an alternative modernism which, in Marshall Berman's words, "assert[s] the presence and the dignity of all the people who have been left out."[17] Although the anti-imperialist rhetoric and the cultural nationalism of the 1960s concealed the term *modernity* under the guises of Marxist theories of dependency and cultural resistance, the issue of modernity was not extraneous to the New Latin American Cinema.[18] Filmmakers problematized either through their films or their writings what has been termed the "discourse of present-ness," a discourse that "takes into account its own present-ness, in order to find its place, to pronounce its own meaning, and to specify the mode of action which it is capable of exercising within this present."[19]

This "discourse of present-ness" is crucial to many of the films of New Latin American Cinema that I have examined in this book. As filmmakers have sought to insert themselves into the social and political spheres, they consciously assumed their role as initiators of change. Through critical writings and manifestos, they proposed modes suitable to distinct forms of creative and political militancy. Their films served to make ideological positions explicit and to intervene ideologically in favor of social change through aesthetic strategies that link interactively the process of production and the moment of reception.

To the extent that a self-declared community of activist filmmakers assumed (through the works of its members) the role of an artistic and political vanguard, the project of the New Latin American Cinema suggests comparisons with groups whose agendas were defined in terms of cultural nationalism. Ambrosio Fornet, for instance, suggests that by the end of the 1960s, the New Latin American Cinema "has definitely acquired the orientation and the physiognomy which, without doubt, will filter through the history of Latin American culture as one of the most innovative and astonishing phenomena of this century. In fact, the only valid precedent could be found in the Mexican muralist movement: the same search for native roots, the same eagerness of decolonization, the same will to create a new language that would be, in the context of world painting, a contemporary language."[20]

This comparison should not be taken as a self-serving accolade, but rather as a critical projection aimed at reclaiming, through parallelisms, the historical legacy of cultural nationalism. Hence, it is useful to recall a statement by Diego Rivera, the most prominent of the Mexican muralists, who wrote: "I had the ambition to reflect the genuine essential expression of the land. I wanted my pictures to mirror the social life of Mexico as I saw it and through the reality and arrangement of the present, the masses were to be shown the possibilities of the future. I sought to be . . . a condenser of the striving and longing of the masses and a transmitter providing for the masses a synthesis of their wishes so as to serve them as an organizer of consciousness and aid their social organization."[21]

Similarly, Robert Stam and Ismail Xavier link the modernist-internationalist inflections of Brazilian tropicalist films, such as *Macunaima* (Joaquim Pedro de Andrade, 1968) and *Red Light Ban-*

dit (Rogerio Szangarela), to Oswald de Andrade's anticolonial metaphor of "anthropophagy" defined in the 1920s. As Stam and Xavier write, tropicalist modernism "was a kind of artistic shock treatment designed to sabotage a falsely optimistic nationalism. The tropicalist allegory presented its diagnosis by mingling the native and the foreign, the folkloric and the industrial, the supermodern and the hyper-archaic, provoking the aesthetic prejudices of the middle class audience by foregrounding all that was incongruous and grotesque in Brazilian society."[22]

The cultural nationalism of the New Latin American Cinema signals an engagement not only with a contemporary anti-imperialist rhetoric but also with the history of movements which, in different countries, sought to radicalize cultural practices. It should not come as a surprise that practitioners of the New Latin American Cinema in the 1960s would reinstate the ideals of cultural nationalism that emerged in the 1920s, a period of intense social and political upheaval. Jean Franco's comments on Brazil are equally applicable to other Latin American countries. She has written that cultural life has been characterized by "the tension between the need for roots and the urge for modernity, between those who want to stress local or regional characteristics and those who want Brazil to be in the forefront of world culture."[23]

For instance, the notion of popular cinema developed by Latin American filmmakers (as an agent of change, requiring political choices and innovative aesthetic options to release popular creativity) reflects this tension between tradition and modernity. Not only has this popular (and reflective) cinema reconstructed the subversive power of popular traditions and historical memory, but deconstructed the representations and discourses that have limited the self-representation of Latin American peoples. Thus, the filmmakers of the New Latin American Cinema have reacted to—but not acquiesced to—hegemonic discourses on modernity. On the contrary, their radical project is characterized by the need to engage critically with the issue of modernity, either as an ideology of progress or an avant-garde aesthetic.

By operating within the dynamic dialectics of modernity, the movement has (like other cultural practices in Latin America) coalesced into formative impulses—what Rama called *impulsos modeladores*—grounded in the search for autonomy, originality, and representativity.[24] These formative impulses constitute precisely the basis upon which the New Latin American Cinema has periodically redefined its ideological and aesthetic project.

To assert the autonomy of cinematographic practices, the filmmakers associated with the movement have identified elements relevant to changing cultural, social, and political conditions. They have drawn upon cinematographic concepts advanced in other historical contexts only to transform them, to make them more suitable to national and continental realities. On the influence of Italian neorealism, for instance, Fernando Birri has said, "Neo-realism was the cinema that discovered amidst the clothing and the rhetoric of development another Italy, the Italy of underdevelopment. It was a cinema of the humble and the offended which could be readily taken up by film makers all over what has since come to be called the third world." [25]

The New Latin American Cinema has also sought to authorize distinct conceptual frameworks through manifestos and critical essays written by its filmmakers. Julio García Espinosa's "For an Imperfect Cinema," for instance, has contributed to the originality of the movement's agenda. The impossibility of practicing art as an impartial activity and popular art conceived as a dynamically active entity have been revolutionary alternatives that "can supply an entirely new response [and] enable us to do away once and for all with elitist concepts and practices in art." [26]

Moreover, the representativity of the movement has been validated by the international and continental circulation of the ideas and films associated with the New Latin American Cinema. Although film historians, critics, and researchers in Latin America and elsewhere are beginning to take a serious look at the cinemas produced before the emergence of the movement, the movement prevails as a referential term of Latin American cinemas. As John King writes, it "show[s] that there is a network of formal and informal contacts that unites film-making practices across and within their national diversities." [27]

To confront the pervasive contradictions of political, social, and economic processes in Latin America, the movement reasserted the role of cinema as a critically interactive space of communication. Insofar as filmmakers began exploring the realities of their countries, as Michael Chanan points out, they discovered "a subjective world, made up of the oral culture that is called folklore, and the amalgam of religious and magical beliefs that are sustained by the misfortune and ignorance of underdevelopment." [28] Rather than forfeiting the militancy of the 1960s, filmmakers sought to remap the intricate dialectics of history and class struggle, memory and representation.

Consistently preoccupied with political agency and social process, and critical of the modernization tendencies of nation-states, the filmmakers of the New Latin American Cinema denounced a modernity based on self-confident promises of progress. Mostly in the 1960s, films stressed class struggle as the only possible way out of social injustice. To restore the subject into history, filmmakers systematically addressed in their writings national identity through the pervading usage of an all-encompassing notion of national reality. Yet the films studied in this book (in contrast to the writings of Latin American filmmakers) problematize the erasure of regional, social, racial, and sexual differences implied by the term *national reality* and privilege subjective and collective identities as embattled sites of representation and discourse. In its project to rearrange the terms that have served to construct national identities, the films of the New Latin American Cinema expose the evolving, rather than foundational, essence of the national. By the 1980s, for instance, filmmakers addressing issues of gender and ethnicity have questioned ahistorical presumptions and romantic celebrations of cultural difference and have freed gender and ethnicity from their problematic appropriation in national allegories.

Once armed with a critical agenda, the movement was capable of projecting its history into the future. Through a self-defined identity, as a regional enterprise, the movement has been able to persist as a valid political endeavor. Throughout the 1970s, for instance, the movement weathered speculations about an impending collapse. As Ana López points out, "The New Latin American Cinema, often forced into exile or silenced by censorship and repression at a national level, assumed an increasingly pan–Latin American character."[29] Moreover, institutional rearrangements and economic growth were promoting commercial trends that affected national practices profoundly. But filmmakers also found in new institutional arrangements the possibility of relocating initiatives, previously supported only by the movement, into national practices. Their initiatives energized rather than weakened the movement and the New Cinema of Latin America integrated these national inflections into its supranational design.

The films of the 1970s opted for narrative and aesthetic strategies (sometimes self-reflexive but always critical) capable of resolving the anachronism of underdevelopment. Moreover, the movement sought to expand its terms of reference and, rather than narrowing itself by prescriptive definitions, set out to disengage its innovational goals from the confining rhetoric of the militant 1960s. The term Third Cinema, for instance, often used to describe the politics of Latin American cinemas, was rearticulated to reflect its original impulse as a critically conscious and experimental agency of signification. In 1979 Fernando Ezequiel Solanas explained again that the Third Cinema "is the way the world is conceptualized and not the genre nor the explicitly political character of a film. . . . Third Cinema is an open category, unfinished, incomplete. It is a research category. It is a democratic, national, popular cinema."[30]

By the 1980s, the New Latin American Cinema identified much more closely with a modernist aesthetic. What Fernando Birri called the "nationalist, realist, critical, and popular" practices of the New Latin American Cinema in the early 1980s are "a poetics of the transformation of reality . . . [that] generates a creative energy which through cinema aspires to modify the reality upon which it is projected."[31] At the basis of this poetics is a critical impulse that can reinvent itself in and through the heterogeneous elements and contradictory discourses of a continent at once unitary and diverse.

The experience of exile, for instance, has been crucial to the production of a new political agency whereby community associations are relocated, cultural specificity is renegotiated, and cultural affiliations are reconstructed. Geographic and cultural displacement has fostered decentered views on identity and nationality, stressed the dialectics of historical and personal circumstance, and validated autobiography as a reflective site. If this aspect is most prominent in films produced in exile, it can also be found in other films of the New Cinema of Latin America studied in this book, which evidence a greater variety of approaches to the political.

While the movement's history provides a framework for understanding the ever-fluctuating situation of filmmaking practices, its conceptual agenda provides insights into the dialectics of representation and cultural politics in Latin America. As Julianne Burton has pointed out, "More than the determination to give expression to new forms and new contents, the most significant aspect of oppositional film movements in the Third World has been their fundamental commitment to transforming existing modes of film production, diffusion and reception."[32]

The movement has sought to integrate culture and politics, to construct instances in which cinematic practices intersect with social change. Therefore, the political and cultural agenda of the New Latin American Cinema has advocated grassroots forms of participation and supported film and video collectives that seek to channel the aspirations of social movements. The movement has contributed to increasing collaborative ventures between filmmakers from countries where the survival of nationally based initiatives has been threatened.

The movement's historical agency—its capacity of self-definition and self-regulation—is grounded in a political and aesthetic agenda (rather than the formal affinity of its national components). As a discursive formation and a cultural practice, the movement has accommodated ideological and contextual realignments. Therefore, it is essential to understand that the movement's specificity resides in the convergence of nationally based practices, including the infrastructural changes affecting filmmakers and their practices, with a pan-continental project.

Insofar as the movement's unified sense of purpose has been capable of controlling the diversity of production strategies, a flexible (rather than a restrictive) approach is required to grasp the impact of infrastructural and organizational changes on the historical consciousness of the New Latin American Cinema. This approach allows an understanding of how the movement's continental orientation, through a process of self-definition, controls the eclecticism of its cinematographic practices.

But in reaction to the movement's singular process of self-definition, Latin American film historians and critics have tended to contest a perceived erasure of contextual considerations.[33] Notwithstanding my agreement with the basic premise of some of these criticisms, I would argue that the New Latin American Cinema emerges as a site of struggle between diverging, and sometimes contentious, processes of historical construction. Latin American identity has been shaped by cultural practices that have sanctioned or contested prevalent forms of representation and social organization. By authorizing different approaches to production, distribution, and exhibition, the movement has endorsed radical forms of filmmaking capable of revolutionizing existing social relations.

By adopting critical realism and advocating modernist aesthetic options, the films of the New Latin American Cinema have served to reinterpret and redefine the place of film, as a cultural and political practice, within the often contradictory, but always material, realities of the continent. In a sense the movement is representative of what Rodolfo Parada calls the *mestizaje definitivo* of Latin America. In other words, the movement originates from an awareness and a sense of belonging produced at that "moment in our history when we acquire the notion of our worth and in which we decide to follow our ambitions. When we decide not to be imitators and followers, we begin to see the world in relation to who we really are, in relation to the Americas, as Latin Americans."[34]

Paulo Emilio Salles Gomes described this process when he wrote about Brazilian cinema: "We are neither Europeans nor North Americans. Lacking an original culture, nothing is foreign to us because everything is. The painful construction of ourselves develops within the rarefied dialectic of not being and being someone else."[35] To the extent that this "not being and being someone else" reasserts the yet untold and multiple narratives of cultural identity and national realities, it is the principle upon which Latin Americans have challenged fixed notions and imagined new utopias.

This principle conforms to "a sense of forever-not-yet being," as Bell Gale Chevigny suggests, "which may constitute an identity in itself."[36] Moreover, this principle implies critique and renewal and is profoundly attached to an unfinished experience of modernity whereby a yet-to-be-constructed modernity can be envisioned. As far as the New Latin American Cinema is concerned, this principle is exemplified in the movement's characteristic logic: its belief that its ideological project remains unfinished.

Notes

1. Convergences and Divergences

1. Ana M. López, "An 'Other' History: The New Latin American Cinema," *Radical History Review* 41 (1988): 104.

2. Ibid., p. 96.

3. Ibid., p. 95.

4. Patricia Aufderheide, "Latin American Cinema and the Rhetoric of Cultural Nationalism: Controversies at Havana in 1987 and 1989," *Quarterly Review of Film and Video* 12, no. 4 (1991): 62.

5. Ana M. López, "Setting Up the Stage: A Decade of Latin American Film Scholarship," *Quarterly Review of Film and Video* 13, nos. 1–3 (1991): 243.

6. This event is highlighted by Alfonso Gumucio Dagrón, *Historia del cine boliviano*, pp. 193–194, and Mario Handler, "Starting from Scratch: Artisanship and Agitprop," in Julianne Burton, ed., *Cinema and Social Change in Latin America: Conversations with Filmmakers*, pp. 17–18.

7. Ambrosio Fornet, *Cine, literatura, sociedad*, p. 18. Unless otherwise indicated, all quotations taken from foreign-language sources are my translation.

8. On the *nueva ola*, see López, "An 'Other' History," pp. 100–103.

9. Ana M. López, "Celluloid Tears: Melodrama in the 'Old' Mexican Cinema," *Iris*, no. 13 (Summer 1991): 29.

10. Fernando Birri, "Cinema and Underdevelopment," translated by Malcolm Coad, in Michael Chanan, ed., *Twenty-Five Years of the New Latin American Cinema*, p. 9.

11. Glauber Rocha, "The Aesthetics of Hunger," translated by Burnes Hollyman and Randal Johnson), in Chanan, ed., *Twenty-Five Years of the New Latin American Cinema*, p. 15.

12. Equally relevant is the point made by Fernando Birri that the New Cinema of Latin America "was born without any kind of, let's say, confabulation between us, but because it was in the air." See "For a Nationalist, Realist, Critical and Popular Cinema," *Screen* 26, nos. 3–4 (May–August 1985): 89.

13. The film program consisted of documentary and fiction films. *Fuelle querido* (Mauricio Berú, 1966), *Greda* (Raymundo Gleyzer and Jorge Preloran, 1966), *Trasmallos* (Octavio Getino, 1964), *Sobre todas las estrellas* (Eliseo Subiela, 1965), and *Las cosas ciertas* (Gerardo Vallejo, 1965) were some of the Argentinian films shown. The only Bolivian film screened was *Revolución* (Jorge Sanjinés, 1963); and Cuba presented *Manuela* (Humberto Solás, 1966), *Now* (Santiago Alvarez, 1965), and *Cerro pelado* (Alvarez, 1966). The Brazilian selection was by far the largest with, among others, *Subterráneos do futebol* (Mauricio Capovilla, 1966), *Memorias do cangaço* (Paulo Gil Soares, 1965), *Maioria absoluta* (Leon Hirzman, 1964), and *Viramundo* (Gerardo Sarno, 1965). *Aborto* (Pedro Chaskel, 1965), *Andacollo* (Jorge di Lauro and Nieves Yankovic, 1967), *Por la tierra ajena* (Miguel Littin, 1965), and *Yo tenía un camarada* (Helvio Soto, 1964) were some of the Chilean films shown. The program also included *Todos somos hermanos* (Oscar Menéndez, 1964) from Mexico, *Forjadores del mañana* (Jorge Volkert) from Perú, *Carlos, cineretrato de un caminante* (Mario Handler, 1965) and *Talvez mañana* (Omar Parada) from Uruguay, and *Arte colonial en Venezuela* and *Colores de la infancia* (Daniel Oropeza) from Venezuela.

14. Alfredo Guevara, "Viña del Mar: Un hito decisivo," *Cine Cubano*, no. 120 (1987): 3. This issue reprints some of the reports presented by national delegations and originally published in *Cine Cubano*, nos. 42–44 (1968).

15. In 1967, as Michael Chanan indicates (*The Cuban Image: Cinema and Cultural Politics in Cuba*, p. 221), the participants of the conference of the Latin American Solidarity Organization held in Havana "declared the political, economic and social unity of Latin America to be far more significant than the political divisions and antagonisms in the continent."

16. John King, *Magical Reels: A History of Cinema in Latin America*, p. 67.

17. Fornet, *Cine, literatura, sociedad*, p. 20.

18. Among the films presented in Mérida were *Asalto* (Carlos Alvarez, 1968) and *The Brickmakers* (Marta Rodriguez and Jorge Silva, 1968) from Colombia; *¡Aysa!* (Jorge Sanjinés, 1965) and *Estampas del Carnaval de Kanas* (Manuel Chambi, 1965) from Bolivia and Perú; *Hasta la victoria siempre* (Santiago Alvarez, 1967) and *David* (Enrique Pineda Barnet, 1967) from Cuba; *Elecciones* (Mario Handler, 1967) and *Carlos, cineretrato de un caminante* (Handler, 1965) from Uruguay; and *La ciudad que nos ve* (Jesús Enrique Guedez, 1967) and *Ceramiqueros detrás de la sierra* (Raymundo Gleyzer and Jorge Preloran, 1966) from Venezuela and Argentina.

19. Julianne Burton, "Democratizing Documentary: Modes of Address in the Latin American Cinema, 1959–1972," in Thomas Waugh, ed., "*Show Us Life*": Towards a History and Aesthetics of the Committed Documentary, p. 378.

20. Walter Achugar, "Using Movies to Make Movies," in Burton, ed., *Cinema and Social Change in Latin America*, p. 228.

21. During my first visit to Cuba in 1979, filmmakers and critics pointed out that the title of my recently published anthology—*Latin American*

Film Makers and the Third Cinema—was misleading in that not all of the New Latin American Cinema should be defined as "third cinema."

22. Fornet, *Cine, literatura, sociedad,* p. 23.

23. Hans Ehrmann, "Encuentro de cineastas," in Aldo Francia, ed., *Nuevo Cine Latinoamericano en Viña del Mar,* pp. 167–168. Ehrmann also remarks that Ché Guevara—the Argentine doctor who played a prominent political and ideological role in the Cuban Revolution and was killed in Bolivia in 1967—was named honorary president of the round-table section of the festival titled "Imperialism and Culture."

24. For a full account, including press reaction, see Francia, ed., *Nuevo Cine Latinoamericano,* pp. 154–170.

25. Among these films were *Ukamau* and *The Blood of the Condor* (Jorge Sanjines and Group Ukamau, 1966 and 1969) from Bolivia, *Brasil Anno 2000* (Walter Lima Jr., 1969) and *Antonio das Mortes* (Glauber Rocha, 1969) from Brazil, *Asalto* (Carlos Alvarez, 1968) and *Camilo Torres* (Diego León Giraldo, 1967) from Colombia, *Memories of Underdevelopment* (Tomás Gutierrez Alea, 1968), *Lucía* (Humberto Solás, 1968), *La odisea del general José* (Jorge Fraga, 1968), *La primera carga del machete* (Manuel Octavio Gómez, 1968), and documentaries by Santiago Alvarez, Octavio Cortázar, Enrique Pineda Barnet, and Alejandro Sanderman (an Argentine filmmaker living in Cuba) from Cuba, *Uruguay 1969: El problema de la carne* (Mario Handler, 1969) from Uruguay, and *Los niños callan* (Jesús Enrique Guedez, 1968), and *TV Venezuela* (Jorge Solé, 1969) from Venezuela.

26. King, *Magical Reels,* p. 69.

27. Pick, ed., *Latin American Film Makers and the Third Cinema,* p. 10.

28. For details see Randal Johnson, "Introduction: Cinema Novo, the State, and Modern Brazilian Cinema," *Cinema Novo × 5: Masters of Contemporary Brazilian Cinema,* pp. 2–3.

29. It is worth mentioning such films as *What Is Democracy?* (Carlos Alvarez, 1971) and *Liber Arce, liberarse* (Mario Handler, 1970), shot in Colombia and Uruguay respectively, and *Third World, Third World War* (Julio García Espinosa, Cuba 1970) and *Mexico, The Frozen Revolution* (Raymundo Gleyzer, Argentina, 1970), filmed in Vietnam and Mexico respectively.

30. Fornet, *Cine, literatura, sociedad,* p. 27.

31. Later three other films appeared: *Os inconfidentes* (Joaquim Pedro de Andrade, Brazil, 1972), *Nobody Said Anything* (Raul Ruiz, Chile, 1972), and *The Days of Water* (Manuel Octavio Gómez, Cuba, 1973).

32. For details see Juan Verdejo, Zuzana M. Pick, and Gastón Ancelovici, "Chili," in Guy Hennebelle, and Alfonso Gumucio Dagrón, eds., *Les cinémas de l'Amérique latine,* pp. 212–227, and Michael Chanan, ed., *Chilean Cinema,* pp. 1–25.

33. Achugar, "Using Movies to Make Movies," pp. 231–236.

34. Ibid., pp. 232–234.

35. Paulo-Antonio Paranagua, "Le nouveau cinéma latino-américain: Entre la répression des dictatures et la tutelle étatique," *Amérique latine: Luttes et mutations/Tricontinental II,* pp. 120–130.

36. Randal Johnson, *The Film Industry in Brazil: Culture and the State,* pp. 104–170.

37. For details see Robert Stam and Ismail Xavier, "Transformation of National Allegory: Brazilian Cinema from Dictatorship to Redemocratization," in Robert Sklar and Charles Musser, eds., *Resisting Images: Essays on Cinema and History,* pp. 279–307.

38. For details see Tim Barnard, "Popular Cinema and Populist Politics," in Tim Barnard, ed., *Argentine Cinema,* pp. 49–55; and Nissa Torrents, "Contemporary Argentine Cinema," in John King and Nissa Torrents, eds. *The Garden of Forking Paths: Argentine Cinema,* pp. 101–105.

39. Alfonso Gumucio Dagrón, "Argentina: A Huge Case of Censorship," in Barnard, ed., *Argentine Cinema,* pp. 84–98.

40. Between 1973 and 1983, exiled Chilean filmmakers produced 50 long feature films and 105 medium- and short-length films. See Zuzana M. Pick, "Chilean Cinema: Ten Years of Exile, 1973–1983," *Jump Cut,* no. 32 (April 1986): 66–70.

41. For details see Chanan, *The Cuban Image,* pp. 257–281.

42. "Declaración final: V Encuentro de cineastas latinoamericanos, Mérida, Venezuela, Abril 1977," *Cine Cubano,* nos. 91–92 (n.d.): 27.

43. During the Second International Festival of the New Latin American Cinema in Havana in 1980, comments made by a German critic and programmer triggered a heated public discussion. Peter Schumann's view about a crisis within the movement was eventually disputed in 1981 by filmmakers and critics who met in Pesaro during a major Latin American retrospective.

44. Fornet, *Cine, literatura, sociedad,* pp. 36–37. This question can be answered only by examining individual films—in other words, by attempting to understand the links between the movement's political agenda and the aesthetic strategies of its constituting cultural practices. The remaining chapters of this book are aimed at addressing some of these links.

45. Alfredo Guevara, "Discurso de clausura: Palabras de clausura pronunciadas por el compañero Alfredo Guevara, presidente del festival," *Cine Cubano,* no. 97 (1980): 9.

46. The promotion of the idea of *mestizaje* would be questioned through films dealing with the historical effects of the violent encounter of indigenous American, African, and European cultures. Chapter 5 deals with issues of ethnicity.

47. The papers presented by filmmakers and critics at the seminars programmed every year during the Havana film festival have been regularly published by *Cine Cubano.* A comprehensive account of these thematic seminars could serve to evaluate to what extent they contributed to an understanding of the New Latin American Cinema as a historical formation.

48. For documents relating to these organizations see Octavio Getino, *Cine latinoamericano, economía y nuevas tecnologías,* pp. 289–297.

49. B. Ruby Rich, "An/Other View of New Latin American Cinema," *Iris,* no. 23 (Summer 1991): 23.

50. Ibid.

51. Getino, *Cine latinoamericano*, p. 243.

52. Among this new generation of scholars are Alfonso Gumucio Dagrón and Carlos Mesa Guisbert (Bolivia), Vicente de Paula Araujo, Jean Claude Bernardet, Maria Rita Galvao, Joao Luiz Viera, and Ismail Xavier (Brazil), Alicia Vega (Chile), Hernando Salcedo Silva (Colombia), Jorge Villacres Moscoso (Ecuador), Marcela Fernández Violante, Gustavo García, Andrés de Luna, and Patricia Vega (Mexico), Luis Trelles Plazaola (Puerto Rico), Luis Elbert (Uruguay), and Rodolfo Izaguirre and Ambretta Marrosu (Venezuela).

53. In this decade there is also a marked expansion of scholarship on Latin American cinema. For a review of this activity (mainly in the United States), see López, "Setting Up the Stage," pp. 239–260.

54. For details see Jesús Salvador Treviño, "Chicano Cinema Overview," *Areíto* 10, no. 37 (1984): 40–43; and Jose Umpierre and Mario Vissepo, "Porto-Rico," in Hennebelle and Gumucio Dagrón, eds., *Les cinémas de l' Amérique latine*, pp. 445–447.

55. For details see John Hess, "Collective Experience, Synthetic Forms: El Salvador's Radio Venceremos," pp. 173–191; Zuzana M. Pick, "Chilean Documentary: Continuity and Disjunction," pp. 124–128; and Karen Ranucci with Julianne Burton, "On the Trail of Independent Video," pp. 193–208, in Julianne Burton, ed., *The Social Documentary of Latin America*.

56. The impact of video on feminist practices has been overwhelming. At the First Meeting of Women Film and Video Makers from Latin America and the Caribbean—called La Cocina de Imágenes—held in Mexico in 1987, for instance, video production overshadowed film.

57. Rich, "An/Other View," pp. 13–14.

58. Aufderheide, "Latin American Cinema and the Rhetoric of Cultural Nationalism," pp. 66–70.

59. P. Leduc, "Nuevo cine latinoamericano y reconversión industrial (una tesis reaccionaria)," translated and quoted in Aufderheide, "Latin American Cinema and the Rhetoric of Cultural Nationalism," p. 69.

60. Julianne Burton, "El próximo tango en Finlandia: Cinemedios y modelos de transculturación" (paper presented at the Ninth International Festival of the New Latin American Cinema, Havana, December 1987).

61. Aufderheide, "Latin American Cinema and the Rhetoric of Cultural Nationalism," p. 71.

62. Ibid., pp. 62–63.

---

2. Creativity and Social Intervention

1. Written in 1954, "A Certain Tendency of French Cinema" was intended as a critique of the literary tendencies of postwar French cinema. See Bill Nichols, ed., *Movies and Methods*, vol. 1, pp. 224–237.

2. Oswaldo Capriles, "Mérida: Realidad, forma y comunicación," *Cine al Día* (Caracus), no. 6 (December 1968): 4.

3. Julianne Burton, "Marginal Cinemas and Mainstream Critical Theory," *Screen* 6, nos. 3–4 (May–August 1985): 21.

4. Ibid., p. 3.

5. Johnson, *The Film Industry in Brazil*, p. 90. (See pp. 91–100 for details on how *cinema nôvo*, as a movement, took a stand against the industrial strategies promoted by government agencies and endorsed by independent producers who believed these measures could solve their chronic financial vulnerability.)

6. Glauber Rocha, *Revisión crítica del cine brasileño*, pp. 21–22.

7. Ibid., p. 64. Cavalcanti's credentials were based on his contributions to the French avant-garde and the British documentary movement. Upon his return in the 1950s, he was commissioned by President Getulio Vargas to outline the constitution of a National Film Institute. But, as Randal Johnson (*The Film Industry in Brazil*, p. 67) points out, Cavalcanti's "decidedly internationalist view . . . would bring him into conflict with the local producers he claimed his project was designed to protect." Although the proposals of the Cavalcanti Commission were never approved, they affected cinematic debates well into the 1960s.

8. Birri, "Cinema and Underdevelopment," p. 11.

9. Burton, "Marginal Cinemas and Mainstream Critical Theory," p. 12.

10. For a historical description of these strategies, see Julianne Burton, "Toward a History of Social Documentary in Latin America," in Burton, ed., *The Social Documentary in Latin America*, pp. 3–30.

11. Although filmmakers themselves have critiqued the recurring tendency in the 1960s to equate reality with cinematic realism, I would argue that most documentaries of this period contradict a naive advocacy of realism. For a discussion of this issue see Burton, "Democratizing Documentary," pp. 344–383.

12. Jorge Sanjinés, "A Militant Cinema," translated by Christina Shantz and Leandro Urbina, in Pick, ed., *Latin American Film Makers and the Third Cinema*, pp. 74–75. Minor corrections in this quote were suggested by Julianne Burton.

13. José Antonio González, "Conversación con Jorge Silva y Marta Rodríguez," *Cine Cubano*, nos. 86–88 (1973): 69–77.

14. Camilo Torres Restrepo (1929–1966) was a priest, sociologist, academic, political activist, and *guerrillero* who was killed in an army ambush. Educated at the Catholic University of Louvain (Belgium), his research was centered on rural and urban development, particularly during the time he was a member of the committee for the implementation of agrarian reform in 1961. He was forced to leave first the university and then the Church, which did not support his radical ideas. He participated in the Popular Unity movement before joining the guerrilla movement.

15. Camilo Torres, *Ecrits et paroles*, translated by Didier Coste, Jean-Michel Fossey, and Henri de la Vega, pp. 67–76, 169–174.

16. Julianne Burton, "*The Brick-Makers*," *Cinéaste* 7, no. 3 (Fall 1976): 38–39.

17. González, "Conversación con Jorge Silva y Marta Rodríguez," p. 71.

18. This cinema was characterized by the inability to resolve in a cinematic and political way the issues it proposed to denounce. Oscar Collazos asks, ". . . when is it possible to work on the events and materials proposed by reality, when the political instruments capable of critically structuring them are lacking?" See "Cine colombiano: ¿Por quién, para quién, contra quienes?" *Cine Cubano*, nos. 76–77 (n.d.): 37.

Although most working filmmakers were formed at film schools in Europe and North America, they were, in the words of Jorge Silva, a "generation of masters" rooted in the tradition of art cinema and hampered by the chronic weaknesses of an underdeveloped infrastructure that relied basically on television (introduced in 1954) and advertising. See González, "Conversación con Jorge Silva y Marta Rodríguez," p. 70.

19. Ibid., pp. 69–77.

20. Burton, "Democratizing Documentary," p. 369.

21. At the end of the film, the still photographs that mark their eviction are punctuated by close-ups of a modest meatgrinder that represents their sole possession.

22. Burton, "Democratizing Documentary," p. 369.

23. Carlos Alvarez, "For Colombia 1971: Militancy and the Cinema," translated by Christina Shantz and Leandro Urbina, in Pick, ed., *Latin American Film Makers and the Third Cinema*, p. 184. I have revised inaccuracies in the original translation.

24. Julianne Burton, "Cine-Sociology and Social Change: Jorge Silva and Marta Rodríguez," in Burton, ed., *Cinema and Social Change in Latin America*, p. 29.

25. For a study of this period from a contemporary perspective see Jenny Pearce, *Colombia: Inside the Labyrinth*, pp. 49–66, 167–170.

26. After being a participant in Nuestro Tiempo, a radical cultural organization formed under the aegis of the University of Havana's student union in the 1950s, Tomás Gutierrez Alea became one of the four founding members of the Cuban Film Institute in the wake of a victorious revolution led by Fidel Castro from the mountains of the Sierra Maestra. As he wrote in an autobiographical piece ("I Wasn't Always a Filmmaker," *Cineaste* 14, no. 1 [1985]: 36), it was while studying law that he discovered film and "came to see filmmaking as an undeniable social responsibility."

27. For a discussion of changes within the Cuban Film Institute see Julianne Burton, "Film and Revolution in Cuba: The First Twenty-Five Years," in Sandor Halebsky and John M. Kirk, eds., *Cuba: Twenty-Five Years of Revolution, 1959–1984*, pp. 134–153.

28. Chanan, *The Cuban Image*, p. 294.

29. A similar argument had already been put forward in Fernando Solanas and Octavio Getino, "Towards a Third Cinema: Notes and Experiences for the Development of a Cinema of Liberation in the Third World," translated by Julianne Burton and Michael Chanan, in Chanan, ed., *Twenty-Five Years of the New Latin American Cinema*, p. 23: "The model of a perfect work of

art, the fully rounded film . . . has served to inhibit the film-maker in the dependent countries, especially when he has attempted to erect similar models in a reality which *offered him neither the culture, the techniques, nor the most primary elements for success."*

30. Julio García Espinosa, "Julio García Espinosa responde," *Primer Plano* (Valparaiso) 1, no. 4 (Spring 1972): 36–42. Reprinted as "Carta a la revista *Primer Plano,"* in Julio García Espinosa, *Una imagen recorre el mundo,* pp. 43–51.

31. Julio García Espinosa, "For an Imperfect Cinema," translated by Julianne Burton, in Chanan, ed., *Twenty-Five Years of the New Latin American Cinema,* pp. 29–30.

32. "We maintain that imperfect cinema must above all show the process which generates the problems. It is thus the opposite of a cinema principally dedicated to celebrating results, the opposite of a self-sufficient and contemplative cinema, the opposite of a cinema which 'beautifully illustrates' ideas or concepts which we already possess. (The narcissistic posture has nothing to do with those who struggle.) To show the process is not exactly equivalent to analysing it. To analyse a problem is to show the problem (not the process) permeated with judgments which the analysis itself generates a priori. To analyse is to block off from the outset any possibility for analysis on the part of the interlocutor." Ibid., p. 32.

33. Burton, "Film and Revolution in Cuba," p. 144.

34. Paulo-Antonio Paranagua, "News from Havana: A Restructuring of Cuban Cinema," *Framework,* no. 35 (1988): 88, 91.

35. Enrique Colina, *"Hasta cierto punto,"* *Cine Cubano,* no. 108 (1984): 88–90.

36. Tomás Gutierrez Alea, "Dramaturgía (cinematográfica) y realidad," *Cine Cubano,* no. 105 (1984): 71–77; Jorge Luis Llopiz, "El talón de Aquiles de nuestro cine," *Cine Cubano,* no. 122 (1988): 6–12.

37. Enrique Colina, "Tomás Gutierrez Alea sobre *Hasta cierto punto,"* *Cine Cubano,* no. 109 (1984): 73–77.

38. Acting problems seem to have pushed the love story to the foreground of the film but, as Paulo-Antonio Paranagua ("News from Havana," p. 91) points out, "without eclipsing the subject which appears to have strongly motivated the director."

39. García Espinosa, "For an Imperfect Cinema," p. 29.

40. "The artistic [spectacle] inserts itself to the sphere of everyday reality (the sphere of what is continuous, stable and relatively calm . . .) as an extraordinary moment, as a rupture. It is opposed to daily life as an unreality, an other-reality, insofar as it moves and relates to the spectator on an ideal plane. (In this being *ideal*—separation from daily life—it expresses its unusual and extraordinary character. Therefore, [spectacle] is not opposed to the typical, but rather it can incarnate the typical as it is a selective process and an exacerbation of outstanding—significant—traits of reality.)" See Tomás Gutierrez Alea, *The Viewer's Dialectic,* translated by Julia Lesage, pp. 33–34.

41. Lesage, "Prologue," ibid., p. 13.

42. Ernesto Ché Guevara, *Escritos y discursos,* vol. 9, p. 355.

43. Torrents, "Contemporary Argentine Cinema," p. 98.

44. In my view, the controversies that have surrounded Peronism have not only induced divergent evaluations of Argentine cinema but have also promoted extended periods of silence on practices that either acknowledge the Peronist agenda or denounce it. Therefore, it should not come as a surprise that the New Cinema of Latin America, as a movement, has been equally affected by the contested impact of Peronism on recent Latin American history.

45. Solanas and Getino, "Towards a Third Cinema," p. 21.

46. Fernando Solanas, "Fernando Solanas: An Interview," translated by James Roy Macbean, *Film Quarterly* 14, no. 1 (Fall 1970): 38–40.

47. Solanas and Getino, "Towards a Third Cinema," p. 20.

48. Ibid., p. 24.

49. Fernando Solanas, "Remarques écrites," *Cinéthique* (Paris), no. 3 (1969): 6.

50. Solanas and Getino, "Towards a Third Cinema," p. 27.

51. Octavio Getino, "Algunas observaciones sobre el concepto del 'Tercer Cine,'" *A diez años de "Hacia un tercer cine,"* pp. 8–9.

52. Fernando Solanas, "Cinema as a Gun: An Interview with Fernando Solanas," translated by Rebecca Douglass with Ruth McCormick, *Cineaste* 3, no. 2 (Fall 1969): 19.

53. Robert Stam, "*The Hour of the Furnaces* and the Two Avant-Gardes," in Burton, ed., *The Social Documentary in Latin America,* p. 253. In an interview Fernando Ezequiel Solanas ("Cinema as a Gun," p. 19) mentions *Los que mandan,* the provisional title of a project turned down by an official financing commission.

54. Solanas and Getino, "Towards a Third Cinema," p. 27. I had the opportunity to attend a full screening of the film in Montreal during the spring of 1971 and in London in the winter of 1977. Although no provisions were made for discussion, the breaks between each section gave rise to all kinds of debates. In Montreal the denunciation of neocolonialism of the first part of *The Hour of the Furnaces* elicited debates on the status of Quebec in view of the events of October of 1970 and the suspension of civil rights by the federal government of Canada. In London the screening was attended mostly by Argentines and Latin Americans who, during the breaks, debated the ideological validity of the film's position on Peronism, one year after the military coup in Argentina.

55. Stam, "*The Hour of the Furnaces,*" p. 255.

56. The *bombo* is an oversized drum that was carried to Peronist political rallies; in the film it gives a rhythmic measure to the movements of the crowd and accompanies all the slogans. It is a rural instrument that belongs to the gaucho tradition.

57. Writing on the auction sequence, Robert Stam ("*The Hour of the Furnaces,*" p. 258) states: "The sequence interweaves shots of the crowned

heads of the prize bulls with the faces of the aristocracy. The bulls—inert, sluggish, well pedigreed—present a perfect analogue to the oligarchs that breed them. Metonymic phrases describing the bulls ("admire the expression, the bone structure") are yoked, in a stunning cinematic xeugma, to the looks of bovine satisfaction on the faces of their owners."

58. Ibid., p. 255.

59. The graphic techniques used by Solanas and Getino are related to those developed by Santiago Alvarez in Cuba during the production of the ICAIC newsreel, but also to the devices used by advertising.

60. See the description in Stam, *The Hour of the Furnaces*, p. 259.

61. John King, "The Social and Cultural Context," in King and Torrents, eds., *The Garden of the Forking Paths*, p. 3, describes this antinomy as follows: "Barbarism was equated with the backward interior, local *caudillos* (military leaders), the *gaucho* as an inferior social type, and introverted nationalism. Civilisation could be found in adopting European patterns in the political, cultural and social spheres. Argentina had to open up its trade to the rest of the world, attract immigrants, and acquire at the same time values of sociability and respectability which would lead the country out of fragmentation caused by excessive individualism, into a well-organized social system."

62. Solanas, "Cinema as a Gun," p. 22. In the same interview Solanas speaks about the censorship of *The Hour of the Furnaces*: "But we are struggling for the legality of our film and the first thing we will do will be to send the film to the commission of censorship for its approval for public distribution. This may seem grotesque but it means demonstrating publicly that we aren't hiding our ideas. This revolutionary action of making a film of liberation was undertaken with the intention that it would be distributed in the widest manner possible and its authors assume complete responsibility for it. On the other hand, and this is the most important thing, we maintain that any actions against us will only serve to clarify and define the situation, i.e. prohibition of the film will explain eloquently that there is not a single culture and there is no possibility for either cultural coexistence or dialogue."

63. An excellent contextualization of the poem has been written by Angeles Cardona de Gilbert in the 1974 edition of *Martin Fierro* (Buenos Aires: Editorial Bruguera).

64. A comprehensive description of these allusions is given by Paulo-Antonio Paranagua, "*Los hijos de Fierro (Les fils de Fierro),*" *Positif*, nos. 208–209 (July–August 1978): 88.

65. The *payada* belongs to the expressive arsenal of traditional gaucho culture; it is a form of popular poetry that consists of improvised verses. In its preliterary form, the *payada* was performed by two famed *payadores* who demonstrated their mastery in front of large audiences. José Hernández gave the *payada* its literary form in *Martin Fierro*. The *milonga* is a folk ballad with tango rhythm indigenous to the Rio de la Plata, a region that includes the lowlands of Uruguay and the northern coast of Argentina. It is sometimes confused with the tango.

66. Paranagua, "*Los hijos de Fierro,*" p. 88.

67. In 1979 Solanas acknowledged that "the anti-Peronist bias which exists is so, so heavy, that there are people who won't even get near the film (to see it). Or they react so epidermically . . . that they cannot even see the humanistic-progressive trend which the film has as its ideology." See Don Ranvaud, "Interview with Fernando Solanas," translated by Cristina Weller, *Framework,* no. 10 (Spring 1979): 36–37.

68. Between 1955 and 1976 Argentine cinema was characterized, in the words of Ana López, by its "outstanding heterogeneity" in a period that "included practices as diverse as a struggling industrial commercial cinema, clandestine political film-making, the cosmopolitan *cinéma d'auteur* of the *nueva ola,* and the socially-conscious documentary work of Fernando Birri in the provinces." See Ana M. López, "Argentina, 1955–1976: The Film Industry and Its Margins," in King and Torrents, eds., *The Garden of Forking Paths,* p. 49.

---

3. Gendered Identities and Femininity

1. Estela Suárez, "The Feminist Movement in Latin America and the Caribbean: Trends and Challenges," translated by Dean Brown, *Aquelarre* (Vancouver), nos. 7–8 (Spring/Summer 1991): 4.

2. For a comprehensive chronology of films made by women in Latin America, see Teresa Toledo, ed., *Realizadoras latinoamericanas/Latin American Women Filmmakers, 1917–1987: Chronology/Cronología.*

3. Julianne Burton, "Latin America," in Annette Kuhn and Susannah Radstone, eds., *Women's Companion to International Film,* p. 234.

4. Women have demanded the whereabouts of the missing through the Association of the Detained-Disappeared (1975) in Chile, the Mothers of Plaza de Mayo (1979) in Argentina, and the Group of Mutual Support (1983) in Guatemala. They have formed such advocacy groups as SOS-Women, Lesbian-Feminist Action Group, and Sexuality and Politics in Brazil to defend women's rights. Women have rallied around such umbrella organizations as the Women's Coordinating Committee (1979) in Peru and such state organizations as the Luisa Amanda Espinosa Nicaraguan Women's Association (1978) in Nicaragua, just to name a few, to lobby for and promote feminist issues.

5. Marjorie Agosin, *Women of Smoke,* translated by Janice Molloy, p. 91.

6. Julia Lesage, "Women Make Media: Three Modes of Production," in Burton, ed., *The Social Documentary in Latin America,* pp. 315–316.

7. Representation in women's films cannot be seen independently from what Janet Wolff (*Feminine Sentences: Essays on Women and Culture,* p. 107) regards as crucial to feminist criticism: "the relationship between textuality, gender and social structure."

8. B. Ruby Rich, "In the Name of Feminist Criticism," in Nichols, ed., *Movies and Methods,* vol. 2, p. 351.

9. Jean Franco, "Beyond Ethnocentrism: Gender, Power and the Third World Intelligentsia," in Cary Nelson and Lawrence Grossberg, eds., *Marxism and the Interpretation of Culture*, p. 514.

10. This quote refers to the work and practice of Alfonsina Storni and Victoria Ocampo (Argentina) and Gabriela Mistral (Chile). See *Women, Culture, and Politics in Latin America*, p. 2.

11. Agosin, *Women of Smoke*, p. 13.

12. Interview with author, Montreal, June 1991.

13. Griselda Pollock, *Vision and Difference: Femininity, Feminism and the Histories of Art*, p. 9.

14. However, following the broadcasting of *A Man, When He Is a Man* on French television, an official of the Costa Rican embassy in Paris wrote a letter to the director of Channel 2 protesting the unfair treatment of Costa Ricans in Sarmiento's film. See Lesage, "Women Make Media," pp. 319–320.

15. The title of the film comes from an interview with an elderly pharmacist who says, "A man is a man when he works and tries to make something of himself. And when he is with a woman, he shows that he's a man by trying to conquer her. If she gives him a chance, he kisses her and wins her over. But if she is willing and he doesn't take her, that woman will think that he isn't a man, she'll feel let down."

16. Nonetheless, the only woman interviewed in the film explains how women have protected themselves from the duplicitous lies of males.

17. Lesage, "Women Make Media," p. 320.

18. The critical distance of the film is not only the result of its modernist strategies. It has a lot to do with Sarmiento's exile in Europe. As the filmmaker has stated (ibid., p. 327), "Now that I have the distance, I can reflect on what it means to be a Latin American. . . . Europe lets me put forth the image of Latin life that I must show."

19. Jean Franco, "Plotting Women: Popular Narratives for Women in the United States and Latin America," in Bell Gale Chevigny and Gari Laguardia, eds., *Reinventing the Americas: Comparative Studies of Literature of the United States and Spanish America*, p. 251.

20. This term is used by Francine Manciello, "Women, State, and Family in Latin American Literature of the 1920s," in *Women, Culture, and Politics in Latin America*, p. 40.

21. The funeral of Jorge Negrete in Mexico in 1954, for instance, was the occasion for massive manifestations of mourning comparable to those that took place at the death of Rudolf Valentino in 1926.

22. Lesage, "Women Make Media," p. 325.

23. The viewer is not at first aware of the fact that these men are in prison since the tight framing of the interviews conceals the surroundings.

24. Lesage. "Women Make Media," p. 324.

25. As Peter Manuel (*Popular Musics of the Non-Western World*, p. 56) points out, the *canción ranchera*, like the Mexican films that popularized it, "tended to extol machismo and an individualistic, self-indulgent life

style; many song texts expressed similar world views, denouncing fickle women and celebrating male independence and drunken self-pity."

26. It is also arguable that this sequence takes on a parodic meaning for North American or European spectators. It is the Latin pastiche "par excellence" for those familiar with the folksy image of pseudomariachi orchestras performing among plastic palm trees in Tex-Mex restaurants.

27. Burton, "Marginal Cinemas and Mainstream Critical Theory," p. 18.

28. *Transparent Woman* is the literal translation of the film's title. The film has not yet been distributed under an English title.

29. Tomás Gutierrez Alea and Manuel Perez headed the other two Creative Groups. This reorganization within the Cuban Film Institute was part of an overall project to change existing production arrangements and prevent stagnation by revitalizing the creative process. See Paranagua, "News from Havana," p. 101.

30. Quoted in ibid., p. 100.

31. "Grupos de Creación: Entrevista con Humberto Solas y Manuel Perez Paredes," *Cine Cubano*, no. 122 (1988): 4.

32. This is a clear reference to the rectification campaign initiated in 1988 to combat corruption and inefficiency.

33. This woman is played by Eslinda Nuñez, one of the best-known Cuban actresses and one of the leads in *Lucía* (Humberto Solas, 1968).

34. B. Ruby Rich, "After the Revolutions: The Second Coming of Latin American Cinema," *Village Voice*, February 10, 1987.

35. Paulo-Antonio Paranagua, "Biarritz 1984: Retour de l'Argentine," *Positif*, no. 288 (February 1985): 51–52.

36. The following year, the award for Best Foreign Film went to another Argentine production, *The Official Story* (Luis Puenzo, 1985).

37. John Lynch, *Argentine Dictator: Juan Manuel de Rosas, 1829–1852*, pp. 239–241.

38. In regard to the last scene of the film, in which the Argentine flag flies on top of the prison's turret, the filmmaker has stated: "This is not the story of what happened 150 years ago; it could happen today with people being tortured and shot for alleged terrorism or defiance of laws that hardly make sense any more. . . . Human rights deserve our attention, and everybody in Argentina is still reeling from the realization we have had these concentration camps and many people have been victimized." See Karen Jaehne, "Love as a Revolutionary Act: An Interview with Maria Luisa Bemberg," *Cinéaste* 14, no. 3 (1986): 24.

39. Ibid., p. 22.

40. Jean Franco, *Plotting Women: Gender and Representation in Mexico*, p. xii.

41. Sheila Whitaker, "Straight to the Heart: Interview with Maria Luisa Bemberg," *Monthly Film Bulletin* 54, no. 645 (October 1987): 5; reprinted in King and Torrents, eds., *The Garden of the Forking Paths*, p. 117.

42. "Every citizen of the Argentine Confederation in Buenos Ayres is obliged to wear a species of uniform, which is a distinctive mark of federal-

ism. His waistcoat must be red, he must wear a red ribbon around his hat, and at his button hole, another red ribbon bearing an inscription of 'Life to the Argentine Confederation' and 'Death to the Savage Unitarians.' The women are likewise bound to wear a knot of red ribbon in the hair." From a letter written by H. Southern to H. J. T. Palmerston in 1848, quoted in Lynch, *Argentine Dictator*, pp. 296–297.

43. This aspect is a clear filmic deviation from the historical record. John Lynch (ibid., p. 240) in his authoritative biography quotes from a letter in which Rosas assumes full responsibility for the execution order.

44. Karen Jaehne, "*Camila*," *Cinéaste* 14, no. 3 (1986): 46–47.

45. As the filmmaker kindly suggested to me, the coach sequence is filled with Flaubertian overtones. I have already commented on culturally specific meanings of beef slaughter in relation to the Argentine documentary *The Hour of the Furnaces*. Maria Luisa Bemberg (Jaehne, "Love as a Revolutionary Act," p. 24) has linked the slaughter to "the harsh social, political and religious side [of the story] that requires slaughter, in every sense of that word. They want blood as revenge; they want to perform rituals; they want to provide food."

46. D. Sommer, "Irresistible Romance: The Foundational Fictions of Latin America," in Homi K. Bhabha, ed., *Nation and Narration*, p. 98.

47. As Doris Sommer (ibid., p. 81) states, "The coherence [of romance narratives] comes, rather, from their common need to reconcile and amalgamate national constituencies, and from the strategy to cast the previously unreconciled parties, races, classes or regions, as lovers are 'naturally' attracted and right for one another."

48. *Una sombra donde sueña Camila O'Gorman*, written by Enrique Molina in 1910 and published in 1982, is the only novel I could trace.

49. Sommer, "Irresistible Romance," p. 90.

50. Although it is beyond the intent of this study to consider reception, the revival of Frida Kahlo in the early 1980s contributed to the film's success with audiences.

51. Joan Borsa, "Frida Kahlo: Marginalization and the Critical Female Subject," *Third Text*, no. 12 (1990): 29.

52. Oriana Baddeley and Valerie Fraser, *Drawing the Line: Art and Cultural Identity in Contemporary Latin America*, p. 92.

53. Denis West, "*Frida*: An Interview with Paul Leduc," *Cinéaste* 16, no. 4 (1988): 55.

54. Haydén Herrera, *Frida: A Biography of Frida Kahlo*, pp. 278–279.

55. Joan M. West and Denis West, "*Frida*," *Cinéaste* 16, no. 4 (1988): 54.

56. Franco, *Plotting Women*, p. 107.

57. Rich, "After the Revolutions," p. 27.

58. This aspect of the film was pointed out to me by María Luisa Bemberg.

59. Gerald Martin, *Journeys through the Labyrinth*, p. 18.

60. Laura Mulvey and Peter Wollen, "The Discourse of the Body," in Rosemary Betterton, ed., *Looking On: Images of Femininity in the Visual Arts and Media*, p. 211.

61. Mulvey and Wollen, "The Discourse of the Body," p. 215.

62. Wolff, *Feminine Sentences*, p. 62.

---

4. Popular Memory and the Power of Address

1. García Espinosa, "For an Imperfect Cinema," p. 30.

2. William Rowe and Vivian Schelling, *Memory and Modernity: Popular Culture in Latin America*, p. 10.

3. Ibid., p. 17.

4. Ibid.

5. Jean Franco, "What's in a Name: Popular Culture Theories and Their Limitations," *Studies in Latin American Popular Culture* 1 (1976): 7.

6. Rowe and Schelling, *Memory and Modernity*, pp. 31–34.

7. Homi K. Bhabha, "DissemiNation: Time, Narrative, and the Margins of the Modern Nation," in Bhabha, ed., *Nation and Narration*, p. 293.

8. Guy Brett, *Transcontinental: An Investigation of Reality. Nine Latin American Artists*, p. 15.

9. Jorge Sanjinés, "Problems of Form and Content in Revolutionary Cinema," translated by Malcolm Coad, in Chanan, ed., *Twenty-Five Years of the New Latin American Cinema*, p. 36.

10. E. Laclau, "Towards a Theory of Populism," *Politics and Ideology in Marxist Theory*, p. 167.

11. Solanas and Getino, "Towards a Third Cinema," p. 21.

12. Birri, "Cinema and Underdevelopment," p. 12.

13. J. Sanjinés, "The Search for a Popular Cinema," in Pick, ed., *Latin American Film Makers and the Third Cinema*, p. 88.

14. This innovative use of found images and sounds is comparable to the Chilean *arpilleras*. The *arpillera* is basically a patchwork of cloth and thread that Chilean women assembled into pictures in order to represent the dramatic experiences of the working class after the 1973 military coup.

15. Joao Luiz Viera and Robert Stam, "Parody and Marginality: The Case of Brazilian cinema," *Framework*, no. 28 (1985): 40.

16. Sanjinés, "The Search for a Popular Cinema," p. 89.

17. The critical task of approaching Birri's film work tends to be weighted down by his pioneering status and pedagogical prestige. Although he lived outside of Latin America during the 1960s, he returned often as teacher and as consultant or guest of universities, institutes, or film festivals, and his films and writings have periodically circulated in the region. After a long exile in Italy Birri took a job at the film school of the Universidad de los Andes in Mérida (Venezuela) in 1982, and later the position of director of the School for Cinema and Television in San Antonio de los Baños (Cuba) in 1987.

18. Birri explained the methodological and political premises of his projects in articles and interviews published first in Argentina and later reprinted in such magazines as *Cine Cubano*. This material was compiled by Settimio Presutto and Fernando Birri in the late 1970s. Whenever possible,

I have checked the original sources for missing information before quoting from this dossier.

19. In an interview with Julianne Burton in 1979, Birri recounts that in the early 1950s he moved from Santa Fé to Buenos Aires to become a film director but soon realized the futility of trying to enter the industry through the back door. See Fernando Birri, "Fernando Birri: The Roots of Documentary Realism," in Burton, ed., *Cinema and Social Change in Latin America*, pp. 2–12.

20. Birri, "Cinema and Underdevelopment," p. 12.

21. As Ana López points out, Domingo di Núbila's history of Argentine cinema, written in 1959, stresses that "if Argentine cinema remained Argentine in its themes, characters, and locales, then it would be able to please not only its national public but also its extensive Latin American audiences." See "A Short History of Latin American Film Histories," *Journal of Film and Video* 37, no. 1 (Winter 1985): 56–57.

22. Fernando Birri, "Nuestro cine, así, es una herramienta útil" (interview by Franco Mongui during the preparation of *Los inundados*), *Ché* (Buenos Aires), June 12, 1960, October 11, 1961; reprinted in *Film Ideal* (Madrid, nos. 69–70 [1961]).

23. Birri, "Cinema and Underdevelopment," p. 12.

24. Ibid.

25. Fernando Birri, "Fernando Birri: Pionero y pelegrino" (interview with Julianne Burton), *C-Cal* (Caracas) 1, no. 1 (December 1985): 60–61.

26. Manuel Horacio Giménez, "Apuntes de filmación de Manuel Horacio Giménez," in Fernando Birri, ed., *La escuela documental de Santa Fé*, pp. 211–214; reprinted in Mario Rodríguez Alemán, "Neorealismo argentino: *Los inundados*," *Cine Cubano*, no. 11 (June 1963).

27. Birri, "Fernando Birri: Pionero y pelegrino," p. 63.

28. Birri (ibid., pp. 64–65) recounts the ironical outcome of the institute's behavior whereby one of its officials had to receive the award because no member of the crew was able to go to Venice. The film disappeared from circulation in 1962, and Birri was forced to leave Argentina in 1964. Its re-release in the late 1970s has enabled limited distribution and exhibition.

29. In spite of protective legislation designed to promote and exhibit Argentine films, exhibitors periodically challenged the policies that the INC was charged to enact after 1957.

30. Quoted in the press book of the film. Dossier compiled by Settimio Presutto.

31. Rich, "After the Revolutions," p. 25.

32. Ibid.

33. For an in-depth study of these two films, see R. Johnson, *Cinema Novo × 5*, pp. 93–99.

34. The *sertao* means literally a deserted place, far from the villages and the cultivated land. This term is used for the western region of the Northeast, which is characterized by periods of drought.

35. Johnson, *Cinema Novo × 5*, p. 93.

36. Anne Marie Gill, "Fiction as Historical Discourse, Political Discourse as Fiction in Brazilian Cinema," Department of Film, University of Iowa, 1988, p. 11. I would like to thank Anne Marie for bringing these texts to my attention. I will endeavor to acknowledge her contribution to the ideas developed in this section, but I also want to apologize for any inadvertent omissions.

37. Roberto Schwarz, "Cinema and *The Guns*," in Randal Johnson and Robert Stam, eds., *Brazilian Cinema*, p. 133.

38. Michel Ciment, "Ruy Guerra," in Ian Cameron, ed., *The Second Wave*, p. 100.

39. This imagery evokes Josué de Castro's description of the Northeast. Therefore, I have taken the liberty of paraphrasing from his book *Una zona esplosiva: Il Nordeste del Brasile*.

40. Schwarz, "Cinema and *The Guns*," p. 131.

41. The sermons of Conselhero are described by Euclides da Cunha, *Rebellion in the Backlands*, translated by Samuel Putman, pp. 133–134.

42. As Rowe and Schelling (*Memory and Modernity*, p. 89) suggest, "Even today, *folhetos* are still valued as vehicles through which everyday life is transfigured by the imagination, critical perception and interpretative depth of the poet."

43. After the suicide of Getulio Vargas, 70,000 copies of a *folheto* detailing this event circulated in the Northeast. See ibid., p. 89.

44. Gill, "Fiction as Historical Discourse," p. 10.

45. Johnson, *Cinema Novo × 5*, p. 105.

46. In 1976, Ruy Guerra and Nelson Xavier produced *The Fall* (*A Queda*). This film brings the former soldiers of the backlands back to Rio de Janeiro. By inserting the black and white images of *The Guns*, the temporal continuity of *The Fall* is disrupted. For a study of this film, see Robert Stam, "Formal Innovation and Radical Critique in *The Fall*," in Johnson and Stam, eds., *Brazilian Cinema*, pp. 234–240.

47. Gill, "Fiction as Historical Discourse," p. 15.

48. The strategy of the state "was a means of mobilizing support and guaranteeing the system's stability, it was also an effective tool for controlling political and social tension." Johnson, *Cinema Novo × 5*, p. 2.

49. Johnson, *The Film Industry in Brazil*, p. 89. For an in-depth analysis of ISEB ideology, see pp. 88–90.

50. Castro, *Una zona esplosiva*, p. 163.

51. For studies of these films, see Robert Stam and Randal Johnson, "The Cinema of Hunger: Nelson Pereira dos Santos's *Vidas Secas*," and Ismail Xavier, "Black God, White Devil: The Representation of History," in Johnson and Stam, eds., *Brazilian Cinema*, pp. 120–127, 134–148.

52. Sanjinés, "Problems of Form and Content," p. 34.

53. Ibid., p. 35.

54. Ibid., p. 36.

55. Sanjinés, "Revolutionary Cinema," pp. 43–46.

56. It is not my intention to justify formal choices the filmmaker has

since discarded, but I will take into account the formal ramifications of the flashback structure to demonstrate the difference between *The Blood of the Condor* and *The Courage of the People*.

57. Before the film was shot, Sanjinés and his crew submitted to the same ceremony in order to let the villagers themselves decide if the filmmakers should stay: "That night, after six hours of enormous tension in which all distractions, even sleep, were impossible because three hundred pairs of eyes, sensitive to any sign of weakness, were fixed on each and every member of our group, the yatiri examined the coca leaves and declared emphatically that our presence was inspired by good, not evil. Neither the intrigues and threats of the neighbouring officials, nor the Indians' traditional distrust of whites and mestizos could overrule this verdict." Sanjinés, "Revolutionary Cinema," p. 46.

58. R. Dalton, "*Yawar Mallku*: Something More Than a Film," translated by Katka Selucky and Will Straw, in Pick, ed., *Latin American Film Makers and the Third Cinema*, p. 97.

59. Sanjinés, "Revolutionary Cinema," pp. 41–42.

60. Following the exile of some of the members of the Ukamau Group, Sanjinés applied the collective mode to *The Principal Enemy* (1976) and *Get Out of Here!* (1977), produced in Peru and Ecuador respectively.

61. Alfonso Gumucio Dagrón, "Product of Circumstances: Reflections of a Media Activist," in Burton, ed., *Cinema and Social Change in Latin America*, pp. 267–268.

62. Rowe and Schelling, *Memory and Modernity*, p. 53.

63. Ibid., p. 122.

64. Sanjinés, "Revolutionary Cinema," p. 42.

65. Achugar, "Using Movies to Make Movies," p. 231.

66. Sanjinés, "Problems of Form and Content," pp. 37–38.

67. As Alfonso Gumucio Dagrón (*Historia del cine boliviano*, p. 294) points out, "The restriction of the film confirmed the weakness of the process of re-democratization, its absence of freedom of expression." For more information about the censoring of this and other films made by Jorge Sanjinés, see Alfonso Gumucio Dagrón, *Cine, censura y exilio en América latina*, pp. 72–76.

68. María Barzola was a woman from Llallagua who led the miners to Cataví in 1942. The people still call the place where she and hundreds of others died the Plain of María Barzola. In published script notations, Jorge Sanjinés uses the name of this historical character for the site where this opening sequence was shot and for the woman who carries the Bolivian flag.

69. Sanjinés, "Revolutionary Cinema," p. 42.

70. The other massacres included Potosí (January 1947), Siglo XX (May 1949), Villa Victoria–La Paz (May 1950), Sora-Sora (October 1964), the occupation of the mining district (May 1965) and Llallagua (September 1965).

71. Domitila Barrios de Chungara has, since the making of this film, become a spokesperson for Bolivian miners. Her testimony is published in *Let Me Speak! Testimony of Domitila, a Woman of the Bolivian Mines*.

72. Ana M. López, "At the Limits of Documentary: Hypertextual Transformation and the New Latin American Cinema," in Burton, ed., *The Social Documentary in Latin America*, p. 425.

73. Ibid., p. 424.

74. Barrios de Chungara, *Let Me Speak!* p. 15.

---

5. Cultural Difference and Representation

1. As Stuart Hall suggests, ethnicity is a useful concept. It "acknowledges the place of history, language and culture in the construction of subjectivity and identity, as well as the fact that all discourse is placed, positioned, situated, and all knowledge is contextual." Quoted in Isaac Julien and Kobena Mercer, "Introduction: De Margin and De Centre," *Screen* 29, no. 4 (Autumn 1988): 6.

2. Rowe and Schelling, *Memory and Modernity*, p. 18.

3. Homi Bhabha defines cultural difference as "a process of signification through which statements *of* culture or *on* culture differentiate, discriminate, and authorize the production of fields of force, reference, applicability and capacity." See "The Commitment to Theory," in Jim Pines and Paul Willemen, eds., *Questions of Third Cinema*, p. 127.

4. Rowe and Schelling, *Memory and Modernity*, p. 231.

5. Quoting the Cuban anthropologist Fernando Ortiz, Rama adopts the term *transculturation* because "it expresses best the different phases of the period of transition from one culture to another, because this process not only consists in acquiring a culture, which is what the Anglo-Saxon term of acculturation means, but the process also implies necessarily the loss or uprooting of a prior culture, what could be a partial deculturation, and, in addition, signifies the subsequent creation of new cultural phenomena that can be called neoculturation." See Angel Rama, *Transculturación narrativa en América Latina*, p. 33.

6. Claudio Solano, "Latin American Cinema: The Non-Realist Side of Reality," *Undercut* (London), no. 12 (1984): 20.

7. Richard Graham, "Introduction," in Richard Graham, ed., *The Idea of Race in Latin America, 1870–1940*, pp. 1–4.

8. Aline Helg, "Race in Argentina and Cuba, 1880–1930: Theory, Policies, and Popular Reaction," in Graham, ed., *The Idea of Race in Latin America*, p. 61.

9. Thomas E. Skidmore, "Racial Ideas and Social Policy in Brazil, 1870–1940," in Graham, ed., *The Idea of Race in Latin America*, p. 28.

10. Lourdes Casal, "Race Relations in Contemporary Cuba," in Philip Brenner, William M. LeoGrande, Donna Rich, and Daniel Siegel, eds., *The Cuban Reader: The Making of a Revolutionary Society*, p. 479.

11. Julien and Mercer, "Introduction: De Margin and De Centre," p. 5.

12. Ibid., p. 3.

13. Esther Mosak, "*Maria Antonia:* Eugenio Hernández's 1967 Play Becomes a 1990 Film by Sergio Giral," *Cuba Update* (New York) 12, no. 3 (Summer 1991): 30.

14. For an analysis of Sara Gómez's documentary work, see Chanan, *The Cuban Image*, pp. 282–284.

15. Ambrosio Fornet, "Trente ans de cinéma dans la Révolution," in Paulo-Antonio Paranagua, ed., *Cinéma Cubain*, p. 96.

16. Carlos Galiano, "*One Way or Another:* The Revolution in Action," *Jump Cut*, no. 19 (December 1978): 33. Originally printed in *Granma Weekly Review* (Havana), English edition, November 20, 1977.

17. Osvaldo Sánchez Crespo, "The Perspective of the Present: Cuban History, Cuban Film Making," in Coco Fusco, ed., *Reviewing Histories: Selections from New Latin American Cinema*, p. 203.

18. Studies of this film (mainly in North America and Europe) have outlined its feminist aspects but downplayed its treatment of race and class.

19. Julia Lesage, "*One Way or Another:* Dialectical, Revolutionary, Feminist," *Jump Cut*, no. 20 (May 1979): 23.

20. I am borrowing the term *mixed* from Julia Lesage. See also López, "At the Limits of Documentary," pp. 417–421.

21. Chanan, *The Cuban Image*, p. 288.

22. Ibid., p. 289.

23. Sánchez Crespo, "The Perspective of the Present," p. 203.

24. Chanan, *The Cuban Image*, p. 291.

25. Lesage, "*One Way or Another,*" p. 22.

26. Sergio Giral, "Cuban Cinema and the Afro-Cuban Heritage," interview by Julianne Burton and Gary Crowdus, in John D. H. Downing, ed., *Film and Politics in the Third World*, p. 269.

27. This quote is attributed to Antonio Maceo by Jorge Ibarra in *Ideología mambisa* and cited in Philip S. Foner, *Antonio Maceo: The "Bronze Titan" of Cuba's Struggle for Independence*, p. 261.

28. Johnson, *The Film Industry in Brazil*, pp. 158–159.

29. Randal Johnson (ibid., p. 159) points out that Bruno Barreto's *Bandit Love* (1978), also mixed in Europe, was not subject to the same limitations as *Iracema.*

30. In 1965 Plinio Doyle listed 106 editions, including translations. See "Pequena bibliografia de *Iracema*," in José de Alencar, *Iracema*, pp. 273–294.

31. Pedro Henríquez Ureña, *Las corrientes literarias en la América hispánica*, pp. 134–135.

32. David T. Haberly, *Three Sad Races: Racial Identity and National Consciousness in Brazilian Literature*, p. 32.

33. Slavery was finally abolished in 1888, one year before the instauration of the republic. Brazil was the last country in the Americas to end slavery following Cuba, where slavery was outlawed in 1880.

34. Sommer, "Irresistible Romance," p. 80.

35. Romance "should contain fantastic and exotic elements, raising the reader above the banalities of daily life. At the same time, the reader should be able to identify with the characters as real people, and the action should remain within the realm of the possible and the moral to maintain involvement and avoid corrupting the innocent." Haberly, *Three Sad Races*, p. 38.

36. Ibid., pp. 16–17. In the period in which Alencar wrote, the Brazilian intelligentsia—including the young emperor Pedro II—were learning the Tupí language and adopting Indian names.

37. Quoted in ibid., p. 48.

38. Johnson and Stam, eds., *Brazilian Cinema*, p. 22.

39. Joao Carlos Rodrigues, "O indio brasileiro e o cinema," *Cinema brasileiro: 8 estudios*, p. 193.

40. Susan Hecht and Alexander Cockburn, *The Fate of the Forest: Developers, Destroyers and Defenders of the Amazon*, p. 8.

41. Ismail Xavier, "*Iracema*: Transcending Cinéma Vérité," in Burton, ed., *The Social Documentary of Latin America*, p. 370. *Iracema* retains this critical function even in light of the contemporary interest in the Amazon. It might remind us that the images and arguments that have been circulated through television, for instance, have a longer history and are not as current as claimed.

42. Ibid.

43. Ibid.

44. This word is used in the novel when Iracema tells Martin that she cannot become his servant. She says, "She holds the secret of jurema and the mystery of dream." In the notes, the writer describes *jurema* as a tree that produces a bitter fruit and from which a hallucinatory drink is prepared. See Alencar, *Iracema*, pp. 16, 89.

45. Johnson, "Carlos Diegues," *Cinema Novo × 5*, pp. 52–90.

46. Paulo-Antonio Paranagua, "Ruptures et continuité: Années 70–80," in Paulo-Antonio Paranagua, ed., *Le cinéma brésilien*, p. 122.

47. David Brookshaw, *Race and Color in Brazilian Literature*, p. 292.

48. Robert Stam, "*Quilombo*," *Cinéaste* 15, no. 1 (1986): 43.

49. Johnson, *The Film Industry in Brazil*, pp. 182–183, 192.

50. Zezé Motta, who plays a leading role in *Quilombo*, for instance, has had to struggle against prejudice. She was blacklisted following *Xica da Silva*, until she was offered a leading role in *Body to Body* in the early 1980s. See Zelbert Moore, "Reflections on Blacks in Contemporary Brazilian Popular Culture in the 1980s," *Studies in Latin American Popular Culture* 7 (1988): 215–216.

51. Charles A. Perrone, *Masters of Brazilian Contemporary Song: MPB 1965–1985*, p. 124.

52. The *afoxé* is both a musical form of Afro-Brazilian *candomblé*, a major syncretic religion, and a procession that adapts religious forms to popular music during the Bahia carnival.

53. Moore, "Reflections on Blacks," pp. 216–217.

54. As historian R. K. Kent points out, "The most apparent significance of Palmares to African history is that an African political system could be transferred to a different continent; that it could come to govern not only individuals from a variety of ethnic groups in Africa but also those born in Brazil, pitch black or almost white, latinized or close to Amerindian roots." See "Palmares: An African State in Brazil," in Richard Price, ed., *Maroon Societies: Rebel Slave Communities in the Americas*, p. 188.

55. Robert Stam, "Samba, Candomblé, Quilombo: Black Performance and Brazilian Cinema," *Journal of Ethnic Studies* 13, no. 3 (Fall 1985): 69.

56. Roberto de Matta, *Carnavals, bandits et héros: Ambiguités de la société brésilienne*, pp. 63–64.

57. The *escolas de samba* are recreational associations, mainly in Rio de Janeiro, that organize and perform in carnival parades, while the *afro-blocos* are neighborhood samba clubs that perform Afro-Brazilian themes.

58. Morton Marks, "Uncovering Ritual Structures in Afro-American Music," in Irving I. Zaretsky and Mark P. Leone, eds., *Religious Movements in Contemporary America*, p. 62.

59. Robert Stam, "Carnival, Politics, and Brazilian Culture," *Studies in Latin American Popular Culture* 7 (1988): 256. In this article, Stam also points out that "in Brazil, the repression of carnival was often linked to anti-Black racism and hostility to Afro-Brazilian religious expression" (p. 258).

60. The Rio de Janeiro carnival is promoted as a quintessential symbol of Brazil. Julie M. Taylor points out that this "visual carnival" has been at the center of controversies because it has been appropriated by middle-class sectors. See "Carnival, Media, and Regional Traditions: Integration and Manipulation," *Studies in Latin American Popular Culture* 7 (1988): 192.

61. Paulo-Antonio Paranagua, "Brésil," *Positif*, nos. 281–282 (July/August 1984): 84.

62. The ancillary position of black characters represents, in my opinion, a waste of the black performers' talents.

63. Robert Stam and Ismail Xavier, "Recent Brazilian Cinema: Allegory/Metacinema/Carnival," *Film Quarterly* 41, no. 3 (Spring 1988): 15–30, 27.

64. Elice Munerato and María Helena Darcy de Oliveira, "Muses derrière la caméra," in Paranagua, ed., *Le cinéma brésilien*, pp. 214–215. (This is an updated version of "When Women Film," in Johnson and Stam, eds., *Brazilian Cinema*, pp. 340–350.)

65. Julianne Burton, "Transitional States: Creative Complicities within the Real in *Man Marked to Die: Twenty Years Later* and *Patriamada*," in Burton, ed., *The Social Documentary of Latin America*, p. 382.

66. Philip Stanford, *Pioneers in the Tropics: The Political Organization of Japanese in an Immigrant Community in Brazil*, pp. 5–8.

67. Thomas E. Skidmore, *Black into White: Race and Nationality in Brazilian Thought*, pp. 130, 197–199.

68. Paranagua, "Ruptures et continuité," p. 117.

69. Tomoo Handa, "Senso estético na vida dos immigrantes," in Hiroshi Saito and Takashi Maeyama, *Assimilaçao e integraçao dos Japaneses no Brasil*, pp. 386–416.

70. Characters speak in their languages of origin, with Japanese and Portuguese being predominant. Yet, as a Japanese-speaking student once remarked to me, the speech patterns and idioms are distinctly Brazilian-Japanese.

71. Victor Casaus, "*Gaijin*: El camino de Tizuka. An Interview with Tizuka Yamasaki, a Brazilian Filmmaker," *Cine Cubano*, no. 99 (1981): 27.

72. Tizuka Yamasaki (ibid.) points out that she is often referred to as a Chinese or a Japanese rather than as a Brazilian.

---

6. Exile and Displacement

1. This process is eloquently reflected in Fernando Birri, "For a Nationalist, Realist, Critical and Popular Cinema," pp. 89–91, which presents an argument for a renewed definition of the movement.

2. See the overview in Gumucio Dagrón, *Cine, censura y exilio en América latina*, pp. 7–15.

3. Sanjinés, "Problems of Form and Content," p. 37. This text also includes comments of people who saw the films of the Ukamau Group in Ecuador.

4. Ibid., p. 38.

5. This chapter elaborates—in the context of the New Cinema of Latin America—some of the ideas I explored in relation to Chilean cinema in "Chilean Cinema (1973–1986). The notion of Exile: A field of Investigation and its Conceptual Framework," *Framework*, no. 34 (1987): 39–57.

6. Burton, "Marginal Cinemas and Mainstream Critical Theory," p. 14.

7. Although I am basically dealing with exile from the perspective of banishment, expatriation, or forced emigration, there are other forms of exile which are the result of censorship and marginalization and which affect individuals and communities inside a country. Each modality of exile has an impact on identity and affiliation.

8. Essayists such as Jose Martí (Cuba), Domingo F. Sarmiento (Argentina), José Carlos Mariátegui (Peru), and Angel Rama (Uruguay) produced some of their most important work in exile. Writers and poets such as Julio Cortázar, Marta Traba and Luisa Valenzuela (Argentina), Jorge Donoso, Gabriela Mistral, and Pablo Neruda (Chile), Gabriel García Márquez (Colombia), Guillermo Cabrera Infante, Alejo Carpentier, and Severo Sarduy (Cuba), Claribel Alegría (Nicaragua), Augusto Roa Bastos (Paraguay), Manuel Scorza and César Vallejo (Peru), Mario Benedetti, Eduardo Galeano, and Christina Peri-Rossi (Uruguay); painters such as Wilfredo Lam (Cuba) and Roberto Matta (Chile) and musicians such as Astor Piazzola (Argentina), Inti-Illimani (Chile), and Rubén Blades (Panamá) have produced distinctively Latin American works away from their countries of origin.

9. Julio Cortázar, "Letter to Roberto Fernández Retamar," in Doris Meyer, ed., *Lives on the Line: The Testimony of Contemporary Latin American Authors*, p. 75.

10. Pick, "Chilean Cinema (1973–1986)," pp. 43–48.

11. José Donoso, "Ithaca: The Impossible Return," in Meyer, ed., *Lives on the Line*, p. 182.

12. Eduardo Galeano, "L'exil: Entre la nostalgie et la creation," in *Amérique latine: Luttes et mutations*, p. 117.

13. Donoso, "Ithaca: The Impossible Return," p. 186.

14. Antonio Skármeta, "La reformulación del status del escritor en el exilio," in *Primer cuaderno de ensayo chileno*, p. 12.

15. Interview with author, Paris, March 1983.

16. Zuzana M. Pick, "Hablan los cineastas," in David Valjalo and Zuzana M. Pick, eds., *Diez años de cine chileno: 1973–1983*, p. 29.

17. Ibid., p. 30.

18. Ibid., p. 29.

19. Bill Nichols, "Embodied Knowledge and the Politics of Power," *CineAction* (Toronto), no. 23 (Winter 1990–1991): 17.

20. In *Thanks to Life, or The Story of a Mistreated Woman (Gracias a la vida, o la pequeña historia de una mujer maltradada*, Finland, 1980) Angelina Vázquez provides an empowering perspective of the difficult choice faced by a pregnant woman who resolves to give birth to a child conceived when she was raped by one of her torturers.

21. The other two films were directed by Jorge Fajardo and Rodrigo González. Although the film has circulated extensively, only Fajardo's *Steel Blues* has been distributed separately in an English version.

22. Interview with author, Montreal, October 1982.

23. Ibid.

24. Because the National Film Board had dropped the freelance program, Mallet approached a small production company that was willing to underwrite the project for script development. With a subsidy from the recently created Institut Québécois du Cinéma (replaced by the Société Générale pour le Développement du Cinéma in 1988), she went to France to work with Valeria Sarmiento. By the time each shot the first letter, the independent producer had gone bankrupt. Unable to continue shooting and having to legalize rights on the footage, the filmmakers suspended production. Ibid.

25. Mallet herself has insisted on this distinction. In her M.A. dissertation (University of Montreal, 1981–1982) and a paper on *Unfinished Diary* (delivered at the New Latin American Cinema Conference, University of Iowa, 1986) Mallet presents the protagonist as "her" rather than "I."

26. M. Mallet, "Notes sur *Journal inachevé*," in Louise Carrière, ed., *Femmes et cinéma québécois*, p. 264.

27. Brenda Longfellow, "Feminist Language in *Journal Inachevé* and *Strass Café*," in William C. Wees and Michael Dorland, eds., *Words and Moving Images: Essays on Verbal and Visual Expression in Film and Television*, p. 88.

28. Pick, "Chilean Cinema (1973–1986)," pp. 49–52.

29. Longfellow, "Feminist Language in *Journal Inachevé* and *Strass Café*," p. 86.

30. S. Feldman, "Circling I's: Some Implications of the Filmmakers' Presence in Michael Rubbo's *Margaret Atwood: Once in August* and Marilú Mallet's *Journal Inachevé*," in Pierre Véronneau, Michael Dorland, and Seth Feldman, eds., *Dialogue: Canadian and Quebec Cinema*, p. 250.

31. Longfellow, "Feminist Language in *Journal Inachevé* and *Strass Café*," p. 89.

32. As I have suggested in Chapter 2, it might be inappropriate to disregard the experimental aspects already present in the films that contributed

to Solanas's status as a militant filmmaker. Although this film is a radical departure from the openly partisan documentary *The Hour of the Furnaces* (and its accompanying manifesto "Towards a Third Cinema"), *Tangos: The Exile of Gardel* shares the same experimental impulse already apparent in *The Sons of Fierro*.

33. See Chapter 2 for details.

34. Fernando "Pino" Solanas, *La mirada: Reflexiones sobre cine y cultura*, pp. 56–57.

35. Solanas mentions in an interview that the earliest version of this film was a script written in 1975, entitled *Adios Nonino*, and was scheduled for production in 1976. He abandoned the project when he left the country after the military coup. See Paulo-Antonio Paranagua, "Entretien avec Fernando E. Solanas," *Positif*, no. 297 (November 1985): 25.

36. Solanas, *La mirada*, pp. 54–55.

37. Alongside Philippe Léotard, founder of the Théâtre du Soleil with Arianne Mouchkinne, Marie Laforet, Marina Vlady, and George Wilson, Solanas engaged an important contingent of Argentine performers, such as Miguel Angel Sola, Gabriela Toscano, Ana Maria Picchio, and Lautaro Murua. The cast also included Chilean and Uruguayan exiles living in Paris, such as Oscar Castro and Jorge Six respectively, and exiled Argentine children, such as Emilio Cedrón, Lorena Gelso, and Victoria Solanas. The Argentine singers Roberto Goyeneche, Susana Lago, and Osvaldo Pugliese and dancers of the Ballet Nucleo Danza of Buenos Aires also participated.

38. Paranagua, "Entretien avec Fernando E. Solanas," p. 26.

39. In France, for instance, film critics were equally fascinated by the film's open-ended structure and formal freedom, but appeared dumbfounded by its most whimsical aspects, such as the visual gags and the apparitions of historical figures. See Vincent Ostria, "Le tutoiement du rêve," *Cahiers du Cinéma*, no. 377 (November 1985): 50–52.

40. Manuel Antín, "Afterword," in King and Torrents, eds., *The Garden of Forking Paths*, p. 129.

41. Solanas, *La mirada*, p. 234.

42. Torrents, "Contemporary Argentine Cinema," p. 106.

43. In an interview Solanas explains that "[critics] would like me to confine myself to being a militant, political documentarian. . . . Then some said, 'Oh, but this film estheticizes exile.' . . . I wanted to take revenge on the system that didn't want me to make any more films with a creative work that is cinematic, pictorial and musical." Coco Fusco, "The Tango of Esthetics and Politics: An Interview with Fernando Solanas," *Cinéaste* 16, nos. 1–2 (1987–1988): 59.

44. Solanas, *La mirada*, p. 231.

45. Ibid., pp. 95, 83.

46. Solanas studied music at the conservatory and worked as a piano teacher. Although primarily interested in classic contemporary music, since 1963 he has composed publicity jingles and made his living making commercials on film. He has also composed and recorded the musical pro-

logue of *The Hour of the Furnaces* using the 6/8 rhythm of Latin American popular dances. Paranagua, "Entretien avec Fernando E. Solanas," pp. 21–22.

47. Fusco, "The Tango of Esthetics and Politics," p. 59.

48. Solanas, *La mirada*, p. 177.

49. These sequences include the November 1981 rally in Paris for artists missing in Argentina, organized by the International Association for the Defense of Artists (AIDA) and recorded on film by Solanas.

50. Solanas (*La mirada*, pp. 62, 63) points out that the shredded papers "are messages, they symbolize ideas. Provoke passions." And he explains further, "My generation hid books for fear of reprisal and we got used to reading between the lines. We burned libraries."

51. Ibid., p. 94.

52. Jean A. Gili, "Le territoire de la nostalgie: *Tangos, l'exil de Gardel*," *Positif*, no. 297 (November 1985): 19.

53. Rowe and Schelling, *Memory and Modernity*, pp. 35–36.

54. Julie M. Taylor, "Tango: Theme of Class and Nation," *Ethnomusicology*, no. 20 (1976): 276–291.

55. Julie M. Taylor (ibid., pp. 273–291) draws some crucial parallels between *Martin Fierro* and the tango by stressing historical and sociocultural filiations between these two texts of Argentine identity.

56. Alicia Dujovne Ortiz, "*Buenos Aires* (An Excerpt)," translated by Caren Kaplan, *Discourse* (Milwaukee), no. 8 (Fall–Winter 1986–1987): 75.

57. For a contemporary review, see Zuzana M. Pick, "Un débat nécessaire: *Diálogo de exilados*," *Positif*, no. 174 (October 1975): 61–62. Even after the critical success of *The Three Crowns of the Sailor* in 1983, Ruiz was still being chastized by Chilean critics for his "lack of generosity"; *Dialogue of Exiles* was judged for its "lack of depth" and for discarding exile as banal scraps of anecdotes. See Jacqueline Mouesca and Carlos Orellana, "El caso Ruiz," *Araucaria* (Paris), no. 23 (1983): 106–112.

58. Interview with author, Paris, July 1983.

59. Waldo Rojas, "Raúl Ruiz: Imágenes de paso," *Enfoque* (Santiago), no. 2 (Summer–Fall 1984): 30.

60. Pascal Bonitzer and Serge Toubiana, "Entretien avec Raoul Ruiz," *Cahiers du Cinéma*, no. 345 (March 1983): 7.

61. Rojas, "Raúl Ruiz," p. 28.

62. Gilbert Adair, "Raúl Sheheruizade, or 1001 Films," *Sight and Sound* 53, no. 3 (Summer 1984): 162.

63. Other comprehensive retrospectives have been organized by the Filmoteca Nacional de España (1978), the National Film Theater in London (1981), the Rotterdam festival (1982), and the Toronto Festival of Festivals (1985).

64. Ronald Melzer, "El realismo de la vocación y los suspensos del chileno Raúl Ruiz," *Cinemateca Revista* (Montevideo), no. 33 (August 1982); Agustín Mahieu, "Los cuadros vivientes o hipótesis de Raúl Ruiz," *Cine Libre* (Buenos Aires), no. 1 (October 1982). The uneven distribution of the

films encouraged highly differing views and entrenched Ruiz's marginality. As a matter of fact, Ruiz is the only major Chilean filmmaker whose films have not been shown at the New Latin American Cinema festival in Havana.

65. The lack of Spanish-language subtitles has hindered the circulation of Ruiz's French films in Chile and contributed to a highly fragmentary reception of his work. But even before 1974, his films never reached a wide audience and only a handful of Chilean critics, like José Román and Hans Ehrmann, appreciated the originality and creative habits of this filmmaker.

66. Ruiz was practically unknown by critics and audiences outside Chile before 1974, although he received an award at the Locarno Film Festival for *Three Sad Tigers*. After the military coup, some of his films were shown in Europe with other Chilean films. The complex reception of this filmmaker's work is an aspect worth exploring in the context of a cinema of exile, since issues of representativity and national origins are involved.

67. For instance, Jonathan Rosenbaum admits to having seen only one of Ruiz's Chilean films. See "Beating the Labyrinth," *Monthly Film Bulletin* 52, no. 612 (January 1985).

On Ruiz's Chilean films, see Zuzana M. Pick, "Le cinéma chilien sous le signe de l'Unité Populaire," *Positif*, no. 155 (January 1974).

68. Zuzana M. Pick, "Raoul Ruiz: De l'exil, du dépaysement et de l'exotisme," *Positif*, no. 274 (December 1983): 33–35.

69. Pick, "Hablan los cineastas," p. 30.

70. David Kehr, "And Now . . . Restructuralism," *Chicago Reader*, April 6, 1984.

71. Robert Stam, "Bakhtin and Left Cultural Critique," in E. Ann Kaplan, ed., *Postmodernism and Its Discontents*, p. 122.

72. *Three Sad Tigers* (based on a play written by the Chilean playwright Alejandro Sieveking) functions as the "Ur-text" of *The Three Crowns of the Sailor*.

73. From a version of this legend written by C. Ducci Claro and compiled in Fernando Emmerich, ed., *Leyendas Chilenas*, p. 67.

74. Gabriela Mistral, "Recado sobre un mito americano: El Caleuche de Chile. (Lisboa. Junio 1936)," in *Gabriela Mistral en el "Repertorio Americano,"* p. 250.

75. Ruiz was born in the southern city of Puerto Montt, and his father worked as navigator steering ships in the straits along the southern Chilean coast. It was his father who, with a group of seafaring colleagues, provided most of the funds to establish Los Capitanes, the company that produced *Three Sad Tigers*.

In an interview Ruiz has pointed out, "[In Chile] I soaked up folklore but I lived popular culture in a nonpolitical way, . . . I experienced it as something that fills up the long winter nights." See Christine Buci-Glucksmann and Fabrice Revault d'Allonnes, "Entretien avec Raoul Ruiz," in Christine Buci-Glucksmann and Fabrice Revault d'Allonnes, eds., *Raoul Ruiz*, p. 98.

76. David Ehrenstein, "Raul Ruiz," in *Film: The Front Line 1984*, p. 95.

77. Jorge Arriagada, an Argentine who has consistently worked with Ruiz, composed the music score in which popular songs (like tangos sung by Reynaldo Anselmi) are inserted to form an evocative tapestry of Latin and Afro-American rhythms.

78. Raúl Ruiz, "Object Relations in the Cinema," *Afterimage* (London), no. 10 (Autumn 1981): 87.

79. Mistral, "Recado sobre un mito americano," p. 249.

80. Christine Buci-Glucksman, "Histoire d'un regard double, allégorique et divin," in Buci-Glucksman and Revault d'Allones, eds., *Raoul Ruiz*, p. 17.

81. David Ehrenstein, "Raul Ruiz at the Holiday Inn," *Film Quarterly* 40, no. 1 (Fall 1986): 6.

82. Paul Willemen, "The Third Cinema Question: Notes and Reflections," *Framework* (London), no. 34 (1987): 8.

83. Ian Christie, "A Secret Cinema: Raúl Ruiz," in Jill Forbes, ed., *INA—French for Innovation: The Work of the Institut National de la Communication Audiovisuelle in Cinema and Television*, p. 32.

84. Gilbert Adair, "The Rubicon and the Rubik Cube: Exile, Paradox and Raul Ruiz," *Sight and Sound* 51, no. 1 (Winter 1981–1982): 42. Ruiz told me recently that he was actually referring to Abraham Valderomar, a turn-of-the-century writer from Peru.

85. In a study on the French cinema of foreign directors, Edgardo Cozarinsky has written that the films of Latin Americans "illuminate France, and consequently its cinema, with a lateral light that emphasizes volume and texture in an elaborate and dramatic way rather than the harsh front-lighting that flattens everything out." See "Les réalisateur étrangers en France: Hier et aujourd'hui," *Positif,* no. 325 (March 1988): 42.

Conclusion. The New Latin American Cinema: A Modernist Critique of Modernity

1. José Luis Abellán, *La idea de América: Origen y evolución*, p. 21.

2. Rama, *Transculturación narrativa en América Latina*, p. 57.

3. Ibid.

4. Ibid., p. 58.

5. Martin, *Journeys through the Labyrinth*, p. 9.

6. Ibid., p. 359.

7. Edward W. Said, *The World, the Text, and the Critic*, pp. 8–9.

8. Andrew Parker, Mary Russo, Doris Sommer, and Patricia Yaeger, eds., *Nationalisms and Sexualities*, pp. 11–12.

9. Baddeley and Fraser, *Drawing the Line*, p. 24.

10. Gabriel García Márquez, "The Solitude of Latin America," in Meyer, ed., *Lives on the Line*, pp. 230–234.

11. Robert Stam, *Subversive Pleasures: Bakhtin, Cultural Criticism, and Film*, p. 123.

12. Carlos Fuentes, *Myself with Others*, p. 205.

13. Carlos Monsiváis, "Cultura: Tradición y modernidad," *La Jornada,* February 21, 1992.

14. Ibid.

15. Pick, ed., *Latin American Film Makers and the Third Cinema,* p. 2.

16. King, *Magical Reels,* p. 69.

17. Marshall Berman, *All That Is Solid Melts into Air: The Experience of Modernity,* p. 8.

18. The Latin American left (particularly the one represented by monolithic communist parties and Marxist-Leninist factions) refused modernity because modernization was presumed and understood as synonymous with capitalism and exploitation. Nonetheless, leftist rhetoric in the 1960s locked into an interpretation of modernity which, according to Monsiváis ("Cultura: Tradición y modernidad," n.p.), went as follows: "The revolution was culture (in abstract or sectarian terms), tradition (significant because it generated in the people) and modernity, without that name, because a revolutionary became, at once, the vanguard of humanity."

19. Michel Foucault, quoted in Gregory Jusdanis, *Belated Modernity and Aesthetic Culture: Inventing National Literature,* p. xv.

20. Fornet, *Cine, literatura, sociedad,* p. 22.

21. Bertram D. Wolfe, *Diego Rivera: His Life and Times,* quoted in Jean Franco, *The Modern Culture of Latin America: Society and the Artist,* p. 89.

22. Stam and Xavier, "Transformation of National Allegory," p. 290.

23. Franco, *The Modern Culture of Latin America,* p. 293.

24. Rama, *Transculturación narrativa en América Latina,* p. 14.

25. Quoted in Chanan, ed., *Twenty-Five Years of the New Latin American Cinema,* p. 2.

26. García Espinosa, "For an Imperfect Cinema," p. 31.

27. King, *Magical Reels,* p. 76.

28. Chanan, ed., *Twenty-Five Years of the New Latin American Cinema,* p. 5.

29. López, "An 'Other' History," p. 325.

30. Quoted in Willemen, "The Third Cinema Question," p. 9; translated from Solanas's "L'influence du troisième cinéma dans le monde," which appeared in *CinémAction* and in *Revue Tiers Monde* 20, no. 79 (July–September 1979): 622.

31. Birri, "For a Nationalist, Realist, Critical and Popular Cinema," p. 90.

32. Burton, "Marginal Cinemas and Mainstream Critical Theory," p. 12.

33. During the 1987 conference on Latin American cinema, held at the University of Iowa, two prominent critics and historians—Isaac León Frias from Peru and Jorge Ayala Blanco from Mexico—explained the inappropriateness of the term "New Cinema" to categorize the cinematographic practices of Latin America. They recalled that the term had historically limited the critical approach to productions reflecting the ideological agenda of the early manifestations of the movement.

34. Roberto Parada Lillo, "Identidad cultural y política," *Literatura chi-*

lena: Creación y crítica (Los Angeles, Madrid), 10, no. 1/35 (January–March 1986): 9–10.

35. Paulo Emílio Salles Gomes, "Cinema: A Trajectory within Underdevelopment," in Johnson and Stam, eds., *Brazilian Cinema*, p. 245.

36. Bell Gale Chevigny, "'Insatiable Unease': Melville and Carpentier and the Search for an American Hermeneutic," in Chevigny and Laguardia, eds., *Reinventing the Americas*, p. 36.

Bibliography

Abellán, José Luis. La idea de América: Origen y evolución. Madrid: Ediciones Istmo, 1972.

Achugar, Walter. "Using Movies to Make Movies." In Julianne Burton, ed., Cinema and Social Change in Latin America. Austin: University of Texas Press, 1986.

Adair, Gilbert. "The Rubicon and the Rubik Cube: Exile, Paradox and Raul Ruiz." Sight and Sound 51, no. 1 (Winter 1981–1982).

———. "Raúl Sheheruizade, or 1001 Films." Sight and Sound 53, no. 3 (Summer 1984).

Agosin, Marjorie. Women of Smoke. Translated by Janice Molloy. Stratford, Ontario: Williams-Wallace Publishers, 1989.

Alea Gutiérrez, Tomás. "Dramaturgía (cinematográfica) y realidad." Cine Cubano, no. 105 (1984).

———. "I Wasn't Always a Filmmaker." Cinéaste 14, no. 1 (1985).

———. The Viewer's Dialectic. Translated by Julia Lesage. Havana: José Martí Publishing House, 1988. Previously published in Jump Cut, nos. 30–32 (1985–1986).

Alencar, José de. Iracema. 2d. critical edition by M. Cavalcanti Proença. Rio de Janeiro: Livros Técnicos e Científicos Editora S.A., 1979.

Alvarez, Carlos. "For Colombia 1971: Militancy and the Cinema." Translated by Christina Shantz and Leandro Urbina. In Zuzana M. Pick, ed., Latin American Film Makers and the Third Cinema. Ottawa: Carleton University. 1978.

Antín, Manuel. "Afterword." In John King and Nissa Torrents, eds., The Garden of Forking Paths: Argentine Cinema. London: British Film Institute and the National Film Theater, 1987.

Aufderheide, Patricia. "Latin American Cinema and the Rhetoric of Cultural Nationalism: Controversies at Havana in 1987 and 1989." Quarterly Review of Film and Video 12, no. 4 (September 1991).

Baddeley, Oriana, and Valerie Fraser. Drawing the Line: Art and Cultural Identity in Contemporary Latin America. London: Verso, 1989.

Bhabha, Homi K. "The Commitment to Theory." In Jim Pines and Paul Willemen, eds., Questions of Third Cinema. London: British Film Institute, 1989.

———. "DissemiNation: Time, Narrative, and the Margins of the Modern Nation." In Homi K. Bhabha, ed., *Nation and Narration*. London: Routledge, 1990.

Barnard, Tim. "Popular Cinema and Populist Politics." In Tim Barnard, ed., *Argentine Cinema*. Toronto: Nightwood Editions, 1986.

Barrios de Chungara, Domitila, with Moema Viezzer. *Let Me Speak! Testimony of Domitila, a Woman of the Bolivian Mines*. New York and London: Monthly Review of Books, 1978.

Berman, Marshall. *All That Is Solid Melts into Air: The Experience of Modernity*. New York: Penguin Books, 1988.

Birri, Fernando. "Nuestro cine, así, es una herramienta útil." Interview by Franco Mongui during the preparation of *Los inundados*. *Ché* (Buenos Aires), June 12, 1960, and October 11, 1961; reprinted in *Film Ideal* (Madrid), nos. 69–70 (1961).

———. "Cinema and Underdevelopment." Translated by Malcolm Coad. In Michael Chanan, ed., *Twenty-Five Years of the New Latin American Cinema*. London: British Film Institute/Channel Four, 1983.

———. "For a Nationalist, Realist, Critical and Popular Cinema." *Screen* 26, nos. 3–4 (May–August 1985).

———. "Fernando Birri: Pionero y pelegrino." Interview with Julianne Burton. *C-Cal* (Caracas) 1, no. 1 (December 1985).

———. "Fernando Birri: The Roots of Documentary Realism." In Julianne Burton, ed., *Cinema and Social Change in Latin America*. Austin: University of Texas Press, 1986.

———, ed. *La Escuela documental de Santa Fé*. Santa Fé: Editorial Documento del Instituto Cinematográfico de la U.N.L., 1964.

Bonitzer, Pascal, and Serge Toubiana. "Entretien avec Raoul Ruiz." *Cahiers du Cinéma*, no. 345 (March 1983).

Borsa, Joan. "Frida Kahlo: Marginalization and the Critical Female Subject." *Third Text*, no. 12 (1990).

Brett, Guy. *Transcontinental: An Investigation of Reality. Nine Latin American Artists*. London and Manchester: Verso/Ikon Gallery, 1990.

Brookshaw, David. *Race and Color in Brazilian Literature*. Metuchen, N.J., and London: Scarecrow Press, 1986.

Buci-Glucksman, Christine. "Histoire d'un regard double, allégorique et divin." In Christine Buci-Glucksman and Fabrice Revault d' Allonnes, eds., *Raoul Ruiz*. Paris: Dis Voir, 1987.

———, and Fabrice Revault d'Allonnes. "Entretien avec Raoul Ruiz." In Christine Buci-Glucksman and Fabrice Revault d'Allonnes, eds., *Raoul Ruiz*. Paris: Dis Voir, 1987.

Burton, Julianne. "*The Brick-Makers*." *Cinéaste* 7, no. 3 (Fall 1976).

———. "Democratizing Documentary: Modes of Address in the Latin American Cinema, 1959–1972." In Thomas Waugh, ed., "*Show Us Life*": *Towards a History and Aesthetics of the Committed Documentary*. Metuchen, N.J., Scarecrow Press, 1984.

———. "Film and Revolution in Cuba: The First Twenty-Five Years." In Sandor Halebsky and John M. Kirk, eds., *Cuba: Twenty-Five Years of Revolution, 1959–1984.* New York: Praeger, 1985.

———. "Marginal Cinemas and Mainstream Critical Theory." *Screen* 26, nos. 3–4 (1985).

———. "Cine-Sociology and Social Change: Jorge Silva and Marta Rodríguez." In Julianne Burton, ed., *Cinema and Social Change in Latin America: Conversations with Filmmakers.* Austin: University of Texas Press, 1986.

———. "El próximo tango en Finlandia: Cinemedios y modelos de transculturación." Paper presented at the Ninth International Festival of the New Latin American Cinema, Havana, December 1987.

———. "Transitional States: Creative Complicities within the Real in *Man Marked to Die: Twenty Years Later* and *Patriamada.*" In Julianne Burton, ed., *The Social Documentary in Latin America.* Pittsburgh: University of Pittsburgh Press, 1990.

———. "Toward a History of Social Documentary in Latin America." In Julianne Burton, ed., *The Social Documentary in Latin America.* Pittsburgh: University of Pittsburgh Press, 1990.

———. "Latin America." In Annette Kuhn and Susannah Radstone, eds., *Women's Companion to International Film.* London: Virago Press, 1990.

———, ed. *Cinema and Social Change in Latin America: Conversations with Filmmakers.* Austin: University of Texas Press, 1986.

———, ed. *The Social Documentary in Latin America.* Pittsburgh: University of Pittsburgh Press, 1990.

Capriles, Oswaldo. "Mérida: Realidad, forma y comunicación." *Cine al Día* (Caracas), no. 6 (December 1968).

Casal, Lourdes. "Race Relations in Contemporary Cuba." In Philip Brenner, William M. LeoGrande, Donna Rich, and Daniel Siegel, eds., *The Cuban Reader: The Making of a Revolutionary Society.* New York: Grove Press, 1989.

Casaus, Victor. "*Gaijin*: El camino de Tizuka. An interview with Tizuka Yamasaki, a Brazilian Filmmaker." *Cine Cubano*, no. 99 (1981).

Castro, Josué de. *Una zona esplosiva: Il Nordeste del Brasile.* Torino: Editorial Einaudi, 1966.

Chanan, Michael. *The Cuban Image: Cinema and Cultural Politics in Cuba.* London/Bloomington: British Film Institute/Indiana University Press. 1985.

———, ed. *Chilean Cinema.* London: British Film Institute, 1976.

———, ed. *Twenty-Five Years of the New Latin American Cinema.* London: BFI/Channel Four. 1983.

Chevigny, Bell Gale. "'Insatiable Unease': Melville and Carpentier and the Search for an American Hermeneutic." In Bell Gale Chevigny and Gari Laguardia, eds., *Reinventing the Americas: Comparative Studies of Literature of the United States and Spanish America.* New York: Cambridge University Press, 1986.

Christie, Ian. "A Secret Cinema: Raúl Ruiz." In Jill Forbes, ed., *INA—French for Innovation: The Work of the Institut National de la Communication Audiovisuelle in Cinema and Television*. London: British Film Institute, 1984.

Ciment, Michel. "Ruy Guerra." In Ian Cameron, ed., *The Second Wave*. New York: Praeger, 1970.

Colina, Enrique. "*Hasta cierto punto*." *Cine Cubano*, no. 108 (1984).

———. "Tomás Gutierrez Alea sobre *Hasta cierto punto*." *Cine Cubano*, no. 109 (1984).

Collazos, Oscar. "Cine colombiano: ¿Por quién, para quién, contra quienes?" *Cine Cubano*, nos. 76–77 (n.d.).

Cortázar, Julio. "Letter to Roberto Fernández Retamar." In Doris Meyer, ed., *Lives on the Line: The Testimony of Contemporary Latin American Authors*. Berkeley and Los Angeles: University of California Press, 1988.

Cozarinsky, Edgardo. "Les réalisateur étrangers en France: Hier et aujourd'hui." *Positif*, no. 325 (March 1988).

Cunha, Euclides da. *Rebellion in the Backlands*. Translation by Samuel Putman. Chicago: University of Chicago Press, 1944.

Dalton, Roque. "*Yawar Mallku:* Something More Than a Film." Translated by Katka Selucky and Will Straw. In Zuzana M. Pick, ed., *Latin American Film Makers and the Third Cinema*. Ottawa: Carleton University, 1978.

"Declaración final: V Encuentro de cineastas latinoamericanos, Mérida, Venezuela, Abril 1977." *Cine Cubano*, nos. 91–92 (n.d.): 27.

Donoso, José. "Ithaca: The Impossible Return." In Doris Meyer, ed., *Lives on the Line: The Testimony of Contemporary Latin American Authors*. Berkeley and Los Angeles: University of California Press, 1988.

Downing, John D. H., ed. *Film and Politics in the Third World*. New York: Autonomedia, 1987.

Dujovne Ortiz, Alicia. "*Buenos Aires* (An Excerpt)." Translated by Caren Kaplan. *Discourse* (Milwaukee), no. 8 (Fall–Winter 1986–1987).

Ehrenstein, David. "Raul Ruiz." In *Film: The Front Line 1984*. Denver: Arden Press, 1984.

———. "Raul Ruiz at the Holiday Inn." *Film Quarterly* 40, no. 1 (Fall 1986).

Emmerich, Fernando, cd. *Leyendas chilenas*. Santiago: Editorial Andrés Bello, 1986.

Feldman, Seth. "Circling I's: Some Implications of the Filmmakers' Presence in Michael Rubbo's *Margaret Atwood: Once in August* and Marilú Mallet's *Journal Inachevé*." In Pierre Véronneau, Michael Dorland, and Seth Feldman, eds., *Dialogue: Canadian and Quebec Cinema*. Montreal: Mediatexte Publications and La Cinémathèque Québécoise, 1987.

Foner, Philip S. *Antonio Maceo: The "Bronze Titan" of Cuba's Struggle for Independence*. New York: Monthly Review Press, 1977.

Fornet, Ambrosio. *Cine, literatura, sociedad*. Havana: Editorial Letras Cubanas, 1982.

———. "Trente ans de cinéma dans la Révolution." In Paulo-Antonio Paranagua, ed., *Cinéma Cubain*. Paris: Centre Georges Pompidou, 1990.

Francia, Aldo. *Nuevo Cine Latinoamericano en Viña del Mar*. Santiago: CESOC Ediciones ChileAmérica, 1990.

Franco, Jean. *The Modern Culture of Latin America: Society and the Artist*. Harmondsworth, England: Penguin Books, 1970.

———. "What's in a Name: Popular Culture Theories and Their Limitations." *Studies in Latin American Popular Culture* 1 (1976).

———. "Plotting Women: Popular Narratives for Women in the United States and Latin America." In Bell Gale Chevigny and Gari Laguardia, eds., *Reinventing the Americas: Comparative Studies of Literature of the United States and Spanish America*. Cambridge: Cambridge University Press, 1986.

———. "Beyond Ethnocentrism: Gender, Power and the Third World Intelligentsia." In Cary Nelson and Lawrence Grossberg, eds., *Marxism and the Interpretation of Culture*. Urbana: University of Illinois Press, 1988.

———. *Plotting Women: Gender and Representation in Mexico*. London: Verso, 1989.

Fuentes, Carlos. *Myself with Others*. New York: Noonday Press, 1990.

Fusco, Coco. "The Tango of Esthetics and Politics: An Interview with Fernando Solanas." *Cinéaste* 16, nos. 1–2 (1987–1988).

———, ed. *Reviewing Histories: Selections from New Latin American Cinema*. Buffalo, N.Y.: Hallwalls, 1987.

Galeano, Eduardo. "L'exil: Entre la nostalgie et la creation." In *Amérique latine: Luttes et mutations*. Paris: Editions François Maspero/Triconti-nental, 1981.

Galiano, Carlos. "*One Way or Another:* The Revolution in Action." *Jump Cut*, no. 19 (December 1978). Originally published in *Granma Weekly Review* (Havana), English version, November 20, 1977.

García Espinosa, Julio. "Julio García Espinosa responde." *Primer Plano* (Valparaiso) 1, no. 4 (Spring 1972). Reprinted as "Carta a la revista *Primer Plano*." In Julio García Espinosa. *Una imagen recorre el mundo*. Havana: Letras Cubanas, 1979.

———. "For an Imperfect Cinema." Translated by Julianne Burton. In Michael Chanan, ed., *Twenty-Five Years of the New Latin American Cinema*. London: British Film Institute and Channel Four, 1983.

García Márquez, Gabriel. "The Solitude of Latin America." In Doris Meyer, ed., *Lives on the Line: The Testimony of Contemporary Latin American Authors*. Berkeley and Los Angeles: University of California Press, 1988.

Getino, Octavio. "Algunas observaciones sobre el concepto del 'Tercer Cine.'" *A diez años de "Hacia un tercer cine."* Mexico: Filmoteca UNAM, 1982.

———. *Cine latinoamericano, economía y nuevas tecnologías*. Buenos Aires: Editorial Legasa, 1988.

Gili, Jean A. "Le territoire de la nostalgie: *Tangos, l'exil de Gardel*." *Positif*, no. 297 (November 1985).

Gill, Anne Marie. "Fiction as Historical Discourse, Political Discourse as Fiction in Brazilian Cinema." Department of Film, University of Iowa, 1988.

Giménez, Manuel Horacio. "Apuntes de filmación de Manuel Horacio Giménez." In Mario Rodríguez Alemán. "Neorealismo argentino: Los inundados." *Cine Cubano*, no. 11 (June 1963).

Giral, Sergio. "Cuban Cinema and the Afro-Cuban Heritage." Interview by Julianne Burton and Gary Crowdus. In John D. H. Downing, ed., *Film and Politics in the Third World*. New York: Autonomedia, 1987.

González, José Antonio. "Conversación con Jorge Silva y Marta Rodríguez." *Cine Cubano*, nos. 86–88 (1973).

Graham, Richard, ed. *The Idea of Race in Latin America, 1870–1940*. Austin: University of Texas Press, 1990.

"Grupos de Creación: Entre vistacon Humberto Solas y Manuel Perez Paredes." *Cine Cubano*, no. 122 (1988).

Guevara, Alfredo. "Discurso de clausura: Palabras de clausura pronunciadas por el compañero Alfredo Guevara, presidente del festival." *Cine Cubano*, no. 97 (1980).

———. "Viña del Mar: Un hito decisivo." *Cine Cubano*, no. 120 (1987).

Guevara, Ernesto Ché. *Escritos y discursos*. vol. 9. Havana: Editorial de Ciencias Sociales, 1977.

Gumucio Dagrón, Alfonso. *Historia del cine boliviano*. La Paz: Editorial Amigos del Libro, 1982. Reprint. Mexico: Filmoteca UNAM, 1983.

———. *Cine, censura y exilio en América latina*. La Paz: Ediciones Film/Historia, 1979. 2d. ed. Mexico City: CIMCA/STUNAM, 1984.

———. "Product of Circumstances: Reflections of a Media Activist." In Julianne Burton, ed., *Cinema and Social Change in Latin America*. Austin: University of Texas Press, 1986.

———. "Argentina: A Huge Case of Censorship." In Tim Barnard, ed., *Argentine Cinema*. Toronto: Nightwood Editions, 1986.

Haberly, David T. *Three Sad Races: Racial Identity and National Consciousness in Brazilian Literature*. New York: Cambridge University Press, 1983.

Handa, Tomoo. "Senso estético na vida dos immigrantes." In Hiroshi Saito and Takashi Maeyama, eds., *Assimilaçao e integraçao dos Japaneses no Brasil*. Sao Paulo: Editora da Universidade de Sao Paulo, 1973.

Handler, Mario. "Starting from Scratch: Artisanship and Agitprop." In Julianne Burton, ed., *Cinema and Social Change in Latin America: Conversations with Filmmakers*. Austin: University of Texas Press, 1986.

Hecht, Susan, and Alexander Cockburn. *The Fate of the Forest: Developers, Destroyers and Defenders of the Amazon*. London: Penguin, 1989.

Helg, Aline. "Race in Argentina and Cuba, 1880–1930: Theory, Policies, and Popular Reaction." In Richard Graham, ed., *The Idea of Race in Latin America, 1870–1940*. Austin: University of Texas Press, 1990.

Henríquez Ureña, Pedro. *Las corrientes literarias en la América hispánica*. Mexico: Fondo de Cultura Económica. 1949.

Herrera, Haydén. *Frida: A Biography of Frida Kahlo.* New York: Harper and Row, 1983.

Hess, John. "Collective Experience, Synthetic Forms: El Salvador's Radio Venceremos." In Julianne Burton, ed., *The Social Documentary of Latin America.* Pittsburgh: University of Pittsburgh Press. 1990.

Jaehne, Karen. *"Camila." Cinéaste* (New York) 14, no. 3 (1986).

———. "Love as a Revolutionary Act: An interview with Maria Luisa Bemberg." *Cinéaste* (New York), 14, no. 3 (1986).

Johnson, Randal. "Introduction: Cinema Novo, the State, and Modern Brazilian Society." In *Cinema Novo × 5: Masters of Contemporary Brazilian Cinema.* Austin: University of Texas Press, 1984.

———. "Carlos Diegues." In *Cinema Novo × 5: Masters of Contemporary Brazilian Cinema.* Austin: University of Texas Press, 1984.

———. *The Film Industry in Brazil: Culture and the State.* Pittsburgh: University of Pittsburgh Press, 1987.

Johnson, Randal, and Robert Stam. "The Cinema of Hunger: Nelson Pereira dos Santos's *Vidas Secas.*" In Randal Johnson and Robert Stam, eds., *Brazilian Cinema.* Austin: University of Texas Press, 1988.

Johnson, Randal, and Stam, Robert, eds. *Brazilian Cinema.* Austin: University of Texas Press, 1988.

Julien, Isaac, and Kobena Mercer. "Introduction: De Margin and De Centre." *Screen* 29, no. 4 (Autumn 1988).

Jusdanis, Gregory. *Belated Modernity and Aesthetic Culture: Inventing National Literature.* Minneapolis: University of Minnesota Press, 1991.

Kehr, David. "And Now . . . Restructuralism." *Chicago Reader,* April 6, 1984.

Kent, R. K. "Palmares: An African State in Brazil." In Richard Price, ed., *Maroon Societies: Rebel Slave Communities in the Americas.* 2d. ed. Baltimore and London, Johns Hopkins University Press, 1979.

King, John. "The Social and Cultural Context." In John King and Nissa Torrents, eds., *The Garden of Forking Paths: Argentine Cinema.* London: British Film Institute and National Film Theater, 1988.

———. *Magical Reels: A History of Cinema in Latin America.* London: Verso, 1990.

———, and Nissa Torrents, ed. *The Garden of Forking Paths: Argentine Cinema.* London: British Film Institute and National Film Theater, 1988.

Laclau, Ernesto. *Politics and Ideology in Marxist Theory.* London: Verso, 1979.

Lesage, Julia. *"One Way or Another:* Dialectical, Revolutionary, Feminist." *Jump Cut,* no. 20 (May 1979).

———. "Women Make Media: Three Modes of Production." In Julianne Burton, ed., *The Social Documentary in Latin America.* Pittsburgh: University of Pittsburgh Press, 1990.

Llopiz, Jorge Luis. "El talón de Aquiles de nuestro cine." *Cine Cubano,* no. 122 (1988).

Longfellow, Brenda. "Feminist Language in *Journal Inachevé* and *Strass*

Café." In William C. Wees and Michael Dorland, eds., *Words and Moving Images: Essays on Verbal and Visual Expression in Film and Television.* Montreal: Mediatexte Publications, 1984.

López, Ana M. "A Short History of Latin American Film Histories." *Journal of Film and Video* 37, no. 1 (Winter 1985).

———. "Argentina, 1955–1976: The Film Industry and Its Margins." In John King and Nissa Torrents, eds., *The Garden of Forking Paths: Argentine Cinema.* London: British Film Institute and National Film Theater, 1987.

———. "An 'Other' History: The New Cinema of Latin America." In Robert Sklar and Charles Musser, eds., *Resisting Images: Essays on Cinema and History.* Philadelphia: University of Temple Press, 1990. An earlier version appeared in *Radical History Review*, no. 41 (1988).

———. "At the Limits of Documentary: Hypertextual Transformation and the New Latin American Cinema." In Julianne Burton, ed., *The Social Documentary in Latin America.* Pittsburgh: University of Pittsburgh Press, 1990.

———. "Setting Up the Stage: A Decade of Latin American Film Scholarship." *Quarterly Review of Film and Video* 13, nos. 1–3 (1991).

———. "Celluloid Tears: Melodrama in the 'Old' Mexican Cinema." *Iris,* no. 13 (Summer 1991).

Lynch, John. *Argentine Dictator: Juan Manuel de Rosas, 1829–1852.* Oxford: Clarendon Press, 1981.

Mahieu, Agustín. "Los cuadros vivientes o hipótesis de Raúl Ruiz." *Cine Libre* (Buenos Aires), no. 1 (October 1982).

Mallet, Marilú. "Notes sur *Journal Inachevé.*" In Louise Carrière, ed., *Femmes et cinéma québécois.* Montreal: Boréal Express, 1983.

Manciello, Francine. "Women, State, and Family in Latin American Literature of the 1920s." In *Women, Culture, and Politics in Latin America: Seminar on Feminism and Culture in Latin America.* Berkeley and Los Angeles: University of California Press, 1990.

Manuel, Peter. *Popular Musics of the Non-Western World.* New York: Oxford University Press, 1988.

Marks, Morton. "Uncovering Ritual Structures in Afro-American Music." In Irving I. Zaretsky and Mark P. Leone, eds., *Religious Movements in Contemporary America.* Princeton, N.J.: University of Princeton Press, 1974.

Martin, Gerald. *Journeys through the Labyrinth.* London: Verso, 1989.

Matta, Roberto de. *Carnavals, bandits et héros: Ambiguités de la société brésilienne.* Paris: Editions du Seuil, 1978.

Melzer, Ronald. "El realismo de la vocación y los suspensos del chileno Raúl Ruiz." *Cinemateca Revista* (Montevideo), no. 33 (August 1982).

Mistral, Gabriela. "Recado sobre un mito americano: El Caleuche de Chile. (Lisboa. Junio 1936)." In *Gabriela Mistral en el "Repertorio Americano."* San José: Editorial Universidad de Costa Rica, 1978.

Monsiváis, Carlos. "Cultura: Tradición y modernidad." *La Jornada,* February 21, 1992.

Moore, Zelbert. "Reflections on Blacks in Contemporary Brazilian Popular Culture in the 1980s." *Studies in Latin American Popular Culture* 7 (1988).

Mosak, Esther. "*Maria Antonia:* Eugenio Hernández's 1967 Play Becomes a 1990 Film by Sergio Giral." *Cuba Update* (New York) 12, no. 3 (Summer 1991).

Mouesca, Jacqueline, and Carlos Orellana. "El caso Ruiz." *Araucaria* (Paris), no. 23 (1983).

Mulvey, Laura, and Peter Wollen. "The Discourse of the Body." In Rosemary Betterton, ed., *Looking On: Images of Femininity in the Visual Arts and Media.* London and New York: Pandora Press, 1987.

Munerato, Elice, and María Helena Darcy de Oliveira. "Muses derrière la caméra." In Paulo-Antonio Paranagua, ed., *Le cinéma brésilien.* Paris: Centre Pompidou, 1987.

Nichols, Bill. "Embodied Knowledge and the Politics of Power." *CineAction!* (Toronto), no. 23 (Winter 1990–1991).

Nichols, Bill, ed. *Movies and Methods.* 2 vols. Berkeley and Los Angeles: University of California Press, 1976 and 1985.

Ostria, Vincent. "Le tutoiement du rêve." *Cahiers du Cinéma,* no. 377 (November 1985).

Parada Lillo, Roberto. "Identidad cultural y política." In *Literatura chilena: Creación y crítica* (Los Angeles, Madrid) 10, no. 1/35 (January–March 1986): 9–10.

Paranagua, Paulo-Antonio. "*Los hijos de Fierro (Les fils de Fierro).*" *Positif,* nos. 208–209 (July–August 1978).

———. "Le nouveau cinéma latino-américain: Entre la répression des dictatures et la tutelle étatique." In *Amérique latine: Luttes et mutations/Tricontinental II.* Paris: Petit Collection Maspero, 1981.

———. "Brésil." *Positif,* nos. 281–282 (July/August 1984).

———. "Biarritz 1984: Retour de l'Argentine." *Positif,* no. 288 (February 1985).

———. "Entretien avec Fernando E. Solanas." *Positif,* no. 297 (November 1985).

———, ed. *Le cinéma brésilien.* Paris: Centre Pompidou, 1987.

———. "Ruptures et continuité: Années soixante-dix–quatre-vingt." In Paulo-Antonio Paranagua, ed., *Le cinéma brésilien.* Paris: Centre Pompidou, 1987.

———. "News from Havana: A Restructuring of Cuban Cinema." *Framework,* no. 35 (1988).

———, ed. *Cinéma cubain.* Paris: Centre Georges Pompidou, 1990.

Parker, Andrew, Mary Russo, Doris Sommer, and Patricia Yaeger, eds. *Nationalisms and Sexualities.* New York: Routledge, Chapman and Hall, 1992.

Pearce, Jenny. *Colombia: Inside the Labyrinth.* London: Latin American Bureau, 1990.

Perrone, Charles A. *Masters of Brazilian Contemporary Song: MPB 1965–1985.* Austin: University of Texas Press, 1989.

Pick, Zuzana M. "Le cinéma chilien sous le signe de l'Unité Populaire." *Positif*, no. 155 (January 1974).

———. "Un débat nécessaire: *Diálogo de exilados.*" *Positif*, no. 174 (October 1975).

———. "Raoul Ruiz: De l'exil, du dépaysement et de l'exotisme." *Positif*, no. 274 (December 1983).

——— "Hablan los cineastas." In David Valjalo and Zuzana M. Pick, eds., *Diez años de cine chileno: 1973–1983.* Hollywood: Edición de la Frontera, 1983. Reprint of materials previously published in *Literatura chilena: Creación y crítica* (Los Angeles) 8, no. 1 (January–March 1984).

———. "Chilean Cinema: Ten Years of Exile, 1973–1983." *Jump Cut*, no. 32 (April 1986).

———. "Chilean Cinema (1973–1986). The Notion of Exile: A Field of Investigation and Its Conceptual Framework." *Framework*, no. 34 (1987).

———. "Chilean Documentary: Continuity and Disjunction." In Julianne Burton, ed., *The Social Documentary of Latin America.* Pittsburgh: University of Pittsburgh Press, 1990.

———, ed. *Latin American Film Makers and the Third Cinema.* Ottawa: Carleton University, 1978.

Pines, Jim, and Paul Willemen, eds. *Questions of Third Cinema.* London: British Film Institute, 1989.

Pollock, Griselda. *Vision and Difference: Femininity, Feminism and the Histories of Art.* London: Routledge, 1988.

Rama, Angel. *Transculturación narrativa en América Latina.* Mexico City: Siglo XXI Editores, 1985.

Ranucci, Karen, with Julianne Burton. "On the Trail of Independent Video." In Julianne Burton, ed., *The Social Documentary of Latin America.* Pittsburgh: University of Pittsburgh Press, 1990.

Ranvaud, Don. "Interview with Fernando Solanas." Translated by Cristina Weller. *Framework*, no. 10 (Spring 1979).

Rich, B. Ruby. "In the Name of Feminist Criticism." In Bill Nichols, ed., *Movies and Methods* vol. 2. Berkeley: University of California Press, 1985.

———. "After the Revolutions: The Second Coming of Latin American Cinema." *Village Voice*, February 10, 1987.

———. "An/Other View of New Latin American Cinema." *Iris*, no. 23 (Summer 1991).

Rocha, Glauber. *Revisión crítica del cine brasileño.* Madrid: Editorial Fundamentos, 1971.

———. "The Aesthetics of Hunger." Translated by Burnes Hollyman and Randal Johnson. In Michael Chanan, ed., *Twenty-Five Years of the New Latin American Cinema.* London: British Film Institute and Channel Four, 1983.

Rodrigues, Joao Carlos. "O indio brasileiro e o cinema." In *Cinema brasileiro: 8 estudios.* Rio de Janeiro: Embrafilme/Funarte, 1980.

Rojas, Waldo. "Raúl Ruiz: Imágenes de paso." *Enfoque* (Santiago), no. 2 (Summer–Fall 1984).

Rosenbaum, Jonathan. "Beating the Labyrinth." *Monthly Film Bulletin* 52, no. 612 (January 1985).

Rowe, William, and Schelling, Vivian. *Memory and Modernity: Popular Culture in Latin America.* London: Verso, 1991.

Ruiz, Raúl. "Object Relations in the Cinema." *Afterimage* (London), no. 10 (Autumn 1981).

Said, Edward W. *The World, the Text, and the Critic.* Cambridge, Mass.: Harvard University Press, 1983.

Salles Gomes, Paulo Emílio. "Cinema: A Trajectory within Underdevelopment." In Randal Johnson and Robert Stam, eds., *Brazilian Cinema.* Austin: University of Texas Press, 1988.

Sánchez Crespo, Osvaldo. "The Perspective of the Present: Cuban History, Cuban Film Making." In Coco Fusco, ed., *Reviewing Histories: Selections from New Latin American Cinema.* Buffalo, N.Y.: Hallwalls, 1987.

Sanjinés, Jorge. "A Militant Cinema." Translated by Christina Shantz and Leandro Urbina. In Zuzana M. Pick, ed., *Latin American Film Makers and the Third Cinema.* Ottawa: Carleton University, 1978.

———. "The Search for a Popular Cinema." Translated by Christina Shantz and Leandro Urbina. In Zuzana M. Pick, ed., *Latin American Film Makers and the Third Cinema.* Ottawa: Carleton University, 1978.

———. "Problems of Form and Content in Revolutionary Cinema." Translated by Malcolm Coad. In Michael Chanan, ed., *Twenty-Five Years of the New Latin American Cinema.* London: BFI/Channel Four, 1983.

———. "Revolutionary Cinema: The Bolivian Experience." In Julianne Burton, ed., *Cinema and Social Change in Latin America.* Austin: University of Texas Press, 1986.

Schwartz, Roberto. "Cinema and *The Guns.*" In Randal Johnson and Robert Stam, eds., *Brazilian Cinema.* Austin: University of Texas Press, 1988.

Skármeta, Antonio. "La reformulación del status del escritor en el exilio." In *Primer cuaderno de ensayo chileno.* Ottawa: Ediciones Cordillera, 1980.

Skidmore, Thomas E. *Black into White: Race and Nationality in Brazilian Thought.* New York: University of Oxford Press. 1974.

———. "Racial Ideas and Social Policy in Brazil, 1870–1940." In Richard Graham, ed., *The Idea of Race in Latin America, 1870–1940.* Austin: University of Texas Press. 1990.

Solanas, Fernando. "Cinema as a Gun: An Interview with Fernando Solanas." Translated by Rebecca Douglass with Ruth McCormick. *Cineaste* 3, no. 2 (Fall 1969).

———. "Remarques écrites." *Cinéthique* (Paris), no. 3 (1969).

———. "Fernando Solanas: An Interview." Translated by James Roy Macbean. *Film Quarterly* 14, no. 1 (Fall 1970).

———, and Octavio Getino. "Towards a Third Cinema: Notes and Experiences for the Development of a Cinema of Liberation in the Third World." Translated by Julianne Burton and Michael Chanan. In Michael Chanan, ed., *Twenty-Five Years of the New Latin American Cinema.* London: British Film Institute and Channel Four, 1983.

————. *La mirada: Reflexiones sobre cine y cultura.* Entrevista de Horacio González. Buenos Aires: Puntosur Editores, 1989.

Solano, Claudio. "Latin American Cinema: The Non-Realist Side of Reality." *Undercut* (London), no. 12 (Summer 1984).

Sommer, Doris. "Irresistible Romance: The Foundational Fictions of Latin America." In Homi K. Bhabha, ed., *Nation and Narration.* London: Routledge, 1990.

Stam, Robert. "Samba, Candomblé, Quilombo: Black Performance and Brazilian Cinema." *Journal of Ethnic Studies* 13, no. 3 (Fall 1985).

————. "*Quilombo.*" *Cinéaste* 15, no. 1 (1986).

————. "Carnival, Politics, and Brazilian Culture." *Studies in Latin American Popular Culture* 7 (1988).

————. "Formal Innovation and Radical Critique in *The Fall.*" In Randal Johnson and Robert Stam, eds., *Brazilian Cinema.* Austin: University of Texas Press, 1988.

————. "Bakhtin and Left Cultural Critique." In E. Ann Kaplan, ed., *Postmodernism and Its Discontents.* London: Verso, 1988.

————. *Subversive Pleasures: Bakhtin, Cultural Criticism, and Film.* Baltimore: Johns Hopkins University, 1989.

————. "*The Hour of the Furnaces* and the Two Avant-Gardes." In Julianne Burton, ed., *The Social Documentary in Latin America.* Pittsburgh: University of Pittsburgh Press, 1990. Originally printed in *Millenium Film Journal*, nos. 7–9 (Fall–Winter 1980–1981).

————, and Ismail Xavier. "Recent Brazilian Cinema: Allegory/Metacinema/Carnival." *Film Quarterly* 41, no.3 (Spring 1988).

————, and Ismail Xavier. "Transformation of National Allegory: Brazilian Cinema from Dictatorship to Redemocratization." In Robert Sklar and Charles Musser, eds., *Resisting Images: Essays on Cinema and History.* Philadelphia: Temple University Press, 1990.

Stanford, Philip. *Pioneers in the Tropics: The Political Organization of Japanese in an Immigrant Community in Brazil.* New York: Humanities Press, 1973.

Suárez, Estela. "The Feminist Movement in Latin America and the Caribbean: Trends and Challenges." Translated by Dean Brown. *Aquelarre* (Vancouver), nos. 7–8 (Spring/Summer 1991). Based on the seminar "Feminism in the 1990s," Fifth Feminist Conference of Latin America and the Caribbean, San Fernando, Argentina, November 1990.

Taylor, Julie M. "Tango: Theme of Class and Nation." *Ethnomusicology*, no. 20 (1976).

————. "Carnival, Media, and Regional Traditions: Integration and Manipulation." *Studies in Latin American Popular Culture*, 7 (1988).

Toledo, Teresa, ed. *Realizadoras latinoamericanas/Latin American Women Filmmakers, 1917–1987: Chronology/Cronología.* New York: Círculo de Cultura Cubana, 1987.

Torrents, Nissa. "Contemporary Argentine Cinema." In John King and Nissa Torrents, ed., *The Garden of Forking Paths: Argentine Cinema.* London: British Film Institute and National Film Theater, 1988.

Torres, Camilo. *Ecrits et paroles.* Translated by Didier Coste, Jean-Michel Fossey, and Henri de la Vega. Paris: Seuil, 1968.

Treviño, Jesús Salvador. "Chicano Cinema Overview." *Areíto* 10, no. 37 (1984).

Truffaut, François. "A Certain Tendency of French Cinema." In Bill Nichols, ed. *Movies and Methods.* vol. 1. Berkeley and Los Angeles: University of California Press, 1976.

Umpierre, Jose, and Mario Vissepo. "Porto-Rico." In Guy Hennebelle and Alfonso Gumucio Dagrón, eds., *Les cinémas de l'Amérique latine.* Paris: Nouvelles Editions Lherminier, 1981.

Valjalo, David, and Zuzana M. Pick, eds. *Diez años de cine chileno: 1973–1983.* Hollywood: Edición de la Frontera, 1983. Reprint of materials previously published in *Literatura chilena: Creación y crítica* (Los Angeles) 8, no. 1 (January–March 1984).

Verdejo, Juan, Zuzana M. Pick, and Gastón Ancelovici. "Chili." In Guy Hennebelle and Alfonso Gumucio Dagrón, eds., *Les cinémas de l'Amérique latine.* Paris: Nouvelles Editions Lherminier, 1981.

Viera, Joao Luiz, and Robert Stam. "Parody and Marginality: The Case of Brazilian Cinema." *Framework*, no. 28 (1985).

West, Denis. "*Frida*: An Interview with Paul Leduc." *Cinéaste* 16, no. 4 (1988).

West, Joan M., and Denis West. "*Frida.*" *Cinéaste* 16, no. 4 (1988).

Whitaker, Sheila. "Straight to the Heart: Interview with Maria Luisa Bemberg." *Monthly Film Bulletin* 54, no. 645 (October 1987). Reprinted in John King and Nissa Torrents, eds., *The Garden of the Forking Paths: Argentine Cinema.* London: British Film Institute and National Film Theater, 1989.

Willemen, Paul. "The Third Cinema Question: Notes and Reflections." *Framework*, no. 34 (1987). Reprinted in Jim Pines and Paul Willemen, eds., *Questions of Third Cinema.* London: British Film Institute, 1989.

Wolff, Janet. *Feminine Sentences: Essays on Women and Culture.* Berkeley: University of California Press, 1990.

Women, Culture, and Politics in Latin America: Seminar on Feminism and Culture in Latin America. Berkeley: University of California Press, 1990.

Xavier, Ismail. "*Black God, White Devil:* The Representation of History." In Randal Johnson and Robert Stam, eds., *Brazilian Cinema.* Austin: University of Texas Press, 1988.

———. "*Iracema:* Transcending Cinéma Vérité." In Julianne Burton, ed., *The Social Documentary of Latin America.* Pittsburgh: University of Pittsburgh Press, 1990.

Index